WILL I MAKE IT TO HEAVEN?

DANIEL DEEDS

Published by Calvary Press Publishing

© Calvary Press Publishing

ISBN: 978-0-9973399-4-9

All Bible quotes are from the English Standard Version 2001 ESV except where stated otherwise.

www.calvarypress.com

PRINTED IN USA

Contents

Introduction

Therefore do not throw away your confidence, which has a great reward. For you have need of endurance, so that when you have done the will of God you may receive what is promised. For, "Yet a little while, and the coming one will come and will not delay; but my righteous one shall live by faith, and if he shrinks back, my soul has no pleasure in him." But we are not of those who shrink back and are destroyed, but of those who have faith and preserve their souls.

(Heb. 10:35–39)

Is perseverance necessary for salvation? Is it possible for a believer to abandon Christ and go back to sin and the world after having been converted? If so, what would the result be? Would such a person remain eternally saved anyway, or would salvation be forfeited? Can someone who is a believer in Christ today know for sure that he or she will continue to be saved forever?

These questions have been around for ages. They have probably crossed the mind of every single Christian. Yet when searching Scripture for answers, Christians don't all reach the same conclusions. Throughout the centuries of Christian history, this issue has led to many debates, and differences have even caused divisions in churches and denominations. In some cases, Bible colleges and ministries were founded for the express purpose of promoting a particular perspective on this point of doctrine.

And what has been achieved through so much debating? Far from coming to a consensus, the subject continues to be the cause of disagreement and fragmentation in the body of Christ. Instead of being remedied, the problem is only exacerbated every time somebody comes along and proposes a new system of interpretation, believing to have finally found the key to overcome the differences and bring an end to the debate. At present, we have more theories disputing over the minds of Christians than at any time in history, and if this is any indication of what lies ahead, viewpoints may just continue to multiply, causing further division, until the return of Christ.

The solution, however, is not to pursue unity by ignoring the issue. Abandoning our efforts toward doctrinal unity and aspiring only to have institutional unity is, in reality, to give up on achieving true unity. If Christ's church does not benefit from division, it profits even less from a disregard for doctrine. External unity, without confessional unity, is merely apparent unity, which becomes an ideal context for the proliferation of error rather than for the proclamation of the truth. After all, the church should function as the pillar and buttress of the truth (1 Tim. 3:15).

A great part of the Bible's message is easily assimilated by the new reader. But the apostle Peter reminds us that it also contains things that are harder to understand, things that the ignorant and unstable twist (2 Pet. 3:16). This manner of speaking shows that there is but one true meaning of the Bible, and that we don't have the freedom to attribute any meaning to the sacred text other than that which was originally intended by the inspired author.

For this very reason, the church should be of assistance in understanding the Scriptures correctly. It should be a secure environment where each disciple of Christ is instructed in sound doctrine. It ought to be a school of Christ, where one learns with teachers who are gifted and capable, so that each believer need not "fend for himself" to understand the doctrines of the Bible. Therefore, it is the duty of every leader and every member of a local church to promote this goal in the church.

Paul repeatedly articulated his concern that biblical doctrine be taught accurately in church. He urged Timothy to remain at Ephesus and admonish "certain persons not to teach any different doctrine" (1 Tim. 1:3). In his second epistle, Paul exhorted Timothy, "Do your best to present yourself to God as one approved, a worker who has no need to be ashamed, rightly handling the word of truth" (2 Tim. 2:15). Writing to Titus, Paul declares that an overseer in the church "must hold firm to the trustworthy word as taught, so that he may be able to give instruction in sound doctrine and also rebuke those who contradict it" (Tit. 1:9). We are not allowed to modify or omit any part of the Bible's teaching. In his own ministry, the apostle Paul did not shrink from declaring the whole counsel of God (Acts 20:27).

We can perceive that this responsibility falls especially, but not exclusively, on the leadership. Each one of us is responsible to study through these matters so as to personally understand what has been divinely revealed, and thus to be able to serve the cause of truth more perfectly. We all help spread those doctrines that we support, even by means of our church affiliation, and we are all responsible for the doctrines that we aid in propagating. If we wish to make the most of our talents and efforts for God's kingdom, we need to be careful about which teachings we endorse. That means we should not fail to properly research, investigate, and examine the Scriptures.

It is this duty that has motivated the writing of this book. Its purpose is to offer biblical answers to the questions above, not under the pretense of bringing the controversy to an end, or of answering the questions involved so that all will be satisfied, but with the intention of supplying one more tool that may be an aid in investigating the topic. It is not a novel approach or the setting forth of an original theological position. Rather, it is an exposition of a doctrine that has been attested to by an innumerable host of outstanding Christians, since the earliest days of Christianity.

In my personal journey, for some time I resisted the doctrine that I here defend. However, as I read my Bible, I saw myself confronted over and over by biblical passages that did not harmonize with my previous conviction, and was forced to reconsider. In the search that ensued, I received enormous benefit from the work of others. It is my conviction that the right answers to these questions have always been available to Christ's church, both in the pages of Scripture and in the voices of capable men whom God has placed in the church down through the ages, to guide it in the midst of the controversies.

The Bible itself states that to avoid doctrinal disunity God has granted the church people who are gifted in the area of teaching,

> To equip the saints for the work of ministry, for building up the body of Christ, until we all attain to the unity of the faith and of the knowledge of the Son of God, to mature manhood, to the measure of the stature of the fullness of Christ, so that we may no longer be children, tossed to and fro by the waves and carried about by every wind of doctrine. (Eph. 4:11–14)

Since the Bible is the only rule of faith, we should study it and allow it to instruct us. We should judge all things in light of what it says but not with an independent spirit that despises what can be learned from those whom God himself placed in the church to guide us along. It would certainly not be wise to reject a teaching that has stood the test of time being attested to by faithful men from generation to generation, without even listening to what they have to say.

It is out of this consideration that I have included quotes, which I deemed to be of value, from various periods of church history, both to shed light on the subject of this book and on the pertinent biblical texts, and to serve as a witness to the antiquity and prevalence of the doctrine of the perseverance of the saints over generations.

We all bring presuppositions to the Sacred Text that can bias our reading. Before having ever read the Bible, new converts typically assume that it is possible for you to experience salvation today but then lose your salvation later on. That men naturally tend to think in this way can be confirmed by the fact that the heretical sects hold to this view, whether they use the Bible or not. In fact, our natural tendency is to believe that salvation is a reward for those who practice good works.

This line of reasoning leads one to believe that salvation can be earned and lost, according to one's conduct. The Bible stands in opposition to all such notions, teaching rather that salvation is by the grace of God alone. But this is a difficult message for us to fully apprehend, and it's possible for our preconceived notions to get in the way of our Bible reading so that we fail to notice just how much of our salvation it attributes to divine grace.

During the Protestant Reformation, the core of the disagreement between the reformers and the teachings that had become widespread in the Catholic Church was precisely about the extent of the role God's grace played in salvation. The reformers raised the motto *Sola Gratia* (grace alone) as their banner, declaring that salvation is, from beginning to end, received by the grace of God alone.

Already at that time, just as today, the Catholic Church was ascribing human works an essential role in salvation and was denying that a Christian can have a legitimate assurance of salvation, apart from some sort of personal special revelation. Furthermore, the Catholic doctrine states that a Christian can fall from a state of grace by committing mortal sin. The lost condition that results from such a sinful act is, nevertheless, reversible, in as much as mortal sins are forgivable through confession and penitence.

Consequently, according to Catholic doctrine, it is possible to fall from a state of grace and be subsequently restored. In this way, the Catholic understanding allows not only for the loss of salvation but also for a second salvation, which may be followed by yet another loss of salvation, then a third restoration, and so on, for as long as one lives.[1] In this manner, the

---

1   In such a system, a person could be in and out of salvation over and over during a lifetime, making it conceivable that an individual who would certainly end up in heaven if death occurred now would end up in hell if only death were delayed until Wednesday of next week, but not if death waited another couple more weeks, by which time this same person would be bound for heaven again—at least until the next major sin, that is!

Catholic dogma maintains that good works carry out a vital role both in the obtaining and in the keeping one's salvation.

On the experiential level, what this means is that the devout follower must live in uncertainty about being accepted before God, both in the present and in the future, but uncertainty is seen as something positive. In traditional Catholic thinking, being sure of one's own salvation is regarded as something dangerous, because it could lead to negligence in the Christian walk. The idea is that whoever has assurance of salvation will not be as motivated and hardworking at doing good in order to please God, as someone who is uncertain as to whether enough has already been done to escape damnation in hell.

This kind of reasoning considers the assurance of remaining eternally secure in salvation as being likewise harmful because it would tend to make Christians even less watchful against temptation. In the Catholic perspective, not only would this detract from holy living but also the overconfidence it would induce could even lead to someone's eternal perdition, assuming salvation actually can be lost.

This Catholic belief reveals a departure from the teaching of the early church. While early Christianity emphatically denied that there would be eternal life for apostates or nominal Christians who persisted in a life of sin, on the other hand, the early church also expressed certainty that every genuine Christian would persevere unto the end in the way of faith and sanctification. Aware of this, and following the Bible as the only infallible authority, the reformers maintained that salvation cannot be lost. They did not mean by this that perseverance is unnecessary. Rather, they held that perseverance in faith and righteousness is just as necessary for someone to enter eternal glory as it is for them to be converted in the first place. The crucial point is that in reformed theology it is God who initially converts the sinner, out of sheer grace, and it is God who, out of pure grace, grants perseverance unto everyone whom he saves.

In the seventeenth century, the Arminian controversy brought about new debates concerning the doctrine of the perseverance of the saints. As he questioned reformed doctrine, although he left the matter unresolved, Arminius seemed to imply that there is a real possibility that saved people could fall and lose their salvation. His followers came to different conclusions so that today we do not find unanimity on this issue among churches that have embraced Arminianism.

In the current state of events, there are four distinct doctrinal positions on the matter of perseverance and security that boast a strong following in terms of evangelical churches, theological seminaries, capable authors, and parachurch ministries:

1. There are evangelicals who believe Christians can lose their salvation when they sin in a way that is serious enough. Those found in this camp may differ as to what kind of sin it would take, whether it be "deliberate" sin (sinning willfully) or sin that ranks in a "more serious" category on other grounds, but what is agreed upon is that sinful conduct of one sort or another can remove true Christians from a state of grace. Salvation is then canceled, or at least suspended, until there is repentance and confession. It is generally agreed that salvation is lost when someone leaves the fellowship of the church, no longer attends services, and goes back to the ways of the world. People in this condition are said to be "backslidden Christians" (i.e., people who have already been saved but are presently in a lost condition and must get right with God to recover their justification). Some individuals believe they have already lost their salvation several times since they first got saved but are confident of having been saved again when they turned back to God.

2. There is a second group of evangelicals that also believes salvation can be lost, but not due to sin (no matter how serious) or backsliding. Instead, advocates of this view argue that saved people can be lost only by committing apostasy—that is, by completely abandoning the faith so that they cease to be believers. As long as someone's faith is in Christ, they would say he or she will remain saved, even if grievous sins are being committed. Sin is a matter of concern, though. We are warned that while sin itself may not sever a believer from Christ, persisting in sin has a way of undermining faith and leading back into incredulity. Once that line is crossed, by becoming once more an unbeliever, salvation is forfeited. A considerable number of those who hold this view consider apostasy irreversible, denying any possibility of a person being saved more than once.

3. There is yet a third view found within evangelicalism that believes, just as the groups above, that saved people do, in some cases, go astray, return to a life of sin, and even deny the faith altogether. The difference, however, is that this view insists that no matter what happens, salvation can never be lost. Those who adhere to this position consider God's justification of the sinner inalterable, but not the transformation wrought in the heart of a

believer. Some even go so far as to deny that a new life is an essential part of true conversion, teaching instead that a person can be saved without ever repenting from sin at all. A distinction is made between receiving Jesus as Savior and receiving him as Lord.

4. Finally, there are those who follow the doctrine of the reformers on this issue. While persuaded that conversion (faith and repentance) and perseverance thereafter are absolutely indispensible for eternal salvation, reformed Christians believe it is God who bestows perseverance unto all those he brings to faith so that none are ever lost.

The proponents of each of these four views are convinced that their doctrine is nothing other than the teaching of the Bible itself, which all regard as the only infallible rule in matters of faith. Nevertheless, the Bible obviously does not contain four contradictory perspectives. The position taken in this book is that the reformers' doctrine expounds the biblical teaching in a precise and balanced way, whereas the other proposals all have their own shortcomings. Though each one contains some aspects of biblical truth, the other three views fail to harmonize all the pertinent biblical material.

The following brief preliminary evaluations attempts to summarize the reasons for this conclusion:

1 —

The belief that salvation can be lost as a result of serious or deliberate sin is the predominant view among churches that teach that salvation can be lost. John Wesley took this position and influenced the Methodist movement toward it. It is also the perspective found in most Pentecostal or charismatic denominations.

Some books that have been important in promoting it are *Kept by the Power of God: A Study of Perseverance and Falling Away* by British scholar I. Howard Marshall (Bethany Fellowship, Minneapolis, 1969), *If Ye Continue* by Guy Duty (Bethany House Publishers, Minneapolis), and *Life in the Son* by Robert Shank (Bethany House Publishers, Bloomington, Minnesota, 1989).

Another author defending this position is the Methodist Steven Harper, whose words surmise the doctrine well:

Involuntary transgressions (i.e., sins we commit without the awareness that we have done so) are not held against us by God, unless we discover them and do nothing about them. Voluntary sins—

deliberate violations of known laws of God—do, however, become mortal if we do not repent of them. The subject of eternal security rests (in both categories of sin) on the matter of ongoing repentance.[2]

STRONG POINTS

The motivation behind this teaching is clearly to oppose sin. Its aim falls equally on sin in the life of believers and on the impenitent life of sin of self-deceived professing Christians. John Wesley certainly favored this doctrine because he saw in it an antidote to abuses he perceived in the church. As Harper explains,

> But Wesley was not a philosophical theologian so much as a practical one, and what he observed in the eighteenth century was a host of people who used Calvinist theology to rationalize inappropriate behavior. To do this, Wesley maintained, was not to honor a doctrine of security but rather to make Christ a "minister of sin and so build on his righteousness as to live in such ungodliness and unrighteousness as is scarce named even among the Heathens.[3]

There can be no doubt that it is this same zeal for holiness that is driving others in such preaching as well. They have, therefore, in their favor the fact that they recognize the need for sanctification and perseverance in the Christian life. Their strongest point is that they do not give any assurance of salvation to those who are living in sin. The backsliders confronted by this sort of teaching are left under no illusion that they will go to heaven in spite of their godless life.

Another good aspect of this doctrinal position is the serious manner in which it handles the biblical warnings against falling away and apostasy. When Christians who hold this view read in their Bibles that we must be faithful unto death or perish, they grow in their determination to persevere, which is the appropriate response to the warning passages.

WEAK POINTS

On the other hand, they go too far when they state that the fact that the Bible contains such warnings against giving up in the Christian race is proof that true Christians do in some cases fall away. That is not a necessary inference, as will be shown in chapter 6. It is also important to note that the Calvinist doctrine should not be blamed for the sinful lifestyles of insincere

2   J. Steven Harper, *Four Views on Eternal Security* (Grand Rapids: Zondervan, 2002), 240.
3   Ibid., 237.

people, since it does not give any assurance of salvation to those who live in sin either. A doctrine should be held responsible for the impact it produces in the lives of those who truly believe and follow it, not for the misuse it may suffer at the hands of those who distort it.

The biblical solution for nominalism and hypocrisy is not to teach that sin causes one's salvation to be lost. The Bible never treats justification as something that occurs repeatedly. Whoever receives justification by faith is saved, for to be justified and lost at the same time is a contradiction in terms. If someone could be saved then lost and then saved again, we would be forced to conclude that such a person would undergo more than one justification (once at conversion and once more at "rededication").

And what are we to say regarding regeneration? Does deliberate sin cause the convert to lose his or her regeneration? Or would it be possible to remain a regenerate person (spiritually alive), even while unsaved and bound for condemnation? Those who defend the possibility of losing salvation find it difficult to offer biblical solutions to these questions. Their view does not square with the definitive character of salvation as found in the Word of God, which states that whoever believes in Christ has passed from death to life (John 5:24) and attributes our being saved in the present to the fact that God made us alive back when we were dead in our trespasses and sins (Eph. 2:1–7).

This evangelical doctrine of losing salvation is much like the Catholic doctrine in its opinion that uncertainty about future salvation is important to keep Christians living the way they should. In some more extreme cases, this point of view has degenerated to the point of making any assurance of salvation impossible. If it were true—as some would lead us to think—that believers lose their salvation every time they sin consciously, then nobody could claim that any departed brother or sister went to heaven, for there is no way of knowing for sure if a sin was not committed and left unresolved at the moment of death.

Neither could we be optimistic about our own eternity, for we all sin. Who could guarantee that we will not be surprised by death or the return of Christ at a moment when we may be committing a sinful act? Who then could really have peace? The chances are that any Christian, no matter how committed, could end up in hell for all eternity. It may seem that dwelling on such a doctrine will keep Christians who believe in it more vigilant, but it is more likely that it will only make them desperate.

The most disturbing element of this particular view, however, is that it establishes a link between salvation and good works that injures the doctrine of justification by faith alone. True faith produces faithfulness, although not perfect faithfulness. Deliberate sins in the life of believers cannot be explained as momentary lapses of Christian faith. Therefore, if we admit the thesis that deliberate sins result in the loss of salvation, we must affirm that there are two types of believers: the believers who would go to heaven if they departed from this world this very moment and those who would not, despite being genuine believers.

This contradicts Paul's axiom that salvation is through faith in Jesus Christ for *all* who believe (Rom. 3:22). We cannot agree with the idea that it is possible to have genuine faith in Christ and still be under condemnation at the same time. If salvation is received through faith but is then maintained by our good conduct, it is difficult to conclude anything other than that final salvation is obtained through faith *and* good works. Maybe that could be called justification by faith *initially*, but not justification by faith *alone*.

Norman Geisler does not share the theological position of this book, but he is right in his critique of the viewpoint we are now evaluating:

> If believers are not eternally secure but can lose their salvation by bad actions, then Arminianism is a tacit form of works salvation. Indeed, Arminian theologian H. Orton Wiley admits so when he says, "Arminians deny the merit of good works but insist upon them as a condition of salvation." He even notes: "Mr. Wesley's formula was, 'Works, not as a merit, but as a condition.'" Why are works a condition? Because according to the Arminian view, one must maintain good works in order to keep one's salvation. In order to guarantee their ultimate salvation, believers must not perform the kind of bad actions that precipitate the loss of salvation after they are saved.
>
> In fact, the Arminian view is similar to the Roman Catholic view, which demands that once one receives initial justification by grace alone, then one must not commit a mortal sin or else one will lose his or her salvation. But if works are necessary for the maintenance of my salvation, then how can I avoid the conclusion that I am saved by my good works?[4]

We need to be mindful of the fact that this first point of view falls short in as much as it loses sight of the implications of the Gospel. By saying so, I do

---

4   Norman L. Geisler, *Four Views on Eternal Security* (Grand Rapids: Zondervan, 2002), 83.

not intend to imply that people cannot be saved as long as they hold such a position. What I do mean is that those who think in this way are unwittingly being inconsistent with the Gospel in which they themselves believe: the Gospel of salvation by grace through faith.

2 —

The doctrine that believers can lose their salvation only by means of apostasy has enjoyed less popularity than the first doctrine of losing salvation. This second position has received support mainly from some Lutherans and Free Will Baptists, but no denomination has unanimously adopted it. Among the authors who have contended on its behalf are Robert E. Picirilli (*Grace, Faith, Free Will*; Randall House, Nashville, Tennessee, 2002) and Stephen M. Ashby (one of the authors of *Four Views on Eternal Security*, Zondervan, Grand Rapids, Michigan, 2002).

Those who take this position agree with the evaluation that the terms of the Gospel are being overlooked when it is believed that salvation can be lost through deliberate sin. For example, Stephen Ashby writes the following:

> Yet one does not receive God's salvation by turning over a new leaf. It is not by quitting sinning that one becomes justified before God. It is, instead, by faith in Christ. Neither does committing sin after one is saved cause one to become unjustified before God.[5]

Ashby even recognizes how Wesley's position can lead to despair:

> I do not know how to interpret such a view other than to say that if a believer commits a single sin, that sin renders him lost—he being once again a child of the devil, until the moment he repents. If this is the view that Wesley espoused, it is a stark view indeed.[6]

In contrast to the Wesleyan view, Picirilli carefully elaborates a different explanation of how he believes it is possible for salvation to be lost:

> If the Bible teaches that apostasy from a truly regenerate state is possible, one must still be very cautious about expressing or formulating such a view....It is extremely important to express our view in such a way that faith, and not works, is the sole condition of salvation. We must not establish salvation by grace through faith with the right hand and take it away with the left...."Saved by faith and

---

5   Stephen M. Ashby, *Four Views on Eternal Security* (Grand Rapids: Zondervan, 2002), 187.
6   Ibid., 186.

kept by works" simply will not accord with Biblical teaching relative to the basis of salvation.[7]

We must not make sinful acts, in themselves, the cause of falling from grace. Likewise we must not give the impression that every time a saved person sins he is lost and needs saving again. Furthermore we must not make the mistake of implying that saved people do not sin. If faith is the condition for salvation, then unbelief is the "condition" for apostasy.[8]

STRONG POINTS

Just like the first view, this system of interpretation has to its credit that it deals seriously with biblical warnings against apostasy and recognizes the need of persevering unto the end. It is actually superior to the first view, though, because it strives to be more consistent with the doctrine of justification by faith alone (*Sola Fide*). In doing so, it recognizes that a converted individual's salvation is not lost by sinning, it avoids teaching repeated regeneration, and it makes assurance of salvation in the present more stable than the first model does.

WEAK POINTS

The leading advocates of this doctrine perceive how fragile the first one is in the way it introduces works as a condition for staying saved. However, since they are persuaded that the Bible teaches that salvation can be lost, they attempt to offer a doctrine that allows for losing salvation *and* avoids attributing part of salvation to human works. Unfortunately, though, it cannot be said that they have succeeded. It is neither a doctrine that is totally free from attributing salvation to human works, nor is it able to stand under biblical scrutiny.

Just as all the other evangelicals who believe that salvation can be lost, so do these accept the thesis that apostates (or at least some of them) are people who were at one point truly regenerated and justified but who lost their salvation. This opinion is simply mistaken for two main reasons. First, because every attempt at proving that apostates (any apostates) had previously experienced true conversion will fail. Second, because it is a theory that is in direct conflict with biblical passages that explicitly teach that Christ will never lose anyone who belongs to him and with passages

---

7   Robert E. Picirilli, *Grace, Faith, Free Will* (Nashville: Randall House, 2002), 204.

8   Ibid., 205.

that state the spurious nature of the faith of all who abandon the way in the most absolute terms. Consequently, our evaluation of an apostate's spiritual condition prior to his or her defection must be informed by what the Bible teaches on the matter.

It is also a mistake to think that true believers fall back into a life of sin. This is a major premise of both views contending that salvation can be lost. However, since the one we are now focusing on maintains that sins (irrespective of what sins or for how long they go on) cannot constitute a sufficient cause for salvation to be revoked, it leads into yet another error, which is the notion that it is possible to be a believer and live in sin simultaneously.

In reality, this manifests confusion about what saving faith is. The contention of the reformers was that God grants and sustains a living faith in the hearts of believers, the kind that will necessarily produce works. Justification is by faith alone, but the faith that justifies is never alone. As a result, living an impenitent life is proof positive that there is no true faith. This implies that when people return to a life of sin externally it is because they do not possess authentic faith internally.

But according to the doctrine on which we are now focusing, having authentic saving faith will not keep someone from returning to sin and becoming a permanently backslidden Christian. We are left speculating as to the spiritual condition of the person who has forsaken the ways of God but has not renounced his profession of faith.

This creates a real dilemma. On the one hand, if those who preach this doctrine defend themselves by saying that returning to a life of sin is precisely what they mean by renouncing one's faith, then we must question if there is any fundamental difference between their own position and the first position from which they try so hard to disassociate themselves. Taking this route would only lead us right back to debating what the grounds are for sins to become mortal.

If on the other hand they go the other way and say that it is possible to go on living in sin and remain saved all the while, the unintended problem of a license to sin is created. In order to avoid this, they start warning us that it is necessary to do good works for one's faith not to collapse. So in the end we find that works continue to play a vital role in keeping the believer saved. Despite all the rhetoric against a doctrine that preaches "Saved by faith and kept by works," Picirilli ends up admitting that in his own doctrinal system works are what keeps a person saved, albeit indirectly.

> One cannot doubt that faithfulness, right conduct, prayer, and obedience to God are required of Christians, or that they are *important for the Christian's spiritual well-being, and thus eventually for his perseverance*. Even so, these must apparently be understood as integrally related to the faith, which is alone the condition of salvation. In other words, these "works"—if that is the right word— are evidences of faith (for the Christian, perhaps even *means of strengthening or sustaining faith*), but it is the faith and not the evidences of it that saves.[9]

Essentially, what he is telling us is that we remain saved exclusively by faith, but he can't help ascribing the role of sustaining faith to works. This inverts the relationship between faith and works. Instead of faith producing works, it makes faith the result of works. Consequently, it is the doing of works that keeps Christians saved, because those who don't perform good works will eventually lose their salvation when their failure to practice good works causes their faith to wilt and die. Picirilli has taken us a longer way around, but we have arrived at the exact same place.

What becomes very clear is that in this form of doctrine it is not God who grants faith and perseverance unto the saved. On the contrary, these things people do for themselves. They are considered man's role, and God will not act in such a way as to infallibly secure these indispensable aspects of salvation. This is the point at which man must come in with his own contribution, and the way in which he carries out his part includes doing good works (faithfulness, right conduct, prayer, obedience to God, etc.).

It is also obvious that this doctrine doesn't afford its adherents any guarantee that they will continue to do "their part" in the future, which means that they must live their entire lives uncertain about where they will ultimately spend eternity, even if they experience assurance of salvation in the present. Just as in Catholicism, this uncertainty is considered important as a way of driving believers to grow spiritually and overcome in the end.

We need to recognize the real effect that believing this way has on Christians. It causes them to take their eyes off God when it comes to the matter of their final salvation and to focus on themselves instead. They will

---

9   Ibid., 205. (Emphasis added.)

not trust that God will actively keep them unless they first do what they see as their own role in keeping themselves. So they exchange confidence in God's immutable faithfulness for a tenuous trust in their own resolve.

There is also the implication that success in actually making it to heaven under these terms depends to some degree on human achievement. The unavoidable conclusion is that the glory of salvation is shared in that same degree with whoever makes it all the way instead of belonging to God exclusively. So this doctrinal proposition fails as it is inconsistent with the biblical principle that salvation is by grace alone (*Sola Gratia*).

3 —

The teaching that declares it possible for a Christian to live in sin, and even abandon the faith without losing salvation, is enjoying great popularity in some segments of evangelicalism. Two statements by R. T. Kendall sum the position up succinctly:

> What if a person who is saved falls into sin, stays in sin, and is found in that very condition when he dies? Will he still go to heaven? The answer is yes....I therefore state categorically that the person who is saved—who confesses that Jesus is Lord and believes in his heart that God raised Him from the dead—will go to heaven when he dies no matter what work (or lack of work) may accompany such faith.[10]

Calvinists have long been falsely accused of teaching this, but only recently has anyone arisen to actually teach this grotesque caricature of Calvinism. Yet this teaching has gained momentum, particularly among those who deny that submission to Jesus as Lord is necessarily involved in conversion.

Perhaps the only groups from the past that would have agreed with this point of view are the antinomian[11] groups that appear from time to time throughout history. The defenders of this point of view are not antinomians in the strict sense of the word, however, because they are not indifferent about matters of sin and holiness. They recognize that God's laws are binding; they seek to live in a godly manner and preach that Christians should persevere as commanded by God. Only they maintain that those who fail to do so will be saved, all the same. This results from attempting to hold on to the motto "Once saved, always saved," while embracing an Arminian understanding of conversion.

---

10 R. T. Kendall, *Once Saved, Always Saved* (Chicago: Moody Press, 1983), 50–53.

11 Antinomians are people who consider it unnecessary to obey God's moral law.

The basic presupposition of this point of view is a doctrine of free will, which teaches that the internal transformation of a person (regeneration) is not necessary for a person to come to Christ. Once conversion has been defined as a human choice that happens apart from an essential change in the individual's nature, the conclusion that the decision can be reversed later on follows naturally.

That is why advocates of this view find themselves in agreement on one key issue with all those who believe that salvation can be lost: they all build upon the presupposition that converted people can (and in some cases do) return to a life of sin, or even apostatize completely from the faith. The distinctive of this latest view is that it holds to the belief that God's forgiveness continues, no matter what the person may do thereafter.

So how can this view account for the biblical exhortations to persevere and the warnings against apostasy? A typical way of handling them is to claim they have nothing to do with salvation but are meant to convey the message that those who do not persevere will lose recompenses and rewards in eternity, which are totally distinct from the salvation of the soul. So once again, they follow the old Arminian reasoning that the existence of warning passages proves that true Christians can fall away, but they've come up with a novel interpretation about what is really at stake. They argue that the loss we are warned about is nothing more than a reduction in the number of rewards to be enjoyed in eternity. In so much, they stand with Arminians in their conviction that the saints do not necessarily persevere and would concede that salvation can be lost, but for the fact that they consider perseverance as unnecessary for entering eternal life.

Because of the great amount of work done to spread this view, it has been gaining ground among evangelicals. In 1986, Robert Wilkin founded the Grace Evangelical Society, a foundation responsible for publications and a website (www.faithalone.org) "to focus worldwide attention on the distinction between the freeness of eternal life and the costliness of eternal rewards."[12]

Some of the main proponents have been Zane Hodges (*The Gospel Under Siege: A Study on Faith and Works*, Rendención Viva, Dallas, 1991; and *Absolutely Free! A Biblical Reply to Lordship Salvation*, Zondervan, Grand Rapids, Michigan, 1989), R. T. Kendall (*Once Saved, Always Saved*, Moody Press, Chicago, 1983), and Michael Eaton (*No Condemnation: A New Theology of Assurance*, InterVarsity Press, Downers Grove, Illinois, 1995).

---

12   Thomas R. Schreiner and Ardel B. Caneday, *The Race Set Before Us* (Downers Grove: InterVarsity Press, 2001), 24–25.

STRONG POINTS

There are two motivating factors behind this theological position that are both noble in themselves. One goal is to do justice to the biblical passages that affirm the eternal security of those who receive Christ. The other goal is to keep human works and merit completely out of the gospel of grace.

> Advocates of this view see themselves as guardians of the gospel, the only consistent preachers of the free grace of the gospel of Jesus Christ and the champions against others who introduce the idea of meriting or earning salvation.[13]

Even so, this doctrine is so weak that it is hard to speak of it as really having strong points. Although it is clear that its proponents seek at all costs to avoid teaching that salvation is by works, they go about it in such a clumsy way that they end up subverting other aspects of the Gospel message while still failing to completely exclude human works from their system.

This is true, first of all, because they do not explain how faith can come about initially without being considered a human work, especially since they so vehemently insist that requiring ongoing faith after conversion is to preach salvation by works. Secondly, their doctrine denies the patent biblical truth that saving faith results in good works. And while it may be true that they try to underscore the biblical teaching that Christ never loses any of his own, they fall into an extremist position by maintaining only one aspect of Calvinistic doctrine in isolation from its complimentary emphasis that the saints persevere, with no exceptions. Praising such a half-truth makes one uneasy. It feels somewhat like congratulating a theological liberal on his Christology for affirming the true humanity of Christ.

WEAK POINTS

It is impossible to contend for this teaching without doing violence to many biblical passages that speak of the need to persevere and the clear warnings addressed to those who live in sin to the effect that they will be excluded from the kingdom of God (1 Cor. 6:9–10; Gal. 5:19–21; Eph. 5:5–6; Rev. 21:8; etc.). Contradicting the Word of God in this way leads to grave dangers.

The most obvious is that it induces a false sense of security. There are people out there today who believe they are saved because one day they made a profession of faith but who do not follow Christ. They may have

---

13   Ibid., 25.

heard that their condition is that of a "carnal Christian" or that they have Christ as Savior and just haven't made him their Lord. With their consciences at ease, they remain unalarmed by the presence of deliberate, ongoing sin in their lives.

Those who live in sin are not saved, and they need to know it. What is at stake is not that of how many rewards they will receive but the eternal destiny of their souls. They need to flee the wrath to come; they must seek the Lord while he may be found, and it is the responsibility of God's people on earth to tell them so. Our role as a church is to warn the wicked to turn from his way (Ezek. 33:8). Otherwise, we will become like blind watchmen or silent dogs that cannot bark (Isa. 56:10).

The Bible says that faith that does not produce works is dead (James 2:17). If someone claims to have faith but does not have works, the real issue is that there is no living faith. Believing that dead faith can save is not believing in justification by faith alone, it is believing in justification apart from faith. Some are willing to go so far as to say that a believer can commit apostasy and remain saved without any kind of faith. By this theory, there are saved unbelievers! As Dr. John Gerstner put it, far from being the perseverance of the saints, this doctrine teaches the preservation of the sinner.[14]

Another danger presents itself in the way the preaching of the Gospel is affected by the persuasion that temporary faith secures eternal life. This opens the doors to all types of manipulation in evangelism and tends to dilute the message, omitting its more offensive elements. Preaching the Gospel is preaching the narrow way; it is preaching repentance for forgiveness of sins; it is calling men and women to deny themselves, take up the cross, and follow Christ to the end. This may not be what the world wants to hear, but it's the Gospel.

Teaching that someone can be saved without following Christ to the end is tampering with the Gospel. Those who do so are preaching faith without works, forgiveness without repentance from sin, security without perseverance, and Christianity without bearing the cross. This type of message only serves to strengthen the hands of evildoers so that no one turns from his evil (Jer. 23:14).

In spite of the claims made by the preachers of this view that they alone are consistent with the gospel of free grace and that they stand as

14   John H. Gerstner, *Wrongly Dividing the Word of Truth: A Critique of Dispensationalism* (Brentwood: Wolgemuth and Hyatt Publishers, 1991), 142ff.

the champions of grace opposing others' attempts to introduce merit into salvation, we will not find in their teaching the biblical doctrine of salvation by grace alone (*Sola Gratia*). The Bible most certainly is opposed to any doctrine of self-salvation. It emphatically teaches that men cannot do anything to save themselves. But this is not incoherent with the biblical teaching that those who enter eternal life are those who believe in Christ and persevere in faith and sanctification.

Understanding how divine grace operates is a key issue. Grace is not only active in the divine court making God's pardon a reality; grace operates within the man himself. It is the working of God's grace that brings the sinner to Christ, converting the heart and granting the gift of faith. This same grace continues to operate in the Christian throughout all his life, producing an ongoing and progressive sanctification. God's plan for his people includes good works—never as criteria for obtaining salvation, of course, but always as its fruit—and no one is an exception. "For we are his workmanship, created in Christ Jesus for good works, which God prepared beforehand, that we should walk in them" (Eph. 2:10).

This is precisely why salvation is by grace, because only the grace of God can transform a sinner into a saint. A fallen human being will never rise up, convert to Christ, and follow Christ unto the end, unless God works to bring this about out of his pure grace. And that is exactly what it means to be saved by God. It means to be reached by divine grace, transformed into a saint, and then be kept by the power of God, through faith, for the salvation that is ready to be revealed in the last time.

> Jesus is "the author and perfecter of our faith." The word *author* (archegos) means that Jesus is the "originator" or "founder" of our faith. In other words, our faith is the gift of God. Not only does our faith come from him, but he also sustains our faith; he is also the "perfecter" or the one who completes our faith. Saying that we must run the race to the end can scarcely be called works-righteousness, since such persevering faith is ultimately the gift of God![15]

These considerations point us toward the fourth view.

---

15 Thomas R. Schreiner and Ardel B. Caneday, *The Race Set Before Us* (Downers Grove: InterVarsity Press, 2001), 314.

4 —

The reformed doctrine of the perseverance of the saints continues to find support in many churches. Historically, it has been the official doctrine of several churches, including the Presbyterian, Baptist, and Congregational denominations.

This book is an attempt to demonstrate that it is correct. It doesn't make the mistake of sacrificing one biblical truth over another. It affirms that only those who persevere in faith until the end will be saved, but it does not fall into the error of teaching that salvation can be lost because it understands that, by the grace of God, all saints persevere. Such is the doctrine of the perseverance of the saints.

The One Who Endures to the End Will Be Saved

Now, however, I am arguing not concerning the beginning of faith...but of that perseverance which must be had even to the end—which assuredly even the saints, who do the will of God, seek when they say in prayer, "Thy will be done." Where the saints pray for this, they are found to be praying for perseverance; since no one attains to that highest blessedness which is in the kingdom, unless he shall persevere unto the end in that holiness which he has received on earth.[16]   (Augustine)

What message are people hearing in churches today on the matter of perseverance? Is there a proper emphasis on the need for perseverance? Judging from what some people are saying, the idea of "Once saved, always saved" is accompanied in some minds by an implicit "whether one perseveres in the faith or not."

We hear a mother asking for prayer, saying, "My son has gone astray from the Lord, but I know that he is saved because I remember the day he asked Jesus to come into his heart." We get news that a church member has left and joined a heretical cult, but the news bearer quickly adds, "I told him that if he doesn't come back he would lose his rewards, although he'd still be saved." A pastor receives a request to speak at a funeral of man he did not know personally, so he asks if he was converted. In reply, he is told, "Oh, yes. He's had nothing to do with church for many years, but he was saved and baptized as a kid."

Cases like these go to show there is a lot of confusion in churches today about the need for perseverance. One would wish it were nothing more than a misunderstanding, which would inevitably be corrected as soon as people

---

16 Augustine, *Augustin: Anti-Pelagian Writings, The Gift of Perseverance*, ed. Philip Schaff, Volume 5 of *The Nicene and Post-Nicene Fathers, Series 1*, The Master Christian Library (Rio, WI: Ages Software Inc., 2000), 1234–1235.

came to realize what is really taught in their churches. But such is not the case. That is exactly what is being taught in a great number of churches nowadays.

It is a very basic principle that true conversion is manifest by its fruits, one of which is perseverance. The belief that persevering unto the end is necessary for salvation was so uniform in the early church that Augustine could declare, without fear of contradiction, that all Christians in his day agreed on that point. He confidently asserts that even a Christian who had served Christ for thirty years would be lost if he apostatized one day before dying.

> For what Christian would dare to deny that the righteous man, if he should be prematurely laid hold of by death, will be in repose? Let who will, say this, and what man of sound faith will think that he can withstand it? Moreover, if he should say that the righteous man, if he should depart from his righteousness in which he has long lived, and should die in that impiety after having lived in it, I say not a year, but one day, will go hence into the punishment due to the wicked, his righteousness having no power in the future to avail him—will any believer contradict this evident truth?[17]

We could not say the same in our days. In our present scenario, there are believers contending against this evident truth. In the 1980s, a controversy broke out among dispensationalists concerning the Lordship of Christ in salvation because some were openly stating that a sinner can be saved without renouncing sin. This error led to the publication of refutations such as *The Gospel According to Jesus* (John MacArthur, Zondervan, 1989, Grand Rapids, Michigan) and *Christ the Lord* (edited by Michael Horton, Baker Book House Company, 1992, Grand Rapids, Michigan).

THE CONTEMPORARY ATTEMPTS TO DENY THE NEED FOR PERSEVERANCE

This misguided doctrine bears directly upon the doctrine of perseverance, for if someone believes that a change of life is not an essential part of salvation, he will naturally believe that going back to the ways of this world after conversion is a matter of no consequence as far as salvation is concerned.

But the confusion is not limited to those who deny the Lordship of Christ in conversion. The concept of unconditional security in salvation has

---

17 Augustine, *Augustin: Anti-Pelagian Writings, The Predestination of the Saints*, ed. Philip Schaff, Volume 5 of *The Nicene and Post-Nicene Fathers, Series 1*, The Master Christian Library (Rio, WI: Ages Software Inc., 2000), 1204.

been gradually spreading throughout the church for decades and is being articulated by an ever greater number of evangelical authors.

Lewis S. Chafer seems to have helped lead the way by weakening the message of texts that declare the need for perseverance. For instance, he argued that Jesus's words "But the one who endures to the end will be saved" (Matt. 24:14) cannot be applied to anyone in our days but only to people who live during a future tribulation period. He claimed, "The verse refers to those who survive the Tribulation and are rescued by Jesus Christ at His second coming."[18]

His interpretation equates the word *endure* (or *persevere*, as in some translations) with *survive*, as if the verse meant simply that whoever makes it through the tribulation alive will be rescued (saved) from the tribulation by Christ's return.

Following this interpretation, it became popular to emphasize that Matthew 24:14 does not mean that the believer must endure unto the end in order to be saved. But that is exactly what the verse says. A comparison with Luke's account reinforces that the meaning of the words Jesus spoke on that occasion can be no other: "By standing firm you will gain life" (Luke 21:19, NIV).

Besides this, the word *but* in Matthew 24:13 points back to the immediate preceding context:

> Then they will deliver you up to tribulation and put you to death, and you will be hated by all nations for my name's sake. And then many will fall away and betray one another and hate one another. And many false prophets will arise and lead many astray. And because lawlessness will be increased, the love of many will grow cold. But the one who endures to the end will be saved.   (Matt. 24:9–13)

The context shows Jesus warning his disciples that many will fall away. He predicts persecution, false prophets, and the increase of lawlessness, factors which will cause many to go astray or grow cold in their love. "But," he adds, "the one who endures to the end will be saved."

Calvin's exegesis of this text brings out this necessary connection with its context:

---

18 Lewis S. Chafer, *Major Bible Themes*, rev. by John Walvoord (Grand Rapids: Zondervan, 1981), 223.

Christ requires from his followers, on the other hand, such courage as to persist in striving against it; as Paul also enjoins us *not to be weary of performing deeds of kindness and beneficence* (2 Thessalonians 3:13). Although, then, the charity of many, overwhelmed by the mass of iniquities, should give way, Christ warns believers that they must surmount this obstacle, lest, overcome by bad examples, they apostatize. And therefore he repeats the statement, that no man can be saved, *unless he strive lawfully,* (2 Timothy 2:5) so as to *persevere to the end.*[19]

Spurgeon's explanation is equally useful:

Again our Savior reminded his disciples of the personal responsibility of each one of them in such a time of trial and testing as they were about to pass through. He would have them remember that it is not the man who starts in the race, but the one who runs to the goal, who wins the prize: *"He that shall endure unto the end, the same."* If this doctrine were not supplemented by another, there would be but little good tidings for poor, tempted, tried, and struggling saints in such words as these. Who among us would persevere in running the heavenly race if God did not preserve us from falling, and give us persevering grace? But, blessed be his name, "The righteous shall hold on his way." "He which hath begun a good work in you will perform it until the day of Jesus Christ."[20]

There is no justification for the attempt at neutralizing the biblical message of the need for perseverance. Indeed, doing so is dangerous. Our Lord's intent is precisely to caution us that whoever fails to persevere unto the end will not be saved. That is his loud and clear warning, directed to Christians of every generation. It is most unfortunate that other voices would attempt to drown it out.

One of the most outspoken voices in this sense has been Zane Hodges, professor of theology for twenty-seven years at Dallas Theological Seminary. Hodges has used all his influence as theology professor, as the author of books and articles, and as a preacher to energetically spread the doctrine of unconditional security, even for "ex-believers."

---

19 John Calvin, *Commentary on Matthew*, Mark, Luke, Vol. 3, *The John Calvin Collection* (Rio, WI: Ages Software Inc., 2000), 97 (emphasis in original).
20 Charles H. Spurgeon, *The Gospel According to Matthew*, The Master Christian Library (Rio, WI: Ages Software Inc., 2000), 352.

A typical example is his recorded message entitled "The Peril of Not Growing" in which he offers an interpretation of the warning passage found in Hebrews 6. His thesis is that the biblical text concerns saved individuals who continue in possession of eternal life even though they abandon the faith. The following personal experience is told to illustrate the point:

> I have a friend, and more than a friend, a man who labored with me side by side in the ministry of God's Word in the little group that has become Victor St. Bible Chapel and this friend has fallen away from the Christian faith....He graduated from Bob Jones University and from Dallas Theological Seminary. And about the time when he and his wife left Dallas his wife contracted a very serious illness which over the years got progressively worse until she was reduced to being a complete invalid, and after the death of his wife I visited my friend (who now lives in the Midwest and who teaches Ancient History in a secular university). And as we sat in the living room together, face to face, he told me very frankly, but graciously that he no longer claimed to be a Christian at all, that he no longer believed the things that he had once preached and taught. And the situation was even worse than he described, because I heard through others that in the classroom on the university campus he often mocked and ridiculed the Christian faith. And as I sat in that living room I was very painfully aware that it was impossible for me to talk that man into changing his mind. It was impossible for me to talk him back to the conviction he had once held. It was impossible for me to renew him to repentance. You want to find someone harder to deal with than an unsaved person? Find a person like that...

> Oh, how disgraceful for a man to have known the truth and proclaimed the truth and then to deny the truth! He has put the Son of God to an open shame! Well you say, "I guess he's headed for hell, right? I guess he's headed for eternal damnation. He's renounced his Christian faith." Wait a minute. I didn't say that, and neither does the writer of Hebrews. Let me remind you that Jesus said, "I am the bread of life. He that cometh to Me shall never hunger and he that believeth on Me shall never thirst." And he also said, "He that cometh to Me I shall in no wise cast out."...God's will is that he lose no one. He has never lost anyone and he never will! And I grieve because my friend and brother has lost his faith but Christ has not lost him. He

has lost his faith, but Christ has not lost him! Do you believe in the grace of God?[21]

The question he asks at the end of the account crystalizes his argument. Salvation is by grace—that is, it is an unmerited favor. The argument runs that requiring the Christian to do anything after conversion to remain saved would make salvation conditioned on human works. Not one thing whatsoever can be required, for "if it is by grace, it is no longer on the basis of works; otherwise grace would no longer be grace" (Rom. 11:6).

From this, he deduces that once someone has believed the Gospel, he or she will never have to do anything else in order to stay saved, not even believe the Gospel. Everyone who rejects this conclusion is then charged with denying that salvation is by grace.

It is surprising that Hodges doesn't recognize how this line of reasoning is inherently inconsistent. If believing in Christ constituted a meritorious work, believing could not be required for a person to be saved at any time, not even at the moment of receiving salvation. Anyone preaching for the unconverted to believe and be saved would be silenced by this same objection.

But of course, only those who believe in Christ as Savior will be saved, and whoever does not believe will be condemned (Mark 16:16). Even Hodges admits this. Just as believing in Christ as Savior in order to get saved is not at odds with salvation by grace, it is not contrary to salvation by grace to require continued faith after conversion either. And since true faith produces works, the one who continues to believe will never cease to produce good fruit, even though this fruit is never the basis for establishing one's righteousness before God.

To be saved, it is necessary to believe in Christ and to persevere in faith. That is why the Bible speaks of our being kept unto our final salvation by the power of God *through faith* (1 Pet. 1:5).

Hodges's position is unsustainable in light of Scripture. In order to defend it, he is forced to come up with unheard of interpretations for several biblical texts. Notice the following texts and his understanding of them:

Do you not know that the unrighteous will not inherit the kingdom of God? Do not be deceived: neither the sexually immoral, nor idolaters,

---

21 Zane Hodges, *The Peril of Not Growing*, accessed October 3, 2016, https://redeeminggod.com/hodges-on-hebrews-part-6/.

nor adulterers, nor men who practice homosexuality, nor thieves, nor the greedy, nor drunkards, nor revilers, nor swindlers will inherit the kingdom of God. (1 Cor. 6:9–10)

Now the works of the flesh are evident: sexual immorality, impurity, sensuality, idolatry, sorcery, enmity, strife, jealousy, fits of anger, rivalries, dissensions, divisions, envy, drunkenness, orgies, and things like these. I warn you, as I warned you before, that those who do such things will not inherit the kingdom of God. (Gal. 5:19–21)

So as not to admit that the texts above exclude those who live in sin from any participation in eternal life, Hodges and his associates argue that there is a distinction between inheriting the kingdom of God and being saved. "There is no difficulty at all in speaking of people who live in the Kingdom of God but who do not inherit that Kingdom...the heirs of the Kingdom, then, are its owners, not merely its residents or citizens."[22]

Along these same lines, Joseph Dillow maintains that "all Christians will enter the kingdom, but not all will rule there, i.e., inherit it....They will, having been justified, be in the kingdom; however, they will not inherit it....There is a difference between being a resident of the kingdom and inheriting it."[23]

This unnatural reading of these passages cannot withstand a comparison with other passages of Scripture, where we find that being an heir of the kingdom of God is synonymous with being saved and that all who are saved inherit the kingdom:

And if children, then heirs—heirs of God and fellow heirs with Christ, provided we suffer with him in order that we may also be glorified with him. (Rom. 8:17)

And if you are Christ's, then you are Abraham's offspring, heirs according to promise. (Gal. 3:29)

So that being justified by his grace we might become heirs according to the hope of eternal life. (Titus 3:7)

And now I commend you to God and to the word of his grace, which is able to build you up and to give you the inheritance among all those who are sanctified. (Acts 20:32)

---

22 Zane C. Hodges, *Grace in Eclipse* (Dallas: Redencion Viva, 1985), 71.

23 Joseph C. Dillow, *The Reign of the Servant Kings* (Miami Springs, Florida: Schoettle Publishing Co., 1992), 62, 64, 78.

> To open their eyes, in order to turn them from darkness to light, and from the power of Satan to God, that they may receive forgiveness of sins and an inheritance among those who are sanctified by faith in Me.　　　　　　　　　　　　　　　　　(Acts 26:18 NKJV)

> Therefore he is the mediator of a new covenant, so that those who are called may receive the promised eternal inheritance, since a death has occurred that redeems them from the transgressions committed under the first covenant.　　　　　　　(Heb. 9:15)

In consideration of these Scriptures, there can be no other conclusion than that people who practice the works of the flesh in an ongoing and impenitent way will go to hell. There is no other possible meaning to the words of Scripture. These verses apply to all people indiscriminately. This means the only way we can believe that all those who experience salvation are saved forever is if we have strong reasons to believe that saved people, regardless of what they may have been in the past, never revert to being sexually immoral, nor idolaters, nor adulterers, nor people who practice homosexuality, nor thieves, nor greedy, nor drunkards, nor revilers, nor swindlers (1 Cor. 6:9–10).

Several parts of John's epistles are an embarrassment to those who take Hodges's position. The apostle John explicitly states that all those who live in sin today have never seen God, nor have they known God, nor have they proceeded from God:

> Beloved, do not imitate evil but imitate good. Whoever does good is from God; whoever does evil has not seen God.　　　(3 John 1:11)

> No one who abides in him keeps on sinning; no one who keeps on sinning has either seen him or known him.　　　　　(1 John 3:6)

To defend his position when faced with these texts, Hodges is obliged to say that seeing God and knowing God must refer to a deeper dimension in the Christian life, which is not reached by every person who possesses eternal life. But in John's writings, eternal life is defined in these very terms: "And this is eternal life, that they know you the only true God, and Jesus Christ whom you have sent" (John 17:3).

When we read 1 John 3:6 in its context, we see that its purpose is to point out the difference that exists between a person who has been born of God and one who is a child of the devil, so that we may tell them apart.

Notice how John makes this plain as he proceeds with the following:

8

Whoever makes a practice of sinning is of the devil, for the devil has been sinning from the beginning. The reason the Son of God appeared was to destroy the works of the devil. No one born of God makes a practice of sinning, for God's seed abides in him, and he cannot keep on sinning because he has been born of God. By this it is evident who are the children of God, and who are the children of the devil: whoever does not practice righteousness is not of God, nor is the one who does not love his brother.   (1 John 3:8-10)

The apostle John's choice of words is too clear to be misunderstood if carefully considered. The one who is born of God does not make a practice of sinning, while the person who does so has not been born of God but is a child of the devil. Having made this point, John concludes by stating that this is how we can tell who the children of God are and who the children of the devil are; by this, he says, it becomes evident. To be born of God is to be born again, to become a child of God. Once more, it could only be true that some saved people live in sin if it were true that some saved people are children of the devil who were never born of God.

Another unprecedented idea we find in Hodges is his thesis that what is described as dead faith in James 2:14 is true saving faith.[24] Interpretations like these have not caused Hodges to be marginalized, though. He is far from being alone. In 1990, Charles Stanley (two-time president of the Southern Baptist Convention and featured speaker on *In Touch* radio and television broadcasts) published a book on the security of the believer, popularizing the same view:

> In his book *Absolutely Free* (Grand Rapids, Mich: Zondervan, 1989), Zane Hodges devotes an entire chapter to the concept of shipwrecked faith. He argues convincingly that Satan can completely shipwreck a believer's faith but that this in no way affects the believer's security.[25]

This kind of reasoning guides Stanley's approach each step of the way. As he puts it, "The Bible clearly teaches that God's love for His people is of such magnitude that even those who walk away from the faith have not the slightest chance of slipping from His hand."[26] Stanley tries to find proof for his point of view in the parables of Jesus. He claims the parable of the prodigal son proves his point as it tells of a son of God who comes back

---

24 Zane C. Hodges, *The Gospel Under Siege* (Dallas: Redencion Viva, 1981), 19–33.

25 Charles Stanley, *Eternal Security, Can You Be Sure* (Nashville: Oliver-Nelson Books, 1991), 91.

26 Stanley, *Eternal Security*, 74.

from the world but never ceased to be a son.

> In his mind, he had forfeited all rights to sonship. He was of the conviction that by abandoning his father and wasting his inheritance, he had relinquished his position in the family. His father, however, did not see things that way at all. In his mind *once a son, always a son*....He did not say, "This was my son and now he is my son again." On the contrary, there is no hint that the *relationship* was ever broken, only the *fellowship*.[27]

It is curious how others have used this same parable in an attempt to prove that salvation can be lost. They point out that the conclusion of the parable says the prodigal son was dead during his rebellion and see this as evidence that he only regained his salvation when he repented and returned to the father. The exact words of Scripture are, "For this your brother was dead, and is alive; he was lost, and is found" (Luke 15:32).

So who is right here? Actually, both interpretations fail because they both start out wrong. The prodigal son is not intended to portray a child of God who rebels and goes astray from the Heavenly Father. Just because he is a son in the symbolism of a parable doesn't necessarily mean he stands for an adopted and redeemed child of God. That is not the analogy.

Keep in mind that the older son stands for people who are full of self-righteousness, namely the Pharisees, who never believed in Christ and who had never been children of God. This parable of our Lord illustrates the conversion of people like the publicans and sinners of the immediate context (Luke 15:1) who finally come to faith and repentance after living in notorious sin. This parable doesn't have anything to say about continuing saved while abandoning oneself to a life of sin, nor about a temporary loss of salvation.

Stanley makes a similar mistake dealing with the parable of the talents (Matt. 25:14–30) by assuming all three characters represent saved people just because they are called "servants." Hence, in his effort to prove that there can be no loss of salvation, he feels compelled to somehow prove that the wicked and slothful servant was saved in the end, even though his condemnation is clearly spelled out: "And cast the worthless servant into the

---

27 Stanley, *Eternal Security*, 51–52 (emphasis in original).

outer darkness. In that place there will be weeping and gnashing of teeth" (Matt. 25:30).

Stanley contends these words do not indicate being sentenced to hell but only to a place within the kingdom of God, which is separate from the place of honor where the faithful men and women will get to stay.

> It certainly does not mean hell in the parable....There is no mention of pain or fire or worms. ...*The kingdom of God will not be the same for all believers*. ...Some will reign with Christ; others will not. Some will be rich in the kingdom of God; others will be poor.[28]

So according to Stanley's interpretation, faithful Christians will enter into the joy of the Lord while others will remain outside, weeping and gnashing their teeth within the bounds of the kingdom.

However, as we examine the Gospels, we discover that in Jesus's use of language, the "outer darkness" where there is "weeping and gnashing of teeth" is the "fiery furnace" where the wicked are burned (Matt. 13:42), it's where the evil are cast (Matt. 13:50), it is the destiny of those who are not clothed in Christ's righteousness (Matt. 22:13), it's the lot of those who are called but not chosen (Matt. 22:14), it's the fate of the hypocrites (Matt. 24:51), it's the end that befalls those who will see Abraham, Isaac, Jacob, and all the prophets in the kingdom of God but will themselves be cast out (Luke 13:28). The sentence pronounced upon the worthless servant is, indeed, eternal condemnation.

What should be readily understood is that the worthless servant was intended to portray a hypocrite, not an authentic Christian. Every true believer bears fruit. It is the tree that does not bear good fruit that is cut down and thrown into the fire. No objection is being raised to the idea that there are Christians who are more faithful than others and that the Bible speaks of rewards for faithfulness in addition to salvation (cf. Luke 19:12–27). Even so, it is an error to consider the privilege of reigning with Christ as something distinct from salvation. Although there will be one who sits at the right hand of Christ and another at his left, none will be poor in the kingdom of heaven.

Stanley produces a few texts in an attempt to support his position. In Luke 12:33, Jesus said that we should provide moneybags for ourselves "that do not grow old, with a treasure in the heavens that does not fail, where no thief approaches and no moth destroys." He sees in this text the inference

---

28 Stanley, *Eternal Security*, 125 (emphasis in original).

that only some will be rich in heaven. He likewise points to 2 Timothy 2:11–13, where we read the following:

> The saying is trustworthy, for: If we have died with him, we will also live with him; if we endure, we will also reign with him; if we deny him, he also will deny us; if we are faithless, he remains faithful—for he cannot deny himself.

It is Stanley's understanding that those who do not persevere in faith make it to heaven, but miss out on reigning with Christ. The phrase "He will also deny us" is explained as nothing more than Christ denying certain rewards and privileges to those who deny him, but which are totally unrelated to salvation itself.

Norman Geisler agrees with this way of interpreting and comments:

> Some Arminians take this to mean that these believers will be denied heaven. However, there is a better way to understand this. The immediate context reveals that Paul is speaking about a denial of *reward*, not of salvation, since the phrase just before he said, "If we endure, we will also reign with him." But reigning is part of a believer's reward (cf. Rev. 20:6; 22:12), not part of salvation, which one receives even if one loses his or her reward (cf. 1 Cor. 3:15). Further, the next verse makes it clear that we cannot lose our salvation, for it declares, "If we are faithless, he will remain faithful, for he cannot disown himself" (2 Tim. 2:13).[29]

Stanley goes so far as to compare salvation with getting a tattoo, which, once it is done, cannot be undone, even if the person who got it regrets it immediately and goes on to hate it for the rest of his or her life.[30] Geisler promotes this same concept by means of a similar illustration:

---

29 Norman L. Geisler, *Four Views on Eternal Security* (Grand Rapids: Zondervan, 2002), 97 (emphasis in original).

30 Charles Stanley, *Eternal Security, Can You Be Sure* (Nashville: Oliver-Nelson Books, 1991), 80. He writes the following: "If I choose to have a tattoo put on my arm, that would involve a one-time act on my part. Yet the tattoo would remain with me indefinitely. I don't have to maintain an attitude of fondness for tattoos to ensure that the tattoo remains on my arm. In fact I may change my mind the minute I receive it. But that does not change the fact that I have a tattoo on my arm. My request for the tattoo and the tattoo itself are two entirely different things. I received it by asking and paying for it. But asking for my money back and changing my attitude will not undo what is done. Forgiveness/salvation is applied at the moment of faith. It is not the same thing as faith. And its permanence is not contingent upon the permanence of one's faith."

12

"Some decisions in life are one way, with no possibility of reversing them—suicide, for example. Saying 'oops' after jumping off a cliff will not reverse the decision."[31]

Geisler recommends Stanley's book but draws back from endorsing his position completely. "Charles Stanley is wrong in affirming that one who ceases to believe in Christ is truly a saved person. This view, originating with Zane Hodges, lacks biblical support,"[32] he asserts. Yet he makes statements that give the idea that a moment of decision for Christ is enough to guarantee eternal salvation, whether accompanied by any lasting faith or not.

> Thus, the act of faith that is the condition for receiving the gift of salvation can be a moment of decision. ...If an initial act of belief were not sufficient for salvation but required a continual process, then there is no way Scripture could pronounce that one has already received the gift of eternal life as a present possession, which it does.[33]

If Geisler's position is not identical to that of Stanley and Hodges, pointing out the differences will prove to be challenging. After all, he clearly believes it is possible to cast off the solemn warnings against apostasy found in the book of Hebrews and go right on to heaven suffering merely the loss of spiritual growth. Note how he deals with the following passages:

> Therefore we must pay much closer attention to what we have heard, lest we drift away from it.   (Heb. 2:1)

> But Christ is faithful over God's house as a son. And we are his house if indeed we hold fast our confidence and our boasting in our hope.
>   (Heb. 3:6)

> For we share in Christ, if indeed we hold our original confidence firm to the end.   (Heb. 3:14)

> Moreover, the context indicates that the author of Hebrews is speaking about practical and progressive holiness, not our positional and perfect holiness in Christ.[34]

> Like the other warnings in Hebrews (see 6:4–7; 10:26–29), the context indicates that these believers are warned about losing their

---

31 Norman L. Geisler, *Four Views on Eternal Security* (Grand Rapids: Zondervan, 2002), 87.

32 Ibid., 198.

33 Ibid., 86.

34 Ibid., 84.

rewards, not their salvation, which is an "eternal redemption." ...To drift away is not a figure of speech indicating a loss of salvation. Later warnings to the same audience indicate that the author is speaking of a loss of "maturity."[35]

Thus, there is no loss of salvation here. Rather, it is a loss of "maturity" (6:1) and growth (5:13−14), which is precisely the context of the discussion.[36]

For if we go on sinning deliberately after receiving the knowledge of the truth, there no longer remains a sacrifice for sins, but a fearful expectation of judgment, and a fury of fire that will consume the adversaries. Anyone who has set aside the law of Moses dies without mercy on the evidence of two or three witnesses. How much worse punishment, do you think, will be deserved by the one who has spurned the Son of God, and has profaned the blood of the covenant by which he was sanctified, and has outraged the Spirit of grace? For we know him who said, "Vengeance is mine; I will repay." And again, "The Lord will judge his people." It is a fearful thing to fall into the hands of the living God.   (Heb. 10:26−31)

As strong as this sounds, like the other warning passages in Hebrews, this too is not a warning about loss of salvation but about loss of rewards.[37]

Geisler's words make it clear that he believes a true Christian can drift away from the truths of the Gospel and fail to hold fast to the end. But what is even more alarming is his opinion that whoever does so will remain saved, notwithstanding. This is not handling biblical texts objectively, but Geisler does it over and over. Here are a few more examples:

And you, who once were alienated and hostile in mind, doing evil deeds, he has now reconciled in his body of flesh by his death, in order to present you holy and blameless and above reproach before him, if indeed you continue in the faith, stable and steadfast, not shifting from the hope of the gospel that you heard, which has been proclaimed in all creation under heaven, and of which I, Paul, became a minister.   (Col. 1:21−23)

---

35 Ibid., 98.
36 Ibid., 99.
37 Ibid., 100.

The reference to continuing steadfastly in the faith in Colossians 1:23 is best taken as implying that, if we so continue walking in the Christian faith, we will be rewarded by Christ when we are presented before his judgment seat. Other passages dealing with continued faithfulness in the Christian life also refer to faithfulness that yields a reward for service, not the gift of salvation. For example, Jesus says, "Be faithful, even to the point of death, and I will give you the crown of life." (Rev. 2:10)[38]

These statements can only mean one thing. In his view, a Christian who doesn't continue in the faith will continue to be saved. A Christian may remain saved even without being faithful to the point of death. Geisler argues that turning away in this manner would only result in missing out on certain rewards that go beyond salvation, such as the "crown of life."

It is sad to find evangelical preachers and authors spreading this idea. The Bible does teach that only those who are faithful to Christ unto death will enter God's eternal kingdom. Biblical interpreters have always identified the crown of life with eternal life itself. Receiving the crown of life is the same as being crowned with eternal life. The attempts to reinterpret the passages above are a mere exercise in futility.

We may admire the effort on the part of these authors at being consistent when faced with these texts, but since they realize that their doctrine can only be reconciled with Scripture by formulating such untenable interpretations, it would be better if they would rethink their doctrinal system instead of proceeding to follow it to the last consequences.

Rendering a different meaning to the Bible's warning passages ends up subverting the intent of the texts. As the Baptist scholar John Gill explains, the words of Colossians 1:23 are meant to push Christians on to persevere by reminding us all that apostates will most certainly not share in salvation:

> But that faith and continuance in it were necessary means of their presentation in unblemished holiness and righteousness; for if they had not faith, or did not abide in it or if the good work of grace was not wrought upon their souls, and that performed until the day of Christ, they could not be presented holy and blameless: this shows the necessity of the saints' final perseverance in faith and holiness,

---

38   Ibid., 85.

and is mentioned with this view, to put them upon a concern about it, and to make use of all means, under divine grace, to enjoy it.[39]

Nothing could be plainer to the reader of Hebrews than that it warns us not to give up our Christian faith in face of adversity on pain of eternal damnation. In the case of those who do not persevere, there no longer remains a sacrifice for their sins; instead, there is a fearful expectation of judgment and a fury of fire that will consume them as adversaries (Heb. 10:26–27).

Although Geisler does not venture into a detailed study of Hebrews, he invites us to examine the larger context of its warning passages. He assures us that in doing so we will find that they invariably seek to prevent a course of action that would result in the loss of spiritual growth and rewards, but not having anything to do with salvation or perdition. We can take him up on this challenge.

The goal of the book of Hebrews is to warn against renouncing or abandoning the Christian faith in the midst of trials and persecution. The specific temptation that presented itself to the Hebrews in the church was that of returning to Judaism. The epistle is an exhortation not to do so and a warning to those who depart as to what they may expect.

As early as in the second chapter, the author says that to turn back is to neglect the great salvation that Christ came to proclaim. Moreover, he states that there will be no escape for those who drift away, just as surely as there was no escape from divine punishment for those who rejected the law given through Moses. We know that as many as rejected the Word of God in the Old Testament were cut off from the covenant community. The language of Hebrews indicates that neglecting the message spoken by Christ will bring on consequences that are even worse.

> Therefore we must pay much closer attention to what we have heard, lest we drift away from it. For since the message declared by angels proved to be reliable and every transgression or disobedience received a just retribution, how shall we escape if we neglect such a great salvation? It was declared at first by the Lord, and it was attested to us by those who heard, while God also bore witness by signs and wonders and various miracles and by gifts of the Holy Spirit distributed according to his will.   (Heb. 2:1–4)

---

39 John Gill, *Exposition of the Old and New Testaments: Colossians, The Collected Writings of John Gill* (Rio, WI: Ages Software Inc., 2002), 40.

In chapter 3, the author of the epistle cautions against hardening the heart like those who rebelled against divine leading in the desert. Their unbelief was punished by being denied entry into the promised land. Likewise, God has also spoken to us regarding a Promised Land where we will find rest. He has prepared us a city, a better country, that is, a heavenly one (Heb. 11:16). Therefore, there remains a Sabbath rest for the people of God (Heb. 4:9), for we have yet to enter into the rest we can only enjoy when we reach our eternal habitation.

But just as unbelief kept many Israelites from entering into the Promised Land of Canaan in the days of Joshua, unbelief will likewise prevent a person from entering into the Promised Land of rest toward which Christ is leading us. A heart that proves to be unbelieving by apostatizing and falling away from the living God will not enter into God's rest. The message being given is that whoever does not persevere will not enter into the Promised Land—that is, such a person will not see eternal life.

> Take care, brothers, lest there be in any of you an evil, unbelieving heart, leading you *to fall away from the living God*. But exhort one another every day, as long as it is called "today," that none of you may be hardened by the deceitfulness of sin. For we share in Christ, if indeed we hold our original confidence firm to the end.
>
> (Heb. 3:12–14; emphasis added)

> Therefore, while the promise of entering his rest still stands, *let us fear lest any of you should seem to have failed to reach it*. For good news came to us just as to them, but the message they heard did not benefit them, because they were not united by faith with those who listened. For *we who have believed enter that rest*, as he has said, "As I swore in my wrath, 'They shall not enter my rest,' ...Let us therefore strive to enter that rest, so that no one may fall by the same sort of disobedience. (Hebrews 4:1–11; emphasis added)

The severe words of chapter 10 are followed by the categorical statement that God has no pleasure in those who turn back and that those who do shrink back do so unto their own destruction.

> Therefore do not throw away your confidence, which has a great reward. For you have need of endurance, so that when you have done the will of God you may receive what is promised. For, "Yet a little while, and the coming one will come and will not delay; but my

righteous one shall live by faith, and if he shrinks back, my soul has no pleasure in him." But we are not of *those who shrink back and are destroyed*, but of those who have faith and preserve their souls.

(Heb. 10:35–39; emphasis added)

One thing is perfectly clear: the result of not persevering is destruction. Consequently, whoever does not persevere in the faith will not see eternal life. The biblical text does not allow for any other conclusion. The word *reward* in verse 35 is not employed to draw a distinction between salvation, which is free, and something extra that can be earned. In this context, it is salvation that is being referred to as a "great reward" in order to highlight its inestimably high value, without entailing any connotation of merit or recompense.

THE ABSOLUTE NECESSITY OF PERSEVERANCE

All this bears out what Christians have historically agreed upon: that the saints must persevere to enter into glory. The phrase "the perseverance of the saints" occurs twice in the book of Revelation:

And it was given to him to make war with the saints and to overcome them; and authority over every tribe and people and tongue and nation was given to him. And all who dwell on earth will worship him, everyone whose name has not been written from the foundation of the world in the book of life of the Lamb who has been slain. If anyone has an ear, let him hear. If anyone is destined for captivity, to captivity he goes; if anyone kills with the sword, with the sword he must be killed. *Here is the perseverance and faith of the saints.*

(Rev. 13:7–10, NASB; emphasis added)

And another angel, a third one, followed them, saying with a loud voice, "If anyone worships the beast and his image, and receives a mark on his forehead or upon his hand, he also will drink of the wine of the wrath of God, which is mixed in full strength in the cup of his anger; and he will be tormented with fire and brimstone in the presence of the holy angels and in the presence of the Lamb. And the smoke of their torment goes up forever and ever; and they have no rest, day and night, those who worship the beast and his image, and whoever receives the mark of his name." *Here is the perseverance of the saints* who keep the commandments of God and their faith in Jesus. (Rev. 14:9–12, NASB; emphasis added)

Both passages use the phrase "*Here is* the perseverance." This structure in Revelation conveys the message that the reality just described calls for or demands perseverance on the part of the saints:

> Because suffering is the church's inevitable path to glory, the saints must demonstrate enduring faith. The "here is" formula in Revelation identifies the response that is called for by the truth that precedes it, as if John were saying, "What is needed in this situation is..." See Rev. 13:18 ("Needed here is wisdom" to calculate the number and name of the beast); 14:12 ("Needed here is the endurance of the saints," for their enemies' [Babylon, beasts] days are numbered); 17:9 ("Needed here is a mind possessing wisdom" to decipher the symbolism of the beast that carried the harlot).[40]

The message of Revelation 13:10 is that Christians cannot succumb to the pressure to worship the beast, no matter how costly resisting may be. Refusing to may very well mean captivity or death, but there is no option. The saints are required to persevere. Revelation 14:12 admonishes in similar fashion that the saints must persevere because whoever caves in and worships the beast will be tormented forever in the lake of fire.

What the Bible is teaching at this point is that God requires believers to persevere even in the harshest circumstances. This does not mean that some saints end up losing their salvation. Those who do worship the beast are identified as the people whose names have not been written in the Lamb's book of life (Rev. 13:8). The need for perseverance goes hand in hand with the biblical truth that every genuine believer does persevere, a point that will be expounded further on in this book.

Obviously, if all true Christians persevere unto the end in faith and sanctification, with no exceptions, the end result will necessarily be that no Christian, at any time, will ever be lost. These two truths combined (the need for perseverance and the certainty of perseverance) form the doctrine called the Perseverance of the Saints, which has been unanimously accepted among Calvinistic Christians and is found in the creeds of several historic evangelical denominations. To teach, as some do today, that there is security apart from perseverance has nothing to do with Calvinism, and Reformed theologians have labored tirelessly to set the record straight on this matter.

---

40 Dennis E. Johnson, *Triumph of the Lamb—A Commentary on Revelation* (Phillipsburg, New Jersey: P & R Publishing, 2001), 194.

19

It is simply not biblical teaching to say that believers are secure regardless of how they live. The doctrine we are considering is the doctrine that believers *persevere*; it is only through the power of God that they are able to persevere, to be sure, but they do persevere. The security of believers is inseparable from their perseverance; did not Jesus say, "He who stands firm to the end will be saved" (Matt. 10:22)? Murray, in fact, puts it as strongly as this: "Perseverance means the engagement of our persons in the most intense and concentrated devotion to those means which God has ordained for the achievement of his saving purpose."[41]

The orthodox doctrine does not affirm the certainty of salvation because we once believed, but certainty of perseverance in holiness if we have truly believed, which perseverance in holiness, therefore, in opposition to all weaknesses and temptations, is the only sure evidence of the genuineness of past experience or of the validity of our confidence as to our future salvation.[42]

While Calvinists have stood united on this issue, Christians in the Arminian camp have gone in different directions on the matter of perseverance and security. There are some who disagree with the Calvinist view of predestination but hold to the Reformed doctrine of the Perseverance of the Saints. Others reject the so-called fifth point of Calvinism[43] as well.

In the Arminian understanding of conversion, an unbeliever cannot come to faith unless assisted by prevenient grace, but the work of grace that operates in conversion is not irresistible. In other words, the role grace plays is to make conversion possible, not certain. Hence, it is not a big step to also believe that it's possible to fall away after conversion, because there is no guarantee that the work of grace will necessarily prevail upon the saved to cause them to persevere.

It has been from this rationale that many have objected to the doctrine of the Perseverance of the Saints and argued that true saints do not always persevere, leaving the door open for the teaching that salvation can be lost. As one Arminian puts it:

---

41 Anthony A. Hoekema, *Saved by Grace* (Grand Rapids: William B. Eermans Publishing Company, 1994), 236.

42 A. A. Hodge, quoted by A. W. Pink, *Eternal Security* (Grand Rapids: Baker Book House, 1979), 102.

43 The doctrine of the perseverance of the saints is known as the fifth point of Calvinism, from the acrostic TULIP.

What has happened to the human will in the process? Do people have free will prior to salvation but lose that *free* will after they are saved?[44]

This same underlying presupposition is at work in the mind of those who teach eternal security apart from the need for perseverance. They build upon the premise that God's grace does not necessarily sustain the saints and that, therefore, some of them choose to leave the narrow path and turn their backs on Christ. However, instead of considering this as fatal, they want to defend a doctrine of unconditional security for such people. This represents an even greater departure from the reformers' doctrine of the Perseverance of the Saints than classic Arminianism (see chart below).

Reformed Faith	1st Arminian Model	2nd Arminian Model
Perseverance is necessary	Perseverance is necessary	Perseverance is not necessary
Apostates perish	Apostates perish	Apostates continue saved
True Saints always persevere	Some true saints apostatize	Some true saints apostatize
Christ never loses his own	Christ loses some of his own	Christ never loses his own

The doctrine of security in salvation cannot hang on air. It can only be consistently sustained in conjunction with a biblical understanding of conversion and providence. Churches that drift away from Reformed soteriology tend to exchange the doctrine of the Perseverance of the Saints for a doctrine of unconditional eternal security or a belief in the loss of salvation. Neither alternative is the solution. Many biblical texts demonstrate conclusively that Christ never loses any of his own. At the same time, other biblical passages teach the need for perseverance.

A careful study will reveal that the whole Bible is in perfect harmony. Rejecting the doctrine of the Perseverance of the Saints will lead to a break (or at least an inconsistency) with several biblical doctrines that are interrelated, such as the doctrines of justification, regeneration, and God's providence. These connections will be examined in the following chapters.

---

44 Stephen M. Ashby, *Four Views on Eternal Security* (Grand Rapids: Zondervan, 2002), 159 (emphasis in original).

HOW SHOULD PERSEVERANCE BE PREACHED?

In light of the biblical warnings regarding the need to persevere, how should we preach about perseverance in church? I have chosen to conclude this chapter by presenting some extracts from real sermons preached in churches by responsible preachers who are doctrinally sound and who can be a model for us all as to how we should take the Bible's message to its hearers.

Albert Martin, preaching, on the Letters to the Seven Churches in Revelation at Trinity Baptist Church, Montville, New Jersey:

> There are some people who wickedly teach that there are two kinds of Christians. Non-overcomers, and you'll just make it in the gates and be a second class citizen forever; and then there are super-duper overcomers and they go strutting down the streets of glory, first class citizens. No, no. Jesus, when he speaks of what will come to overcomers, speaks of things that are of the essence of the final consummate glory of heaven. Beginning with this first one: "To him that overcomes I will give to eat of the tree of life." Which is where? "In the paradise of God." And when we turn to the latter chapters of the book of the Revelation, the redeemed are seen in the paradise of God; they have access to the tree of life. There's no other second class, non-overcomers, who still make it to the paradise of God. You overcome or you'll miss paradise. That's the thrust of the words of our Lord Jesus.

> Chapter 2 and verse 11: "He that has an ear let him hear what the Spirit says to the churches. He that overcomes shall not be hurt of the second death." He won't go to hell. That's the second death, according to Revelation 20:15. You want to escape hell? Then you've got to overcome. If you don't overcome, you go to hell. That's the teaching of the passage.
>
> …

> Chapter 3 and verse 5: "He that overcomes shall thus be arrayed in white garments and I will in no wise blot his name out of the Book of Life and I will confess his name before my Father and before his angels." On the Day of Judgment, Jesus will either confess you before his father, or deny you. This is not a matter of extra rewards, folks, it's a matter of life and death. Would you have Christ to confess you to be one of his? Then you must overcome.
>
> …

THE ONE WHO ENDURES TO THE END WILL BE SAVED

You see, when I'm convinced in the depths of my being that if I don't overcome I'll go to hell, that makes me ruthless with so called little sins that I know can flower into big sins and can draw me away from Christ. That makes me merciless on those things that would erode the vital life-giving context of a sensitive conscience. As John Owen said, "We see in every sin not only the modest proposal of its beginning, but the maximum expression of its end." And not only will the world think us overly scrupulous, and overly fastidious, but dead, half-converted fellow Christians will think you extreme. But when you are persuaded: "I must overcome or be damned! I must overcome or be cut off from the promises!" Nothing is too precious to be spared the acts of mortification. Dear people, I fear some of you don't really believe this. The marks of ruthlessness in dealing with yourself are not prominent in your Christian life.

Michael Phillips, in his introduction to a message on perseverance preached at Grace Baptist Church, Fremont, California, on August 27, 2003:

The Bible teaches that all saints persevere. That is, we endure the hardships of life and live for God until we die. Our devotion to God is never perfect and often it's not very consistent, but it is real and we never give it up. The saved believers must persevere. The Lord says, "He who endures to the end, the same shall be saved." The others won't be saved. People who profess Christ and then fall away from the Lord, fall away from obedience, from prayer and Bible reading, and who no longer have any meaningful communion with him, will not go to heaven when they die. No matter how warmly they started their Christian life.[45]

…

If you want to go to heaven, you must persevere. What you did twenty years ago, fifty years ago, no matter how sincere you were at the time, is not enough. To be with Christ in heaven you must first live for Christ on earth. Whether your Christian life is a long one, like Noah's, or a short one, like the thief on the cross, you must persevere in order to be saved. This is what the Bible teaches, and it is what our study is about.[46]

45 Albert N. Martin, *The Book of Revelation (2 of 2)* (min. 43:16–51:58), accessed October 3, 2016, http://www.sermonaudio.com/sermoninfo.asp?SID=1080283757.
46 Michael Phillips, *Thomas Watson #3 Perseverance of the Saints* (min. 0:28–2:19), accessed October 3, 2016, http://www.sermonaudio.com/sermoninfo.asp?SID=9210304340.

Stuart Johnston, preached on January 2, 2000, at Grace Reformed Baptist Church in Mebane, North Carolina:

> It is simply a fact that God's sovereign, triumphant grace works through means. God does not bring people to heaven no matter what they choose to do. And our assurance, if we are Christians, is not that no matter what we do, God is going to bring us to heaven. Rather, he brings his own to heaven by means of choices that we make, actions that we engage in. That does not mean that in the final analysis our salvation is dependent upon our actions and our choices. It simply affirms that the God that is committed to bringing his people to glory brings them along one specific trail to glory. There are not many ways to heaven, there's only one way to heaven. It is a narrow way, and yes, it is a difficult way. God himself will see to it that all of his own will be brought down that way to himself, but it is down that way. It is through means that he has appointed, through which his own appointed end shall be reached. God's sovereign grace provides for and secures the elects' continuance in that narrow way. But that provides no comfort for us, unless we live that way.[47]

May God grant that more churches hear this kind of biblical clarity. Salvation is in Christ. There is no salvation outside of Christ. The person who is not in Christ will not see life. The Bible doesn't afford any hope to the one who abandons Christ, giving into sin. Instead, it solemnly testifies that such a person will not see life. It exhorts us to "strive for peace with everyone, and for the holiness without which no one will see the Lord" (Heb. 12:14).

The only ones who will enter God's eternal kingdom are those who are in Christ by faith, who follow the way of sanctification, and who persevere therein unto the end. This is what the Bible teaches, and this is what we should be preaching.

---

47 Stu Johnston, *Assurances for the Perseverance of the Saints* (min. 43:05–44:35), accessed October 3, 2016, http://www.grmi.8k.com/reformed_sermons_search_results.htm.

2

The Irreversible Character of Justification

> Righteousness comes from faith, which means that it too is a gift of God. For since this righteousness belongs to God, it is an unmerited gift. And the gifts of God greatly exceed any achievements of our own zeal.[48]　　　　　　　　　　　　(Chrysostom, AD 347–407)

> The blessed Paul argues that we are saved by faith, which he declares to be not from us but a gift from God. Thus there cannot possibly be true salvation where there is no true faith, and, since this faith is divinely enabled, it is without doubt bestowed by his free generosity. Where there is true belief through true faith, true salvation certainly accompanies it.[49]　　　　　　　　　　　(Fulgentius, AD 520)

What does the term *justification* mean? One day, we will all appear before God in judgment. The unjust will go away into eternal punishment, but the righteous into eternal life (Matt. 25:46). How can we be righteous in God's eyes? This question of eternal importance was at the very heart of the controversy in the sixteenth-century Protestant Reformation. The reformers, who insisted on returning to apostolic Christianity, sought to answer this question by going back to what the Bible teaches about justification and accepting it as the final authority. In doing so, they noted that Catholicism had largely strayed from the doctrine of justification we find in Scripture. They were reformers, not innovators. They did not come up with a new doctrine; neither did they set forth a new interpretation of the Bible. The view they arrived at on the matter of justification proves to be none other than the doctrine of the early church, as found in the writings of the early church

---

48　John Chrysostom, *Homilies on the Philippians* 12 3:7–9, *Galatians, Ephesians, Philippians: Ancient Christian Commentary on Scripture*, NT vol. 8, ed. Mark J. Edwards (Downers Grove, IL: InterVarsity Press, 1998), 270.

49　Fulgentius, *On the Incarnation 1, Galatians, Ephesians, Philippians: Ancient Christian Commentary on Scripture*, NT vol. 8, ed. Mark J. Edwards (Downers Grove, IL: InterVarsity Press, 1998), 133–34.

2

fathers, even those celebrated by the Catholic Church as its own historical link to Jesus and the apostles.[50]

The concept of justification we subscribe to has many ramifications. While the Catholic Church came to believe that salvation could be lost precisely due to the erroneous concept of justification it eventually adopted, it was their biblical understanding of justification that led the reformers to believe that salvation cannot be lost. It is, therefore, fundamental to understand both the Catholic and the Protestant doctrines of justification if we wish to understand what took them in opposite directions on the issue of security and the loss of salvation.

THE DOCTRINE OF JUSTIFICATION IN THE MEDIEVAL CATHOLIC CHURCH

The sinner's natural tendency is to think that salvation must be achieved by one's own merit. We naturally suppose that we can make up for offending our Creator by doing something for him in exchange for forgiveness, whether it be by doing good deeds, or, as a last recourse, by suffering for our own mistakes until we have sufficiently paid for them. This is how people attempt to earn salvation in pagan religions. They strive to do good works, they participate in religious rituals, and they impose suffering upon themselves, believing that by these means they may prove themselves worthy and attain salvation. This is all contrary to the Gospel.

The truth is that as sinners we can never save ourselves (Rom. 3:23). We are not worthy of eternal life, and we never will be, no matter what we do. There is nothing we could do that would truly compensate for our errors. Consequently, we are utterly unable to earn our own salvation through our efforts, and we are left totally at God's mercy. Our guilt is such that God would be perfectly just in condemning us all and saving no one. Our only hope is being saved by God's unmerited grace. That is why the Gospel is good news. Its message is that Jesus came into the world to save sinners. Out of his amazing grace, God saves sinners.

Catholicism never denied that God's grace is absolutely necessary for sinners to be saved; even so, it has degenerated into a system that seeks to reconcile two opposites: grace and merit. On the one hand, it maintains that salvation depends on divine grace, for it would be impossible for anyone

---

50 See appendix for documentation of the early-church fathers' view on justification.

to reach salvation unassisted by divine grace. However, at the same time, it holds that everything also depends on possessing a certain amount of individual merit, which comes from one's own works.

According to traditional Catholic teaching, for a sinner to obtain salvation, there are a number of steps that must be followed. First, it is necessary to be baptized, receiving the beginning of spiritual life. At this moment, justification begins, as original sin and all past sins are forgiven.

But from that moment on, justification must be maintained. Every new sin that is committed throughout life is immediately put to the person's account. However, that does not mean that Christians necessarily become lost again every time they sin, because Catholic doctrine divides sins into the categories of mortal sins and venial sins.

Venial sins do not compromise the individual's salvation. To die in a state of grace, it is not necessary to have a clean slate, containing no sins at all. So long as there are only venial sins on their accounts, baptized Christians will not go to hell; instead, they will go to purgatory to receive a temporary punishment that is proportional to their guilt.

As all Christians commit more venial sins than they are diligent to confess for absolution, it is practically unavoidable to spend some time in purgatory, which is why masses are performed for those who pass away.

On the other hand, mortal sins are so called because they kill the soul, destroying the grace of justification and leaving the sinner lost once more.

For mortal sins to be absolved, the formula is confession and penitence, which includes works of propitiation, whereby the sinner can prove to be contrite and penitent and can make up, to some degree, for his wrongdoing. In this manner, good works assume a vital role in salvation. Salvation, which is initially acquired by participating in a God-pleasing rite, is thereafter kept by performing good deeds and avoiding bad ones.

Finally, works come once more into play as part of the process to restore salvation, if it has been lost. The Council of Trent (1545–1563), section 6, chapter 14 explains this:

> Those who through sin have forfeited the received grace of justification, can again be justified when, moved by God, they

exert themselves to obtain through the sacrament of penance the recovery, by the merits of Christ, of the grace lost.[51]

This is deemed necessary for a sinner to be worthy of God's forgiveness.

It is interesting to note how Catholic theologians use the word *merit* in this context. In one sense, they admit that as sinners we cannot deserve to be justified, but in another sense, they insist that we must deserve it. Be it a paradox or a contradiction, they appeal to a distinction that they themselves make between two types of merit: (1) what they call *meritum de condigno* (condign merit, or merit of the deserving) and (2) *meritum de congruo* (congruous merit).

Meritum de condigno is the name reserved for the kind of merit that would obligate God to reward whoever had it in order to not be unjust. The Catholic Church denies that a sinner could deserve salvation in this way. However, the second type of merit is inferior because, strictly speaking, it does not render the sinner actually worthy of salvation. *Meritum de congruo* only makes the sinner sufficiently deserving of salvation when human merit is added to a measure of divine grace. It is maintained that having this kind of merit is essential for the salvation of a sinner to be reasonable, although not enough to confer it as a right.

Notice how a contemporary Catholic Catechism argues that it is impossible to obtain merit in God's eyes apart from his grace but that cooperating with his grace produces real merit:

With regard to God, there is no strict right to any merit on the part of man....The merit of man before God in the Christian life arises from the fact that God has freely chosen to associate man with the work of his grace. The fatherly action of God is first on his own initiative, and then follows man's free acting through his collaboration, so that the merit of good works is to be attributed in the first place to the grace of God, then to the faithful. Man's merit, moreover, itself is due to God, for his good actions proceed in Christ, from the predispositions and assistance given by the Holy Spirit.[52]

In medieval Catholic thinking, this kind of merit came to play such an indispensable role that no sinner could be saved without having it. This

51 H. J. Schroeder, trans., *Canons and Decrees of the Council of Trent: Original Text with English Translation* (London: Herder, 1941), 39.
52 *Catechism of the Catholic Church* (Liguori, MO: Liguori, 1994), 486.

merit is obtained by practicing good works, especially those associated with penitence after confession. So the individual who makes good use of divine assistance to accumulate enough merit will be declared just, because he or she will have become righteous by possessing an inherent justice that stems from his or her good works.

In theological terms, this view of justification is referred to as "analytical justification" to denote that it is a justification that occurs on the basis of an analysis of the individual. The person who actually proves to be righteous under divine scrutiny is then proclaimed to be just. According to the Vatican, a pronouncement on God's part declaring the sinner to be just is only admissible once God can truly perceive the presence of an objective inherent righteousness in the person by virtue of his or her deeds.

A justification that rests on such an unstable criterion will obviously be subject to ongoing revision and potential cancelation, thereby eliminating any certainty as to the future. What is more, such a system doesn't leave any room for present assurance of salvation either. Since a sinner does not know for sure how much good is really needed to be personally judged righteous in God's eyes, one can never know if enough has already been done to stand justified today. This comes out very clearly in the words of Gregory I (bishop of Rome from AD 590 to 604):

> The greater our sins the more we must do to make up for them.... Whether we have done enough to atone for them we cannot know until after death....We can never be sure of success....Assurance of salvation and the feeling of safety engendered by it are dangerous for anybody and would not be desirable even if possible.[53]

The conclusion that assurance would be undesirable, even if possible, is quite revealing. It indicates that in this life a person should never come to the point of resting and trusting. On the contrary, each Christian should constantly entertain doubts about being truly saved. Of course, it would be argued that this is not the same as doubting God because it is a lack of confidence in oneself. Nevertheless, it is undeniably true that the only reason a lack of trust in self is even relevant is because there is no trust that God has accomplished all that is necessary for salvation apart from the contribution of our own merit. Supposing that God does his part and that we must do our part, the fear is as to whether we have done our own part well enough.

---

53 Gregory I, quoted by Joel Beeke, *The Quest for Full Assurance* (Carlisle, PA: The Banner of Truth Trust, 1999), 13.

A man of this mindset is persuaded that it would be arrogant to consider himself saved and that it would be presumptuous to affirm that he will continue to be faithful unto the end. He does not count on a divine provision on his behalf to make him righteous before God nor to infallibly keep him unto the end, because he doesn't believe God acts in such a way as to ensure these aspects of his salvation. He is convinced that these things constitute his own contribution to his salvation.

It is in these matters that God puts him to the test, and it is where he must achieve a passing mark. Therefore, he is reluctant to proclaim his own success, because on these matters he may not look to God and trust but must provide for himself. His lack of assurance also means that he will never be in a position to thank God for being saved, for each time he thinks about where he will spend eternity he cannot look up in peaceful gratitude, because he can never take his worried eyes off himself.

The main criticism that needs to be brought against this model of salvation is that it does not teach people to trust in Christ alone as their Savior. It presents Jesus as the one who makes salvation possible through his death on the cross and by granting a measure of grace to work in us, all of which is vital but insufficient. To be saved and to stay saved depends on achieving enough merit to make salvation reasonable, besides going on to suffer in purgatory for unconfessed venial sins. This ultimately turns out to be a process of divinely assisted self-salvation. The medieval church strayed from biblical teaching and from its roots by embracing a man-centered doctrine of salvation.

For the reformers, the biblical teaching that most urgently needed to be restored to its rightful place in the church was the sufficiency of Christ as Savior. We are not inherently righteous, but Christ lived a perfect sinless life in our place, gaining a perfect righteousness for us. We are sinners who deserve condemnation, but by his substitutionary death on the cross, Christ took our sins upon himself, and we do not need to expiate them ourselves.

Salvation is God's work from beginning to end. We are, no doubt, involved in conversion and perseverance, but not in a way that would justify calling it our contribution to our own salvation, because the conversion of the sinner is the work of the Holy Spirit (Titus 3:5), who then inhabits the Christian to ensure perseverance until the day of final salvation (Eph. 1:13–14; 4:30). Believing in God as Savior means trusting in him exclusively for salvation without dividing our trust between two saviors. Above anything else, it was the loss of this truth that made the reformation necessary.

THE REFORMED DOCTRINE OF JUSTIFICATION

The Bible consistently presents justification as the opposite of condemnation in God's judgment. The language it uses in connection with justification comes straight out of the legal process in a courtroom setting (judgment, accuse, the judge, a lawyer, guilty, condemned). Therefore, to justify does not mean to make someone righteous in practice.

Justification "is never taken for an infusion of righteousness, but as often as the Scriptures speak professedly about our justification, it always must be explained as a forensic term."[54] This means that justification occurs when God pronounces someone to be righteous, even while that person is still a sinner!

Luther observed that in the Bible the righteous is someone who is "simultaneously just and sinner" (*simul iustus et peccator*). In other words, it is someone who in practice still sins but who judicially has already been forgiven and is treated as being perfectly righteous. This is what is called "forensic justification" (or judicial justification) because it has to do with a pronouncement on God's part regarding the condition or position of the sinner before the law.

In contrast to "analytical justification," which needs to be maintained and renewed through works, the Bible asserts that the only criterion for justification is true faith in Christ. This justification is not a process but a single act that is decisive and final, and which occurs at the moment of true conversion. This is the doctrine of justification as taught in Scripture itself.

Biblically speaking, it is impossible to be both justified and condemned at the same time. In Romans, the apostle Paul repeatedly draws a contrast between justification and condemnation, showing them to be opposites.

> And the free gift is not like the result of that one man's sin. For the judgment following one trespass brought **condemnation**, but the free gift following many trespasses brought **justification**.
> (Rom 5:16; emphasis added)

> Therefore, as one trespass led to **condemnation** for all men, so one act of righteousness leads to **justification** and life for all men.
> (Rom 5:18; emphasis added)

---

54 Francis Turretin, *Institutes of Elenctic Theology*, Vol 2, Eleventh Through Seventeenth Topics, trans. George Musgrave Giger (Phillisburg, NJ: P&R, 1994), 634.

Who shall bring any charge against God's elect? It is God who **justifies**. Who is to **condemn**? Christ Jesus is the one who died-more than that, who was raised- who is at the right hand of God, who indeed is interceding for us.   (Rom 8:33–34; emphasis added)

In Acts 13:38–39, justification is synonymous with having the forgiveness of sins:

Therefore let it be known to you, brethren, that through this Man is preached to you the forgiveness of sins; and by Him everyone who believes is justified from all things from which you could not be justified by the law of Moses.   (Acts 13:38–39, NKJV)

This last passage promises justification—that is, forgiveness of sins—to everyone who believes. The promise is not conditioned on proving oneself worthy through works, much less can it be made to mean that the person who believes instantly becomes righteous in practice. There is not a single verse in Scripture where it would be possible to interpret justification as a transformation of the person into someone who is inherently righteous. The meaning is always that the justified person is rendered free from any guilt in judgment.

When a person truly believes in Christ, there is sincere repentance from sin, but that is nothing close to being a truly righteous person in practice. Romans 4:5 goes so far as to says that "God justifies the ungodly." He does not pronounce justification because he perceives that the person has truly become just; he rather justifies the one he still perceives in practice as being ungodly.

Martyn Lloyd-Jones has very ably explained this concept:

We tend to think that justification means that we are made righteous or good or upright or holy. But that is quite wrong. In justification we are not made righteous, we are declared to be righteous—the thing is quite different. To say that in justification you are made righteous is to confuse it with sanctification. Justification is something legal or forensic. It is God, as the Judge, who is responsible for administering His own law, saying to us that as regards the law He is satisfied with us because of the righteousness of Christ. Justification is a declaratory act. It does not do anything to us; it says something about us. It has no reference to my actual state or condition inside; it has reference to my standing, to my position, to my appearing in the presence of God. Now that is the biblical doctrine of justification.[55]

It can be demonstrated that this is the proper biblical definition of the term *justify* by looking at some biblical texts that speak of human judgments. For example, in Deuteronomy 25:1 (NASB), we find the following instruction given to human justices:

If there is a dispute between men, and they go to court, and the judges decide their case, and they justify[56] the righteous and condemn the wicked ...

In this passage that deals with a dispute between two men, the Bible recognizes that the obligation of the human authorities is to justify the righteous and condemn the wicked. This is obviously a purely legal matter. By justifying the righteous, the judges would not be changing anything in the man himself. They would merely be making a statement about him. They would be making a pronouncement to the effect that the man could not be punished for any crimes of which he may have been accused.

Another example is found in Proverbs 17:15: "He who justifies the wicked and he who condemns the righteous are both alike an abomination to the LORD." Notice once more how justifying someone is the opposite of condemning the person. It refers to a legal action. Whether someone condemned the righteous or justified the wicked, in neither case would that involve effecting a change in the person. If justification were the same as making someone become righteous, God would certainly not prohibit the justifying of the wicked. There wouldn't be anything immoral about transforming a bad person into a better one. On the contrary, that would be a good thing to do. But justifying the wicked is an abomination to the Lord because the term *justification* is forensic in its nature.

Moreover, the Greek word used in the New Testament for justification is the same word that would have been used in court to pronounce the acquittal of a defendant. There is, however, an important distinction. To acquit typically means that the defendant is innocent; but when used in a soteriological context, justification involves the recognition that the accused is actually guilty.

---

55 D. Martyn Lloyd-Jones, *Great Doctrines of the Bible, Volume II, God the Holy Spirit* (Wheaton, IL: Crossway, 2012), 169 (emphasis in original).

56 The word in the Septuagint is the same Greek word as used by the New Testament authors for justification.

God justifies the wicked. This in itself raises an interesting question. The phrase "justifies the wicked" occurs twice in the Bible. The first time is in Proverbs 17:15, where we read that whoever justifies the wicked is an abomination to the Lord. The second is in Romans 4:5, where it states that God justifies the wicked.

How can this be? Could God be doing wrong in justifying the wicked? Certainly not. There is no error on the part of God. God justifies people who have real guilt but whose sins have been blotted out (Acts 3:19) and who now have a perfectly and perpetually clean slate due to the fact that their penalty has already been paid. That is exactly what Paul sets forth in Romans chapter 3:

> For all have sinned and fall short of the glory of God, and are justified by his grace as a gift, through the redemption that is in Christ Jesus, whom God put forward as a propitiation by his blood, to be received by faith. This was to show God's righteousness, because in his divine forbearance he had passed over former sins. It was to show his righteousness at the present time, so that he might be just and the justifier of the one who has faith in Jesus.   (Rom 3:23–26)

In these verses, Paul sums up what he had just been saying about all humanity's guilt and just condemnation in the words: "For all have sinned and fall short of the glory of God." He then proceeds to explain how people can be justified.

Justification is a free gift—that is, it is not given as in exchange for any price or as a payment for anything good a person has done. Justification is through what Jesus did on the cross. When he died shedding his blood, he did it as a propitiation. The word *propitiation* signifies an offering or sacrifice that is made to placate God's wrath.

Jesus offered himself as a sacrifice to expiate sins, suffering the penalty of the law in the place of all who take refuge in him. So it is not as if sinners were declared innocent by some mistake or by a lapse in justice. Sinners redeemed by Christ are justified because their sins are paid for. In this way, the substitutionary death of Christ satisfies the demands of divine justice that sinners be punished.

If God justified us (the wicked) without our sins being paid for, he would be our justifier, but he would cease to be a just God. If he punished us as we deserve, he would remain just, but he would not be our justifier. Through the substitutionary death of Jesus, he found a way to be both just and the justifier of the wicked who have faith in Jesus.

The Bible consistently teaches this concept of substitution, showing that God saves his people by not imputing their sins *unto them*:

> That is, in Christ God was reconciling the world to himself, *not counting their trespasses against them*, and entrusting to us the message of reconciliation. (2 Cor. 5:19; emphasis added)

The just are those who escape condemnation because their sins are laid to Christ's account, imputed to Christ:

> For our sake he made him to be sin who knew no sin, so that in him we might become the righteousness of God. (2 Cor. 5:21)

There is a transfer that takes place for justification to occur: the sinner's sins are imputed to Christ, put to his account as if they were his own to pay for. He bears them in the sinner's place, suffering the penalty the sinner deserves and leaving his debt paid in full:

> He himself bore our sins in his body on the tree, that we might die to sin and live to righteousness. By his wounds you have been healed. (1 Pet. 2:24)

These words of Peter reflect the prophecy of Isaiah that the Messiah would justify the many by bearing their iniquities:

> Surely our griefs He Himself bore, and our sorrows He carried; yet we ourselves esteemed Him stricken, smitten by God, and afflicted. But He was pierced through for our transgressions, He was crushed for our iniquities; the chastening for our well-being fell upon Him, and by His scourging we are healed. All of us like sheep have gone astray, each of us has turned to his own way; but the LORD has caused the iniquity of us all to fall on Him. ...As a result of the anguish of his soul, He will see it and be satisfied; by His knowledge *the Righteous One, my Servant, will justify the many, as He will bear their iniquities*. (Isa. 53:4–11, NASB; emphasis added)

Jesus suffered the punishment that brought us peace. Once Christ has paid for someone's sins, it would be unjust to require another payment or impose more punishment. According to the Bible, the justified are sinners who have nothing in themselves but shame and who escape condemnation only because they are not made to bear their own sins. They escape punishment because Someone who was able to save them loved them enough to take their place and personally undergo the immense punishment their sins deserve. Now that their sins have been paid for, never again will they be charged with them so that they are now free.

Since the correct understanding of justification puts it in contrast with condemnation, nobody can be both justified and condemned at the same time and all who are not justified stand condemned. This also means that nobody can be in a state of partial justification. To justify someone is to remove *all* the offenses from the record. If a single transgression of God's law is outstanding on our account we are not justified; we are not declared to be just (or righteous).

But writing to the Colossians, Paul emphatically states that the forgiveness we have received as Christians encompasses all our trespasses, without exception, and that our debt is entirely removed, having been settled at the cross:

> And you, who were dead in your trespasses and the uncircumcision of your flesh, God made alive together with him, having forgiven us *all* our trespasses, by canceling the record of debt that stood against us with its legal demands. This he set aside, nailing it to the cross.
> (Colossians 2:13–14; emphasis added)

Further, the biblical comprehension of justification includes more than just forgiveness, as is indicated by the phrase "So that in him we might *become the righteousness of God*" (2 Cor. 5:21; emphasis added). In Christ, we also gain a righteousness that is foreign to us. We become the righteousness of God. We become righteous by receiving a righteousness that is not our own but of God that is imputed to us. It is called "the free gift of righteousness" in Romans 5:17. It is the righteousness that Christ gained for us by living a perfect life in our stead and dying to pay for our sins.

Those who receive the free gift of righteousness have the righteousness of Christ himself imputed to their accounts, as if they themselves had performed it. Clothed in this perfect righteousness, a person could not be condemned, just as surely as nothing worthy of condemnation could be found in the person of Christ.

But it must be understood that this justified person is still a sinner. The imputation of righteousness causes the believer to be treated as a just person by divine justice in spite of not being an inherently just person, just as the imputation of our sins to Christ caused him to be treated as if he were a sinner at the hands of divine justice although he was not inherently sinful.

The fact that Christ's righteousness is imputed unto the believer is an important concept that cannot be ignored. If justification were nothing more than the forgiveness of sins and lacked this element of being clothed with the righteousness of Christ, we could imagine that once sins were removed from someone's account it would be the good things henceforth done by the person living a godly life that would be the reason why God could call such a person "righteous." If this were the case, the person would be "righteous" on the basis of his or her own righteousness that God would take into account to his or her credit.

But it is not the good that believers do that God imputes to them as righteousness. The good works of believers do not contribute at all to their justification. On the contrary, the righteousness that they possess is a righteousness that is infinitely superior to that of the Pharisees (Matt. 5:20). They have the perfect righteousness of Christ imputed to their accounts.

This is one of the crucial differences between the Catholic and the Evangelical understanding of justification. Both the Catholic (analytical justification) and the Protestant teaching (forensic justification) affirm that God declares the sinner to be righteous, but there is a world of difference in what is perceived as the righteousness that the sinner possesses and which constitutes the basis for God to make such a declaration. It is an integral part of the Catholic concept that the sinner possesses his own righteousness, coming from doing good works. Nothing is added to or imputed to the Christian that is not properly his own, and God only declares Christians to be righteous in view of this righteousness, *after* he detects that they possess it.

The Protestant perspective is that Christians do not possess any righteousness that is inherently their own that comes from their good works. When the reformers spoke of forensic justification, they sought to emphasize this very point, that justification is a judicial declaration made by God in view of the imputation of Christ's righteousness unto the believer. The only righteousness that the righteous possess is the righteousness of Christ, which is put to their account when they believe. Christ's righteousness is the basis for God to declare them to be righteous.

The idea of Christ's righteousness being imputed to the sinner comes from the Bible itself and cannot be dismissed as if it were some kind of legal fiction. If the imputation of righteousness did not exist, neither could there be the imputation of our sins to Christ, which would mean his death could not procure our redemption.

The concept of imputation permeates the whole book of Romans. In chapter 4, it becomes explicit. Paul there refutes any notion that Abraham may have been justified by works and declares that the righteousness he had was that which was imputed unto him when he believed. He next proves that David also believed in a salvation that was based on the idea of God not imputing sins to the account of the guilty sinner, while instead imputing a righteousness to the sinner's account that was not based on that individual's own good works:

> What then shall we say that Abraham our father has found according to the flesh? For if Abraham was justified by works, he has something to boast about, but not before God. For what does the Scripture say? "Abraham believed God, and *it was accounted to him for righteousness*." Now to him who works, the wages are not counted as grace but as debt. But to him who does not work but believes on Him who justifies the ungodly, his faith is accounted for righteousness, just as David also describes the blessedness of *the man to whom God imputes righteousness apart from works*: "Blessed are those whose lawless deeds are forgiven, And whose sins are covered; *Blessed is the man to whom the LORD shall not impute sin*." (Rom. 4:1–8, NKJV; emphasis added)

"God imputes righteousness." What an important phrase! It means that God imputes or credits righteousness to the individual's account. If the righteousness of Christ is imputed to somebody's account, it is perfectly admissible for that person to be declared righteous, apart from any works of his or her own.

As Paul proceeds, it is noteworthy how many times he speaks of righteousness being imputed:

> Does this blessedness then come upon the circumcised only, or upon the uncircumcised also? For we say that *faith was accounted to Abraham for righteousness*. How then *was it accounted*? While he was circumcised, or uncircumcised? Not while circumcised, but while uncircumcised. And he received the sign of circumcision, a seal of the righteousness of the faith which he had while still uncircumcised,

that he might be the father of all those who believe, though they are uncircumcised, *that righteousness might be imputed to them also...* And therefore *"it was accounted to him for righteousness."* Now it was not written for his sake alone that *it was imputed to him,* but also for us. *It shall be imputed to us* who believe in Him who raised up Jesus our Lord from the dead, who was delivered up because of our offenses, and was raised because of our justification.

(Rom. 4:9–25, NKJV; emphasis added)

We shouldn't miss how Paul emphasizes that righteousness is received as a gift:

If, because of one man's trespass, death reigned through that one man, much more will those who receive the abundance of grace and *the free gift of righteousness* reign in life through the one man Jesus Christ. (Rom. 5:17; emphasis added)

He argues as well that this righteousness that God grants was foretold in the older Scriptures of the law and the prophets, waiting only to be fully revealed and made known in the Gospel of Christ:

But now *the righteousness of God* has been manifested apart from the law, although *the Law and the Prophets bear witness to it—the righteousness of God through faith in Jesus Christ* for all who believe. For there is no distinction.

(Rom. 3:21–22; emphasis added)

For I am not ashamed of *the gospel,* for it is the power of God for salvation to everyone who believes, to the Jew first and also to the Greek. *For in it the righteousness of God is revealed* from faith for faith, as it is written, "The righteous shall live by faith."

(Rom. 1:16–17, emphasis added)

In chapter 4, Paul supports his claim that this free gift of righteousness is indeed the teaching of the Old Testament, a fact that could easily be proven by a host of other passages besides the ones that he cites. We shall examine a few other Old Testament passages.

They will say of Me, *"Only in the LORD are righteousness and strength."* Men will come to Him, and all who were angry at Him shall be put to shame. *In the LORD all the offspring of Israel will be justified,* and will glory." (Isa. 45:24–25, NASB; emphasis added)

Isaiah 45:25 calls attention to the fact that the justification of the saved is something that is realized "in the Lord."

> The preceding verse (45:24) states the other respect in which the truth is expressed, that it is in the Lord righteousness resides: "Only in the Lord, it is said of me, is righteousness and strength."… There need be no question but Israel is represented as righteous or justified in the Lord because the righteousness that resides in the Lord is brought to bear upon Israel.[57]

> I will greatly rejoice in the LORD; my soul shall exult in my God, for he has clothed me with the garments of salvation; he has covered me with the robe of righteousness, as a bridegroom decks himself like a priest with a beautiful headdress, and as a bride adorns herself with her jewels.
>
> (Isa. 61:10)

In this second passage, Isaiah refers to God covering his people with a robe of righteousness. The parallelism he makes between clothing them with the garments of salvation and covering them with the robe of righteousness confirms that the righteousness contemplated is that which pertains to salvation.

It also signifies that the righteousness whereby the righteous are saved is not properly their own. It is rather a righteousness that comes to them from without and is given to them by God as a gift. This righteousness from God is placed over them, and once they are covered by it, they can stand before God in judgment. By this, we can understand how God's people are justified in the Lord (Isa. 45:25) and how their righteousness is in the Lord.

> Behold, the days are coming, declares the LORD, when I will raise up for David a righteous Branch, and he shall reign as king and deal wisely, and shall execute justice and righteousness in the land. In his days Judah will be saved, and Israel will dwell securely. And this is the name by which he will be called: *The LORD is our righteousness.*
>
> (Jer. 23:5)

This marvelous messianic prophecy of Jeremiah resonates that "The LORD is our righteousness" is a name by which the Messiah is to be called. He himself is our righteousness toward God. In other words, instead of God considering his people as righteous because he perceives that there

---

57 John Murray, *The Epistle to the Romans, Volume I* (Grand Rapids: William B. Eerdmans Publishing Company, 1997), 344.

is a measure of righteousness in them, he sees them covered in the righteousness of the Divine Messiah himself, who is their righteousness. Such an arrangement is only possible due to the transfer that takes place when the righteousness of Christ is imputed unto them.

JUSTIFICATION IS THROUGH FAITH ALONE

If righteousness is a free gift, how does one receive this gift from God? The texts from Romans cited above answer this question in the following terms: "salvation to everyone who believes" (Rom. 1:16); "the righteousness of God is revealed from faith for faith, as it is written, 'The righteous shall live by faith'" (Rom. 1:17); "to be received by faith" (Rom. 3:25); "the justifier of the one who has faith in Jesus" (Rom. 3:26); "Abraham believed God, and it was accounted to him for righteousness" (Rom. 4:3); "to him who does not work but believes" (Rom. 4:5); "his faith is accounted for righteousness" (Rom. 4:5); "the righteousness of the faith" (Rom. 4:11); "all those who believe" (Rom. 4:11); "shall be imputed to us who believe" (Rom. 4:24).

All this leads up to this conclusion: "Therefore, since we have been justified *by faith*, we have peace with God through our Lord Jesus Christ" (Rom. 5:1; emphasis added).

The repetition is such that not even the most distracted reader could miss the point. Paul is less concerned about sounding redundant than he is about stressing the fact that justification is through faith. This truth is corroborated by dozens of other biblical texts, a few of which are here collected:

> For God so loved the world, that he gave his only Son, that *whoever believes in him* should not perish but have eternal life.
> (John 3:16, NKJV; emphasis added)

> *Whoever believes in the Son* has eternal life; whoever does not obey the Son shall not see life, but the wrath of God remains on him.
> (John 3:36, NKJV; emphasis added)

> Truly, truly, I say to you, *whoever believes has eternal life*.
> (John 6:47, NKJV; emphasis added)

> To him all the prophets bear witness that *everyone who believes in him receives forgiveness of sins* through his name.
> (Acts 10:43, NKJV; emphasis added)

And by Him *everyone who believes is justified* from all things from which you could not be justified by the law of Moses.

> (Acts 13:39, NKJV; emphasis added)

What would the Roman Church have to say in response to this? The Catholic Church concedes that justification is by faith but not by faith *alone*. We can find in the canons of the Council of Trent (1545–1563) what the official position of the Catholic Church still is on this matter:

> We are therefore said to be justified by faith, because faith is the beginning of human salvation, the foundation and root of all justification, "without which it is impossible to please God" (Heb. 11:6) and to come to the fellowship of His sons; and we are therefore said to be justified gratuitously, because none of those things that precede justification, whether faith or works, merit the grace of justification.[58]

This declaration shows that the Catholic Church holds faith to be necessary for there to be justification, but that it is only the beginning or foundation of justification. It is insufficient to secure a permanent justification. Justification remains incomplete without works of righteousness performed by the individual, as other statements from Trent go on to clarify:

> If anyone says that by faith alone the sinner is justified, so as to mean that nothing else is required to cooperate in order to obtain the grace of justification...let him be anathema.　　　　(Section 6, canon 9)

> If anyone says that men are justified either by the imputation of the righteousness of Christ alone, or by the remission of sins alone, to the exclusion of the grace and love that is poured forth in their hearts by the Holy Spirit and is *inherent in them*; or even that the grace by which we are justified is only the favor of God—let him be anathema.　　　　(Section 6, canon 11; emphasis added)

> If anyone says that the justice received is not preserved and also not increased before God *through good works*, but that those works are merely the fruits and signs of justification obtained, but not the cause of its increase, let him be anathema.[59]

> (Section 6, canon 24; emphasis added)

If anyone says that the guilt is remitted to every penitent sinner after

---

58 H. J. Schroeder, trans., *Canons and Decrees of the Council of Trent: Original Text with English Translation* (London: Herder, 1941), 34–35.

59 Ibid., 45 (emphasis added).

the grace of justification has been received, and that the debt of eternal punishment is *so blotted out that there remains no debt of temporal punishment* to be discharged either in this world or in the next in Purgatory, before the entrance to the kingdom of heaven can be opened—let him be anathema.

(Section 6, canon 30; emphasis added)

What must be noted is that these declarations maintain that faith is insufficient for justification; that justification is based on a righteousness that is inherent in the righteous person; that the sinners own good works are instrumental in obtaining and preserving justification; and that a person who is justified is still liable to punishment in purgatory. The Vatican's position in this regard has not changed since Trent[60]:

> The Canons and Decrees of Trent are not merely the archaic opinion of some medieval bishops. They represent the official position of the Church to this day. All subsequent Catholic councils have uniformly reaffirmed Trent's pronouncements. In fact, the Second Vatican Council in the 1960s declared these doctrines "irreformable." All faithful Catholics are commanded to receive them as infallible truth. Therefore, to understand Roman Catholic doctrine on justification, we must go back to the Council of Trent.[61]

The Council of Trent constitutes an important historical landmark because it is from that date that the Catholic Church officially rejected the doctrine of justification by faith alone. It was the culminating point of a long, drifting process. What had been energetically preached in the first centuries of Christianity had been largely neglected so that it gradually became a rarity as centuries went by.

Finally, the Catholic Church's rejection of salvation through faith alone became official. From that point on, according to its own testimony, the Catholic Church considers anyone who maintains that justification is by faith alone to be anathema, accursed, separated from Christ. It should be clarified that the division in Christianity that took place in the sixteenth century was not due to the Protestants breaking with the church but due to the Roman

---

60 Second Vatican Council, Document 3, *LUMEN GENTIUM*, I:25: "Bishops...proclaim Christ's doctrine infallibly...when, gathered together in an ecumenical council, they are teachers and judges of faith and morals for the universal Church, whose definitions must be adhered to with the submission of faith."

61 John MacArthur, *Justification by Faith Alone*, ed. Don Kistler (Morgan, PA: Soli Deo Gloria Publications, 1995), 8.

Church breaking with the tradition of early Christianity and disassociating itself from the apostolic faith.

JUSTIFICATION BY FAITH PLUS WORKS IS INCOMPATIBLE WITH BIBLICAL TEACHING

Any attempt to combine faith and works for justification needs to be emphatically rejected. The biblical texts above do not allow for any other conclusion than that faith alone is sufficient for justification. To say that justification is by faith plus something else does not do justice to the Sacred Text since "everyone who believes is justified."

If it were possible to believe and still not be justified for lack of some additional element, we would be forced to say that "not everyone who believes is justified." The result would be that only some of those who believe would be justified. The saved would be those who not only have faith but also possess the other necessary element.

Faith is in no way the mere beginning of justification, which awaits completion through good works; faith is the beginning and the end of justification. In addition to teaching that justification is by faith, the Bible emphatically negates the possibility that human works may have the slightest role or make any contribution whatsoever to our salvation:

> He saved us, *not because of works done by us* in righteousness, but according to his own mercy, by the washing of regeneration and renewal of the Holy Spirit.   (Titus 3:5; emphasis added)

> Who saved us and called us to a holy calling, *not because of our works* but because of his own purpose and grace, which he gave us in Christ Jesus before the ages began.
> (2 Tim. 1:9; emphasis added)

> Yet we know that *a person is not justified by works of the law* but through faith in Jesus Christ, so we also have believed in Christ Jesus, in order to be justified by faith in Christ and *not by works of the law*, because *by works of the law no one will be justified*.
> (Gal. 2:16; emphasis added)

> What then shall we say that Abraham our father has found according to the flesh? For if Abraham was justified by works, he has something to boast about, but not before God. For what does the Scripture say? "Abraham believed God, and it was accounted to

him for righteousness." Now to him who works, the wages are not counted as grace but as debt. But *to him who does not work* but believes on Him who justifies the ungodly, his faith is accounted for righteousness, just as David also describes the blessedness of the man to whom God imputes righteousness *apart from works*.

(Rom. 4:1–6, NKJV; emphasis added)

For by grace you have been saved through faith. And this is not your own doing; it is the gift of God, *not a result of works*, so that no one may boast.   (Ephesians 2:8–9; emphasis added)

But if it is by grace, *it is no longer on the basis of works*; otherwise grace would no longer be grace.   (Rom. 11:6; emphasis added)

Then what becomes of our boasting? It is excluded. By what kind of law? By a law of works? No, but by the law of faith. For we hold that one is justified by faith *apart from works* of the law.

(Rom. 3:27–28; emphasis added)

The denials are so many and so clear that any doctrinal system which incorporates works as part of the criteria for justification cannot be considered biblical. Works have been totally excluded, not only perfect works or works that are good enough to make us deserving of eternal life. The Bible excludes works of any kind. Whether they be works done before we believe or afterward, whether they be works in conformity to the ceremonial law or to the moral law of God, they all fall together when confronted by this all-inclusive pronouncement: "Apart from works."

Salvation being by faith alone does not mean, of course, that the Bible is opposed to our performing good works in obedience to God's commandments. It is quite the contrary. The grace of God instructs us to renounce ungodliness and worldly passions, and to live self-controlled, upright, and godly lives in the present age (Titus 2:12).

Saving faith is a living faith that results in sanctification. There are no saved people who are not transformed. The one who has been forgiven of much, loves much. Whoever loves God keeps his commandments. True faith invariably produces works, but the works are the fruit of faith and do not constitute the reason for justification.

The difference between the Catholic doctrine and the Reformed faith can be thus summarized: In Catholicism, faith plus works result in justification;

in the Reformed faith, it is faith that results in justification and works. This difference is crucial, as will be explained ahead.

There are at least two reasons why salvation cannot be through works:

1 —

In the mind of the biblical authors, salvation through works would contradict salvation by grace. This is the driving force of the contrasts, "not because of works done by us in righteousness, *but* according to his own mercy" (Titus 3:5; emphasis added), and "not because of our works *but* because of his own purpose and grace" (2 Tim. 1:9; emphasis added).

Paul's reasoning focuses on the difference between a free gift and wages. Wages are earned by merit. They are gained as a right by fulfilling the requirements of a contract. Whoever works fulfilling the terms of an agreement has the right to receive the stipulated payment. Therefore, wages are paid as a debt, as an obligation. "Now to the one who works, his wages are not counted as a gift but as his due" (Rom. 4:4).

An employer who refuses to pay the agreed wages can be sued and forced to pay. This means that if God awarded salvation to the one who works, salvation would become a payment of sorts. In this case, God would be bound to grant salvation to all those who sufficiently performed the works he prescribed. If he did not, people could rightly protest.

Salvation on these terms is the opposite of salvation by grace. Grace, by definition, is unmerited favor. Grace is not the recompense for noble deeds. Grace can never be earned or bought. It is only grace if it is granted freely. Only that which could be retained without violating the rights of the receiver can be called grace.

In other words, grace is that which may be withheld leaving no room for somebody to allege injustice. Anything that God gave us in recognition for our works could be rightfully called wages, but not grace. But as sinners, the only wages we can hope to earn from our works is eternal death: "For the wages of sin is death, but the free gift of God is eternal life in Christ Jesus our Lord" (Rom. 6:23).

Eternal life is not in the category of wages. It is a free gift. If God set a goal for humanity and then promised salvation to those of us who achieved it by our own efforts, eternal life would be earned as wages, not received as a free gift. That is exactly why Paul insists that salvation is received by those who do not work for it *at all*:

But to him who does not work but believes on Him who justifies the ungodly, his faith is accounted for righteousness. (Rom. 4:5, NKJV)

This is a vital understanding. The free nature of salvation is at stake. The Bible says we are "justified by his grace as a gift" (Rom. 3:24). The same Greek word translated "gift" (δωρεὰν) is used in John 15:25, where we read that Jesus was hated "without a cause." The meaning is the same. God justifies his people freely, apart from our having given him any reason or cause for it, just as those who hated Jesus did so gratuitously, apart from him having supplied them with any cause or reason to hate him.

If God saved people according to their works, salvation would not be a free gift granted without a cause, that is, by grace. Grace and merit are opposites. We must choose between one and the other. Any attempt to combine the two will inevitably cancel out grace the moment works get included, no matter what works they may be, for "if it is by grace, it is no longer on the basis of works; otherwise grace would no longer be grace" (Rom. 11:6).

The only way to preserve the teaching that salvation is by grace is to exclude human works completely and, in so doing, exclude human merit as well. And since it is an irrefutable axiom that biblical salvation is by grace, any notion of our works contributing to salvation must be rejected. It is for this reason that the apostle Paul considers justification through faith alone as the only soteriology that is compatible with salvation by grace: "For this reason it is by faith, that it might be in accordance with grace" (Rom. 4:16, NASB).

The various systems that try to blend salvation by faith and by works all have essentially the same profile. They recognize that the sinner does not possess perfect righteousness, but they believe God considers it acceptable to condescend to sinners by establishing a lower standard of righteousness that is within their reach and promising to save those who succeed in at least living up to this inferior alternate standard.

The Jews in the time of Christ preached that the standard was to keep the law adequately (circumcision, the rituals of Judaism, the observance of holy days, obedience to the moral laws, etc.). In Catholicism, the required works became baptism, confirmation, going to mass, observing confession and penance, a good moral conduct, etc. Other standards could be proposed. It could be more rigorous, requiring decades of impeccable conduct; or it could be more lenient, demanding nothing more than regular church attendance. It could even be, as many in society today suppose, that to be right with

God it is enough to be a good person by contemporary social standards, not engaging in crimes of theft, murder, or the like. In any such model, salvation is always a reward for attaining a specified level of goodness, which is not reached by all people.

The Bible is radically opposed to all this, teaching instead that salvation is a free gift received through faith. The person who is saved cannot congratulate himself or herself for having done a single thing toward salvation, not even believing. The faith that brings justification itself is not something produced by the sinner and for which he or she is rewarded, for saving faith is a gift from God brought about by the work of the Holy Spirit in the heart (Eph. 2:8; John 6:29, 45):

> Jesus answered them, "This is the work of God, that you believe in him whom he has sent." (John 6:29)

> It is written in the Prophets, "And they will all be taught by God." Everyone who has heard and learned from the Father comes to me. (John 6:45)

Instead of believing and receiving grace for it, the Bible teaches that it is necessary to receive grace in order to believe (Acts 18:27; Phil. 1:29). We cannot invert this order without transforming faith into a human work and grace into its reward.

Once it has been understood that faith is a gift from God and that justification is through faith alone, it becomes evident how salvation is truly by grace alone. In light of this, it makes perfect sense for Paul to contend that "for this reason it is by faith, that it might be in accordance with grace" (Rom. 4:16, NASB).

Dr. Lloyd-Jones has put it very well:

> What is the relationship between faith and justification? This is important because some people think it means that we are justified on account of our faith. But that is the very essence of heresy and must be condemned root and branch. If I am justified on account of my faith, or because I exercise faith, then my salvation is definitely by works and God justifies me because of this work that I have done which I call faith. But the Scripture does not say that I am justified on account of my faith or because I am exercising faith, it says that I am justified *by* faith, which means that faith is the instrument—and

nothing but the instrument—by which I am enabled to receive the righteousness which God gives me.[62]

To better understand this concept, we need to ask ourselves the following questions: What is the righteousness by which we are made righteous in the eyes of God? Is it our act of believing, or is it something else? And if it is something else, what relation does our faith have to our justification?

In answering these two questions, we must realize that faith is not the righteousness that makes a person righteous. As John Murray explains,

If faith itself is the righteousness contemplated and is that *on account of which* God justifies the ungodly, then the question poses itself: how is this to be reconciled with what is the burden of New Testament teaching in this connection, namely, that the redemption which is in Christ, the propitiation and reconciliation through his blood, and his obedience unto death constitute that on the basis of which sinners are justified? If faith is itself the righteousness, how does the redemptive work of Christ come into direct relation to our justification, as the teaching of Paul in particular indicates?[63]

Nobody becomes righteous by his or her own obedience. Those who become righteous do so by the obedience of another, specifically the obedience of Christ.

For as by the one man's disobedience the many were made sinners, so *by the one man's obedience the many will be made righteous.*
(Rom. 5:19; emphasis added)

The biblical teaching is that faith, our faith, is not the grounds of our justification. The grounds of our justification is the righteousness of the Lord Jesus Christ imputed to us. Christ, and not my faith, is my righteousness. It is not my believing in Him that saves me. It is He who saves me. So you see the subtle danger of regarding my faith as the grounds of salvation?[64]

---

62 D. Martyn Lloyd-Jones, *Great Doctrines of the Bible, Volume II, God the Holy Spirit* (Wheaton, IL: Crossway, 2012), 176 (emphasis in original).

63 John Murray, *The Epistle to the Romans, Volume I* (Grand Rapids: William B. Eerdmans Publishing Company, 1997), 353 (emphasis in original).

64 D. Martyn Lloyd-Jones, *Great Doctrines of the Bible, Volume II, God the Holy Spirit* (Wheaton, IL: Crossway, 2012), 176.

Faith does not have the power to justify us, because to be righteous, we need a perfect righteousness. That is something that only the righteousness of Christ can supply. Believing in Christ could never be equated with being perfectly righteous. If God graciously accepted faith as righteousness, the truth would be that he would accept that which is not righteousness as if it were righteousness and salvation would end up being the recompense for an imperfect life.

The comments of puritan Obadiah Grew are particularly insightful:

> Faith itself, as an inherent quality, does not justify. A man is not justified because of faith, but by it; not for it, as a cause of, but by it, as an instrument in justification....faith is only that in us which God makes use of in our justification—not as meritorious of it, but as instrumental in it....Indeed, if faith itself were our righteousness, as some mistakenly think, then we would be justified by an imperfect righteousness.[65]

> For this is to make our faith our Christ, and to thrust out His righteousness from being the reason and matter of our justification.[66]

So we must deny that our faith is our righteousness and affirm that the obedience of Christ is our righteousness. Now as to the question of the relation our faith has to our justification, we should conclude that faith serves as an instrumental means by which the righteousness of Christ is put to our account. This important understanding of the relation between faith and justification is carefully delineated by Francis Turretin (1623–1687) in his classic book on justification:

> We are not justified except by a perfect righteousness....Nor can it be said that it is not indeed a perfect righteousness of itself, but is admitted as such by God and considered such by a gratuitous lowering of the law's demands....If faith is counted for righteousness, we will be justified by works because thus faith cannot but have the relation of a work which justifies.[67]

> Thus the antithesis of the apostle between works and faith would not hold good, since faith would always justify like a work....Thus we could be said to be justified "on account of faith" (*dia tēn pistin*). The Scripture never says this, but always either "by faith" (*pistei*) or "through faith" (*dia tēs pisteōs, ek pisteōs*) as by and instrument.[68]

---

65 Obadiah Grew, *The Lord Our Righteousness* (Morgan, PA: Soli Deo Gloria Publications, 2005), 20.
66 Ibid., 74.
67 Francis Turretin, *Justification* (Phillipsburg, NJ: P & R, 2004), 76.
68 Ibid., 79.

In our language, the preposition *by* can be ambiguous. It can indicate the agent or the instrument employed. Consider, for instance, these two phrases: "I was told by Peter" and "I was told by phone." In New Testament Greek, however, there is no room for this kind of ambiguity. For this reason, even if translations to other languages fail to make this fact apparent, it is perfectly clear in the original Greek text that faith serves an instrumental role each time we encounter the words *by faith* or *through faith* (dia with the genitive and never with the accusative).

The point is that faith does not constitute the righteousness of the righteous or the reason why they are righteous. Instead, it is the mere instrument by means of which the righteousness of Christ is imputed. It is not as though in the Gospel God accepted faith as making the believer righteous enough to be saved. God has not lowered his standard. Perfect righteousness is still needed. It would be inappropriate to reward faith with salvation because faith does not constitute a righteousness that is worthy of salvation and because doing so would transform salvation into a reward for obedience, violating everything the Bible teaches about salvation being by grace apart from works.

> Faith or the act of believing is not considered as our righteousness with God by a gracious acceptation: because what is only the instrument for receiving righteousness cannot be our righteousness itself formally....This is alluded to by Paul in Rom. 3:24 where faith cannot sustain any other meaning than that of an instrument, since the grace of God holds the relation of an efficient principle and the redemption of Christ that of the meritorious cause.[69]

Essentially, Turretin is explaining that having been brought to faith by the Spirit of God, we exert the faith that we received as a gift. In this manner, faith is the instrumental cause of salvation. Just as the act of eating does not nourish the body but rather the food which is ingested, so the act of believing does not justify but rather the perfect righteousness of Christ which is imputed unto the one who believes. Therefore, the believer is not justified by the merit of faith or as a reward for having believed, but through faith.

2 —

The second concern in the minds of the biblical authors when they exclude human works from the plan of salvation is that including them would give people room to boast in themselves. Paul raises this objection repeatedly:

---

69 Ibid., 75.

For *if Abraham was justified by works, he has something to boast about,* but not before God.   (Rom. 4:2; emphasis added)

For by grace you have been saved through faith. And this is not your own doing; it is the gift of God, *not a result of works, so that no one may boast*.   (Eph. 2:8–9; emphasis added)

Then *what becomes of our boasting? It is excluded. By what kind of law? By a law of works? No, but by the law of faith*. For we hold that one is justified by faith apart from works of the law.
(Rom. 3:27–28; emphasis added)

In the biblical perspective, salvation being a free gift, the people who God saves do not contribute in any way to their own salvation, so there is nothing about which they could boast or glory in themselves. Here too we may ponder Paul's questions:

For who makes you differ from another? And what do you have that you did not receive? Now if you did indeed receive it, why do you boast as if you had not received it?   (1 Cor. 4:7, NKJV)

And what could we answer? Only silence. However, if we could claim to have something that we did not receive, then we would have a right to boast and glory in ourselves for our accomplishment. But such is not the case. So there is nothing more inappropriate than for man to glory in himself.

Apart from God's grace, we are incorrigible sinners. The Bible describes our condition in eyes of God in the bleakest terms:

The LORD looks down from heaven on the children of man, to see if there are any who understand, who seek after God. They have all turned aside; together they have become corrupt; there is none who does good, not even one.   (Ps. 14:2–3)

For the intention of man's heart is evil from his youth.   (Gen. 8:21)

We have all become like one who is unclean, and all our righteous deeds are like a polluted garment. We all fade like a leaf, and our iniquities, like the wind, take us away.   (Isa. 64:6)

It is not as if we were only slightly imperfect, we are truly abominable in the eyes of God. To him, even our righteous deeds are polluted, even the very best of our works that we would look upon as our virtues. The Bible says we provoke God's wrath every day (Ps. 7:11) and attributes our survival to the daily renewed mercy of God:

> Through the LORD'S mercies we are not consumed, because His compassions fail not. They are new every morning; Great is Your faithfulness. (Lam. 3:22–23, NKJV)

Such a vile creature in such a deplorable moral condition has nothing to boast about and can only be saved if God, in his grace, shows pity. In the event that God does so, the sinner will have to recognize that none of his or her "good" works (like polluted garments) make a contribution. Nothing would be more repugnant than a man glorying in self-righteousness when his sole "contribution" toward salvation was to render it necessary! It is absolutely imperative that all gratitude be directed toward God. There can be no congratulations to the sinner because it would be both immoral and dishonoring to God to whom everything is owed.

This is what Paul has in mind when he says, "Not a result of works, so that no one may boast" (Eph. 2:9). Salvation by grace through faith leaves no room for sinners to boast (Rom. 3:27); it exalts God's grace and causes God, and God alone, to be glorified in the salvation of sinners. God's glory is, after all, the ultimate goal of creation and redemption.

> Your people shall all be righteous; they shall possess the land forever, the branch of my planting, the work of my hands, *that I might be glorified.* (Isa. 60:21; emphasis added)

> To grant to those who mourn in Zion—to give them a beautiful headdress instead of ashes, the oil of gladness instead of mourning, the garment of praise instead of a faint spirit; that they may be called oaks of righteousness, the planting of the LORD, *that he may be glorified.* (Isa. 61:3; emphasis added)

> *So that we* who were the first to hope in Christ *might be to the praise of his glory.* (Eph. 1:12; emphasis added)

God will not allow for a counterfeit salvation plot that robs him of his glory, transferring it to man:

> For my own sake, for my own sake, I do it, for how should my name be profaned? *My glory I will not give to another.* (Isa. 48:11; emphasis added)

Turn to me and be saved, all the ends of the earth! For I am God, and there is no other. By myself I have sworn; from my mouth has gone out in righteousness a word that shall not return: "To me every knee shall bow, every tongue shall swear allegiance. *Only in the LORD, it shall be said of me, are righteousness and strength*; to him shall come and be ashamed all who were incensed against him. *In the LORD all the offspring of Israel shall be justified and shall glory.*
(Isa. 45:22–25; emphasis added)

He is the source of your life in *Christ Jesus, whom God made* our wisdom and *our righteousness* and sanctification and redemption. Therefore, as it is written, *"Let the one who boasts, boast in the Lord."*
(1 Cor. 1:30–31; emphasis added)

"Or who has given a gift to him that he might be repaid?" For from him and through him and to him are all things. *To him be glory forever.* Amen.
(Rom. 11:35–36; emphasis added)

This leads up to a crucial issue. Every belief system that divides the glory of salvation between God and the sinner is offensive to God. Some people may suppose it is better to believe in salvation through a combination of faith and works, just in case, because it would make them more zealous of good works.[70] They imagine it is safer to believe this way, because they will be better insured if it turns out that works are indeed taken into account for salvation; and in any case, if on the Last Day salvation proves to be by faith alone, they feel that they won't have lost anything because they will still have had faith, besides their leftover good works.

There is, however, a serious flaw in this way of thinking. Those who believe in salvation by works inevitably deposit their faith in themselves, trusting in their own achievements for salvation. But God only saves those who place their faith and trust in Christ. Doing good works under the guise of securing one's own salvation is unbelief in the work of Christ as redeemer. It turns out that instead of having faith and good works, those who look to their own works for eternal salvation do not have the faith of which the Bible is speaking and are, therefore, unsaved. The Bible makes this abundantly clear, such as where Jesus denounced trusting in oneself as a hindrance to justification:

---

70 Love and gratitude are actually greater motivations to obedience than ambition (1 Cor. 15:10; 2 Cor. 5:14; Luke 7:41–43), whereas believing that salvation can be secured by good works taints the noble character of every good deed with a degree of self-interest.

He also told this parable to some who trusted in themselves that they were righteous, and treated others with contempt: "Two men went up into the temple to pray, one a Pharisee and the other a tax collector. The Pharisee, standing by himself, prayed thus: 'God, I thank you that I am not like other men, extortioners, unjust, adulterers, or even like this tax collector. I fast twice a week; I give tithes of all that I get.' But the tax collector, standing far off, would not even lift up his eyes to heaven, but beat his breast, saying, 'God, be merciful to me, a sinner!' I tell you, this man went down to his house justified, rather than the other. For everyone who exalts himself will be humbled, but the one who humbles himself will be exalted." (Luke 18:9–14)

Luke informs us that the parable is directed at some who were trusting in themselves, considering themselves to be righteous. There is no doubt that the Pharisees counted on a measure of divine mercy to be saved, but Jesus makes it irrefutably plain that they also counted on their own works.

The Pharisee described here makes no mention of ceremonies. The things he refers to as he reveals why he is confident of his justification are his works of obedience to God's commandments that are moral in nature ("You shall not steal" and "You shall not commit adultery," etc.). Jesus made His point extremely clear. He explicitly states that the Pharisee, trusting in his own works for salvation, was not justified, despite praying to the one true God, while the publican, who recognized his spiritual bankruptcy, went home justified. For what reason? Because everyone who exalts himself will be humbled, but the one who humbles himself will be exalted (v. 14).

Paul knew the mind of a Pharisee very well, having been one himself. Writing to the Philippians, he gives his testimony as to how he left the Pharisee system, which he describes as a legalistic religion of salvation by works, to trust in the grace of God in Christ:

For we are the real circumcision, who worship by the Spirit of God and glory in Christ Jesus and put no confidence in the flesh—though I myself have reason for confidence in the flesh also. If anyone else thinks he has reason for confidence in the flesh, I have more: circumcised on the eighth day, of the people of Israel, of the tribe of Benjamin, a Hebrew of Hebrews; as to the law, a Pharisee; as to zeal, a persecutor of the church; as to righteousness, under the law blameless. But whatever gain I had, I counted as loss for the sake of Christ. Indeed, I count everything as loss because of the surpassing worth of knowing Christ Jesus my Lord. For his sake I have suffered the loss of all things and count them as rubbish, in order that I may gain Christ and be found in him, not having a righteousness of my own that comes from the law, but that which comes through faith in Christ, the righteousness from God that depends on faith.   (Phil. 3:3–9)

Paul draws a contrast between those who "glory in Christ" and those who "put confidence in the flesh." He confesses that before coming to Christ, as one who practiced Judaism, he used to put his trust in the flesh. He portrays his experience in Judaism as that of a man full of self-righteousness who believed that he was increasing his chances of salvation by his obedience to God's commandments. He calls this "trusting in the flesh." So as to help others not commit the same mistake, he lists his impressive credentials, which start back when he was no more than eight days old. But he reveals that he later came to reject all of his credentials. He ceased to trust in the flesh and began to trust only in Jesus as his Savior.

Paul's choice of words is very radical at this point: "But whatever gain I had, I counted as loss for the sake of Christ....For his sake I have suffered the loss of all things and count them as rubbish, in order that I may gain Christ" (verses 7–8). Paul does not add Christ to his own array of works. He totally discards all his confidence in his own works and replaces it with Christ. After all, the true children of God are not those who glory in Christ and also in the flesh, but those who glory in Christ and put no confidence in the flesh (v. 3). Paul concludes by saying that he desires to be found in Christ *"not having a righteousness of my own that comes from the law,* but that which comes through faith in Christ, the righteousness from God that depends on faith" (v. 9; emphasis added).

We must pay careful attention to this conclusion. Paul emphatically renounces any righteousness of his own. He doesn't wish to have any of this kind of righteousness, not even just a little. He desires not to have any righteousness except that which comes through faith in Christ, because for him that is enough. While rejecting righteousness of his own, he embraces the righteousness that comes from God. This righteousness of divine origin does not proceed from works; it comes through faith in Christ. Paul replaces all trust in himself for trusting exclusively in Christ, because that is the only way he can be one of those who "glory in Christ" and "put no confidence in the flesh" (v. 3).

Just like Paul, we all must choose either to cling to our own righteousness or to renounce it in order to trust and glory in Christ alone as Savior. It's a choice between two saviors. Those who choose to trust in themselves are not trusting fully in Christ. Those who wish to trust in Christ must give up depending on what they do for themselves.

Writing to the Romans, Paul demonstrates that a belief in salvation by works was the spiritual downfall of his fellow Jews who remained in Judaism:

> What shall we say, then? That Gentiles who did not pursue righteousness have attained it, that is, a righteousness that is by faith; but that Israel who pursued a law that would lead to righteousness did not succeed in reaching that law. Why? Because they did not pursue it by faith, but as if it were based on works. They have stumbled over the stumbling stone, as it is written, "Behold, I am laying in Zion a stone of stumbling, and a rock of offense; and whoever believes in him will not be put to shame." (Rom. 9:30–33)

> Brothers, my heart's desire and prayer to God for them is that they may be saved. I bear them witness that they have a zeal for God, but not according to knowledge. For, being ignorant of the righteousness that comes from God, and seeking to establish their own, they did not submit to God's righteousness. For Christ is the end of the law for righteousness to everyone who believes. (Rom. 10:1–4)

In this passage, we again come across the idea of two opposing methods of becoming righteous: by trusting in Christ or by means of one's own works. Referring to Gentiles who were converted by the Gospel, Paul tells us that they were people who previously had not even been pursuing righteousness, yet they attained righteousness when they trusted in Christ. Next, he tells of people who pursued righteousness but failed. He is speaking of those caught up in Judaism. They did not succeed, Paul assures us, because of the means by which they sought to become righteous. "Why? Because they did not pursue it by faith, but as if it were based on works" (Rom. 9:32).

It matters that we pay attention to how the first-century Jews are described by the divinely inspired author. They pursued a law that would lead to righteousness, but they did not succeed (Rom. 9:31). They had zeal for God, but not according to knowledge (Rom. 10:2). They were ignorant of the righteousness that comes from God (the righteousness of Christ received by trusting him), so they went about establishing their own righteousness through their works (Rom. 10:3; 9:32).

Each one of these phrases proves that they were not saved in spite of all their religiosity and fervor. Paul is deeply grieved by this fact and prays to God for them, that they may be saved (Rom. 10:1). But these verses do more than just tell us that they were lost; they tell us why they were lost. The message that comes through repeatedly as Paul reinforces it is that they were not saved due to their own attempts at saving themselves by means of their own works. By doing so, they were refusing to submit to the righteousness that comes from God as a gift (Rom. 10:3).

How do we submit to the righteousness that comes from God? The only way is recognizing that we are totally incapable of saving ourselves and abandoning all trust in our own works or merits. Until we do so, we may be zealous of good works, but our righteousness will never be anywhere near what we need to stand before God, and all our efforts will be nothing more than a testimony of our refusal to trust in Christ alone as a sufficient Savior. We only seek to establish our own righteousness when we do not trust in the righteousness of God that is provided freely in Christ. That, in essence, is to reject the Gospel.

How difficult it is to accept the Gospel. Nothing seems more logical to us than salvation by works. Our natural tendency is to think that salvation must be a reward for those who prove themselves worthy. It doesn't make sense to the unregenerate mind that a religious person that strives to do good works during a whole lifetime can be condemned, while a notorious sinner can be justified instantly by depositing his or her faith in Christ as Savior. Salvation by grace through faith seems like something immoral, even subversive to good conduct. "For the word of the cross is folly to those who are perishing, but to us who are being saved it is the power of God" (1 Cor. 1:18).

For this reason, Jesus is called "a stone of stumbling, and a rock of offense" (Rom. 9:33). The Jews stumbled on this stone. We too should beware, lest we also stumble! The only remedy against stumbling is to profoundly understand the truth that we are all likewise condemned sinners. In the words of Scripture, "There is no distinction: for all have sinned and fall short of the glory of God" (Rom. 3:23).

This is an understanding that is reached when proper use is made of the law of God. It exposes us for who we really are so that nobody under its light can harbor any hopes of being saved by works. To take the law of God as a "Do it yourself" guide to salvation is to misuse it. The law's end is to show us how sinful we are so that every mouth may be stopped by the recognition of guilt before God (Rom. 3:19–20). If God graciously uses the law to awaken a heart to this reality, the sinner will despair of trusting in his or her own righteousness and be compelled to seek salvation in terms of pure mercy, putting the person on the right track to find the needed Savior in Christ. "For Christ is the end of the law for righteousness to everyone who believes" (Rom. 10:4).

If we are made uncomfortable by the Gospel, we need to rethink our beliefs. Our works cannot save us, nor can they help save us. We must understand that salvation by works exalts the sinner who does his or her part in salvation. That is what would actually be immoral. Salvation through faith in Christ alone exalts God's grace. That is what is truly appropriate.

Paul's epistle to the Galatians was written for the express purpose of refuting a distortion of Christianity that taught salvation by faith in Christ *plus* works. Paul called such a doctrine a perversion of the Gospel. He completely threw out any possibility of associating the two and insisted that it was a contradiction of grace and a cancellation of faith in Christ:

> I am astonished that you are so quickly deserting him who called you in the grace of Christ and are turning to a different gospel—not that there is another one, but there are some who trouble you and want to distort the gospel of Christ. But even if we or an angel from heaven should preach to you a gospel contrary to the one we preached to you, let him be accursed.   (Gal. 1:6–8)

These strong opening words of Paul are more than a mere rebuke or admonition; they are the pronouncement of a curse. Paul saw himself as opposing nothing less than a fatal heresy. As he writes, he exposes the character of the error he is so against. The Judaizers did not deny that the cross of Christ was essential for salvation. What they denied was that salvation was by faith in Christ alone. The "gospel" they preached went beyond that which Paul preached by adding the works of the law as a condition for salvation. They taught a legalistic version of Christianity. It was Christianized Phariseeism, which sought justification by keeping the law (circumcision, keeping of days, and other works of the law).

Paul rejected works completely in favor of justification by faith alone:

> Yet we know that a person is not justified by works of the law but through faith in Jesus Christ, so we also have believed in Christ Jesus, in order to be justified by faith in Christ and not by works of the law, because by works of the law no one will be justified.   (Gal. 2:16)

Paul considers it impossible to mingle grace and works because the one cancels out the other. There can be no halfway compromise. For him, it must be either all of grace or all of works. Thus he concludes that if works could save there would be no need for the death of Christ at all:

I do not nullify the grace of God, for if justification were through the law, then Christ died for no purpose. (Gal. 2:21)

In chapter 3, Paul divides people into two categories: those of faith and those of works:

Those of faith who are the sons of Abraham. (Gal. 3:7)

Those who are of faith are blessed along with Abraham the man of faith. (Gal. 3:9)

All who rely on works of the law are under a curse. (Gal. 3:10).

That is Paul's unyielding stance. He reinforces it in chapter 5:

Look: I, Paul, say to you that if you accept circumcision, Christ will be of no advantage to you. I testify again to every man who accepts circumcision that he is obligated to keep the whole law. You are severed from Christ, you who would be justified by the law; you have fallen away from grace. (Gal. 5:2–4)

Those who attempt to establish their own righteousness pursue salvation in a way that makes it impossible for Christ to be of any benefit to them. The salvation plan they buy into will only work if they succeed in keeping the whole law perfectly without ever sinning (which is impossible). Doing works to attain salvation is choosing to be either saved or damned on that basis. It amounts to severing oneself from Christ and from grace as the operating principle in salvation.

As Paul approaches the end of the epistle, the true motivation of the Judaizers is unmasked: "It is those who want to make a good showing in the flesh who would force you to be circumcised" (Gal. 6:12). A legalistic system of salvation appealed to the Judaizers because it would give them grounds to boast in their own achievements in the flesh. To state it another way, a salvation that includes works makes it possible for man to glory in what he has done for himself.

The great difference between the Gospel Paul preached and the false gospel of the Judaizers is that in Paul's proclamation all the glory of salvation went to God, while in the message of the Judaizers it was possible to glory in the flesh. That leads Paul to make the most definitive statement in the whole epistle: "But far be it from me to boast except in the cross of our Lord Jesus Christ, by which the world has been crucified to me, and I to the world" (Gal. 6:14).

To boast in the cross means to give God the glory for our salvation. It is to say, "I will have eternal life because of what Christ did for me on the cross." We should note that Paul doesn't simply boast in the cross; he will not boast in *anything* except the cross.

By contrast, it would be possible to attribute salvation to many things besides Christ. We could think that eternal life is the result of what Jesus does plus what we do for ourselves by keeping the law of God. But all who go the way of trusting in their own works will be judged according to their works and will receive from God what their works really deserve, while it is those who trust in Christ alone who will be saved. So Paul abhors the idea of boasting in anything else to the point of saying, "Far be it from me!"

It is not enough to say, "Salvation is through faith in Christ." We must say, "Salvation is through faith in Christ alone." We cannot trust in Christ to accomplish part of our salvation and trust in ourselves to complete it. We need to trust in Christ as our only and sufficient Savior.

Finding this message in the Bible, it is not surprising that the reformers were so alarmed by the belief that we can gain merit through good works, which contribute to our salvation. Even if we attempt to circumvent the problem claiming that the merit we can achieve is not the merit of actually deserving salvation, it continues to be our merit and our righteousness, and this is the very antithesis of the doctrine of salvation by grace taught in the Bible. It is nothing less than teaching another gospel that goes beyond that which was taught by the Lord and his apostles. As Luther put it, justification by faith alone is "the article on which the church stands or falls" (*articulus stantis et cadentis ecclesiae*).

THE LOSS OF SALVATION IN CATHOLIC DOCTRINE

As was stated at the beginning of this chapter, the Catholic concept of justification is the source of its doctrine of the loss of salvation. Justification is seen as a process that depends on works, so it can be lost according to one's works.

The Canons of Trent, section 6, canon 15 states the following:

It must be maintained that the grace of justification...is lost not only by infidelity, whereby also faith itself is lost, but also by every other mortal sin, though in this case faith is not lost; thus defending the teaching of the divine law which excludes from the kingdom of God not only unbelievers, but also the faithful [who are] "fornicators, adulterers, effeminate, liers with mankind, thieves, covetous, drunkards, railers, extortioners" (1 Cor. 6:9f.; 1 Tim. 1:9f.), and all others who commit deadly sins, from which with the help of divine grace they can refrain, and on account of which they are cut off from the grace of Christ.[71]

As R. C. Sproul has pointed out, the implications of this canon are quite significant:

Trent indicates that the grace of justification can be lost in two ways. The first is by infidelity, in which case faith is lost and justification with it. The second and more significant way is by mortal sin, in which case one may have faith but lose justification. If it is possible to have true faith but not have justification, then it is clear, by resistless logic, that justification is not by faith alone.[72]

The two ways by which salvation can be lost according to this declaration should be analyzed separately. As Sproul noted, it is a rejection of justification by faith alone to teach that salvation depends upon one's daily *conduct* and that it can be lost by sinning even when there is genuine faith. This, of course, is no matter of difficulty for the Roman Catholic Church since it openly rejects the doctrine of justification by faith alone. But an evangelical church that claims to preach justification by faith alone falls into a serious contradiction by saying that a *believer* may lose his salvation by sinning.

Believers do sin; that is not a matter of dispute. It is a fact attested to in Scripture both in didactic passages (such as Romans 7:15–23) and in narrative passages. The Bible is very frank about the sins of the saints. But sinning is not the same as renouncing the faith. Even when Peter denied the Lord in a moment of weakness, he did not cease to be a believer in Christ. The biblical formulation *"Whoever* believes has eternal life" (John 6:47; emphasis added) necessarily implies that as long as a person has genuine faith in Christ, that person is saved, even while committing a sin. Salvation is

---

71 H. J. Schroeder, trans., *Canons and Decrees of the Council of Trent: Original Text with English Translation* (London: Herder, 1941), 40.

72 Sproul, *Faith Alone* (Grand Rapids: Baker Books, 2006), 123.

not kept through good works, nor is it lost by committing a sinful act. Those who are in Christ by faith have the righteousness of Christ and are righteous. They are simultaneously righteous and sinners.

The Bible deals with the issue in this manner:

My little children, I am writing these things to you so that you may not sin. But if anyone does sin, we have an advocate with the Father, Jesus Christ the righteous. He is the propitiation for our sins, and not for ours only but also for the sins of the whole world.

(1 John 2:1–2)

John is speaking about believers. His words demonstrate that when believers sin they do not fall into condemnation. They continue to be defended by Jesus, their advocate. This is nothing more than the outworking of justification by faith. Teaching otherwise is essentially to teach justification by works and can only be done by consciously rejecting justification by faith alone or by having such a weak understanding of it that we fail to grasp its implications.

Underlying a doctrine of progressive justification is the idea that each new sin is put to the Christian's account and stays there until it too is forgiven or brought to judgment. That would mean that we would all accumulate sins on a daily basis, many of which would go unconfessed. To face God's just judgment, we need for all our sins to have been removed from our account. One sin is enough to condemn a person. As the psalmist noted, "If you, O LORD, should mark iniquities, O Lord, who could stand?" (Ps. 130:3).

The Catholic Church tries to find a way out of this problem with its doctrine of mortal and venial sins, along with its doctrine of purgatory. According to their teaching, only mortal sins incur the loss of salvation while venial sins can only add to the time one spends in purgatory. But according to the Bible, every sin is worthy of condemnation so that any sin from which one has not been justified would prevent that person from entering into eternal glory. If we reject the doctrines of venial sins and purgatory as unbiblical but still insist on the idea that justification is a progressive process, we can only conclude that the salvation of a justified person is lost each time a new sin is committed, no matter what sin it may be.

Following such a theory, we would be led to believe that losing one's justification is an everyday occurrence. And how could it be regained? By confessing each sin by name? If so, what would happen if one is overlooked and never confessed? Or would it be enough to just have a general attitude of repentance and a sincere purpose to please God?

If that were the case, what would happen if we died before we came to repentance of a particular sin? It would certainly mean that everything hangs on the moment of a Christian's death. If one is "lucky," death will come at a good moment or with ample warning time to allow for a last-minute "getting right with God."

But the "unlucky" Christians, who are caught by surprise at a moment of sin, will be in hell by the time they realize what happened. Such a perspective would make it impossible to affirm that a departed brother or sister is with the Lord, apart from knowing the person's last thoughts.

Frankly, such a view is absurd. Nobody can determine to never sin again. Neither can we vow to not sin moments before we die. This is by no means merely theoretical. Many Christians have died in the very act of sin. Who can be sure that it will not be the same with us? Believing in this way will lead to an absolute uncertainty as to where we will spend eternity. Some may think that this kind of pressure will promote more zeal in fighting sin (although it would still not ensure salvation), but it is more likely that it will only be effective in causing Christians to despair.

In fact, many evangelicals today live in this insecurity. They believe they are going back and forth, in and out of salvation all the time. I have personally known brothers and sisters who were living under this kind of pressure. On one occasion, I even heard a young lady share her testimony telling everybody that she had already lost her salvation several times while, at the same time, assuring us that she was ready in case Jesus came back at that moment. We cannot stand for such a teaching. The biblical passages examined above teach us to reject every doctrine that makes salvation dependent upon our good behavior.

JUSTIFICATION IS AN ACT, NOT A PROCESS

Furthermore, the Bible doesn't treat justification as a process but as a single act. The reformed tradition has shown a great precision on this point, as can be seen in the definition of justification found in the *Westminster Shorter Catechism*:

Question 33. What is justification?

Answer. Justification is an act of God's free grace, wherein he pardoneth all our sins, and accepteth us as righteous in His sight, only for the righteousness of Christ imputed to us, and received by faith alone.

A proof of this is that the Bible always links justification with what occurred at conversion. The Bible never treats justification as something that is ongoing or that occurs repeatedly after conversion.

The question could be stated in terms of when justification takes place. Is it at the moment a person believes, is it repetitive throughout one's lifetime, is it at the moment of death, or is it on the Day of Judgment after a scrutinizing a person's whole life?

The Bible consistently teaches that justification takes place once for all, at the moment a person believes:

> For what does the Scripture say? "Abraham believed God, and it was counted to him as righteousness." (Rom. 4:3)

Of course, Abraham sinned after that point in time, but when Paul recalls the case of Abraham, he pinpoints the moment when he believed God as the instant in which the matter was settled. The justification that he received on that occasion never expired or required a renewal. When he was circumcised years later, it was a sign of the righteousness he had had since that day:

> He received the sign of circumcision as a seal of the righteousness that he had by faith while he was still uncircumcised. (Rom. 4:11)

In his parable of the Pharisee and the publican, Jesus answered the question about when justification takes place: "I tell you, this man went down to his house justified" (Luke 18:14). He did not have to wait until he had performed works of penitence, much less until the Day of Judgment. That same day, he went home a justified man. Similarly, the narrative of Zacchaeus's conversion closes with our Lord, proclaiming, "Today salvation has come to this house" (Luke 19:9).

JUSTIFICATION IS A SINGLE UNREPEATABLE ACT

Every time the Bible speaks of salvation, it is treated as something that takes place instantaneously, not as a process. In addition, justification is treated as a definitive act. We never find the idea in the Bible that a person could be justified more than once. The words of Jesus in John 5:24 presuppose this once for all character of salvation:

> Truly, truly, I say to you, whoever hears my word and believes him who sent me has eternal life. He does not come into judgment, but *has passed from death to life.* (John 5:24; emphasis added)

The verb tense employed here looks back to something that has already occurred in the past. At a specific moment in time, whoever believes (presently) has passed (in the past) from death to life. In like fashion, Paul writes the following:

> Therefore, if anyone is in Christ, he is a new creation. *The old has passed away*; behold, the new has come.
> (2 Cor. 5:17; emphasis added)

Much of 1 Corinthians was written in a tone of rebuke. Paul was seeking to correct errors in the church. Among these were divisions, disrespect for the Lord's Supper, abuses in the realm of spiritual gifts, complacency in face of ongoing immorality, and lawsuits among church members.

The Corinthians were still sinners, nobody can deny that. Yet Paul does not speak of their justification as something that was being revised; he refers to it as having been settled once for all on the day that they believed, with permanently enduring results:

> And such were some of you. But you were washed, you were sanctified, *you were justified* in the name of the Lord Jesus Christ and by the Spirit of our God.　　(1 Cor. 6:11; emphasis added)

If any of them had ever lost their justification since conversion, what would matter now would not be their original justification but rather their more recent renewal of it. It is clear that the Bible treats the justification of believers as an act that has been concluded since the day the Gospel was believed, not as an ongoing process.

JUSTIFICATION IS AN IRREVERSIBLE ACT

Lastly, we should note that justification is an irreversible act. The act of justification is not the doing of a person; it is an act of God. It is a declaration on God's part affirming that a certain person is just, or righteous, in the court of divine justice. That is to say that when God justifies a person, he has already pronounced his verdict declaring that person to be justified, even before the Judgment. Justification cannot be revoked nor repeated, because once God has made a pronouncement, he will never go back on his word.

Francis Turretin expresses this truth succinctly:

> It's certainty is twofold: one of the object in itself by the immutability and perseverance by which God never recalls the pardon once

given (on account of the immutability of his grace, justice and promise confirmed by an oath, Heb. 6:17–18). For the gifts of God bestowed upon the elect and the calling according to his purpose (*kata prothesin*) are without repentance (*ametamelēta*, Rom. 11:29). Hence God never condemns and disinherits those whom he has once justified and made heirs.[73]

THE IMMUTABILITY OF GOD

The reality of God's immutable nature weighs in on this issue. If everything depended on our consistency, God would certainly find an abundance of motives to disinherit and destroy us. He doesn't do so for one good reason:

> For I the LORD do not change; therefore you, O children of Jacob, are not consumed. (Mal. 3:7)

Paul tells us in Romans 11:29 that the gifts and the calling of God are irrevocable. Paul is dealing with another subject in the context, but the truth of those words applies just as much here because Paul appeals to that statement as an absolute principle that is applicable to all of God's gifts. His whole point is that the gifts and calling of God are always irrevocable, which makes it so in the case of which he is speaking.

If there were cases in which the gifts and calling of God were revocable, Paul's argument would be invalid. We are, therefore, obliged to recognize that God never revokes the gift of eternal life once it has been granted to someone.

With this in mind, we can go back to the words of James:

> Every good gift and every perfect gift is from above, coming down from the Father of lights with whom there is no variation or shadow due to change. Of his own will he brought us forth by the word of truth, that we should be a kind of firstfruits of his creation. (James 1:17–18)

James teaches us that every good gift and every perfect gift comes from God, a God who never changes. There can be no variation or hint of change in God. Our salvation became a reality because he brought us to himself of his own will, by the word of truth (v. 18). Seeing it was a work of God, we can be sure that it will never be undone, for God does not change. What has been done is definitive.

---

73 Francis Turretin, *Justification* (Phillipsburg, NJ: P & R, 2004), 111.

It would truly denigrate God to portray him as one who forgives today and is sorry for having done so tomorrow, reneging on his own pronouncement. That is not the God we find in the Bible:

> God is not a man, that He should lie, Nor a son of man, that He should repent. Has He said, and will He not do? Or has He spoken, and will He not make it good? Behold, I have received a command to bless; He has blessed, and I cannot reverse it. He has not observed iniquity in Jacob, Nor has He seen wickedness in Israel. The LORD his God is with him, And the shout of a King is among them.
>
> (Num. 23:19–21, NKJV)

Some have sought to find contrary evidence in the Bible, arguing that God can go back on his Word They especially appeal to 1 Samuel 2:30 (NIV), where God pronounces judgment upon the house of Eli:

> "Therefore the Lord, the God of Israel, declares: 'I promised that members of your family would minister before me forever.' But now the Lord declares: 'Far be it from me! Those who honor me I will honor, but those who despise me will be disdained.'"

For those unfamiliar with this text, it may really seem like God changed here, but those who understand the context of the promise know better. God had given the priesthood in the Old Covenant to the tribe of Levi, more specifically to the descendants of Phinehas, who was Aaron's grandson (Num. 25:11–13). Eli and his sons were from that lineage, but they were not the only ones.

God's curse on Eli and his descendants did not in any way annul his previous promise to Phinehas, whose other descendants continued to serve in the priesthood. There is a similarity between this case and the curse pronounced on Jehoiakim in Jeremiah 36:30, which disallowed any of his descendants from the throne of David but did not undo God's promise to David.

Another text that is often cited is 1 Samuel 13:13–14, in which Samuel tells Saul that the Lord would have established Saul's kingdom over Israel forever if only he had obeyed God. But this text is not really pertinent because the Lord had never actually promised such a thing to Saul. Therefore, nothing was granted by God, which was later revoked. It goes without saying that God would have kept his word if he had given Saul the promise of a perpetual kingdom.

It has also been objected that if the immutability of God implies that justification is irreversible, it would imply that the sinner can never be forgiven either, because consistency would necessitate a doctrine of once under the wrath of God, always under the wrath of God. It would make God unable to change so as to forgive, it is claimed. However, that comparison is invalid since condemnation is not a gift from God and because in the case of the lost God has not pronounced individual sentences in advance of the Day of Judgment. It is not that God cannot change in his dealings with his creatures; it is that God cannot go back on his word.

It is equally futile to claim that saved individuals could lose the gift of eternal life according to how they changed so that God would be the same, but the loss of justification would only indicate a change occurring in the person. If a change in the individual could bring about the loss of justification, the question we should ask is whether or not God knew beforehand that he was dealing with somebody who would later fall away.

If we deny that he knew it, we deny his omniscience. If we admit he must have known, we are left with a scenario in which God declares a person to be righteous and grants him the gift of eternal life, even while he knows that he will be revoking it at a later time. This involves God in treating justification as a sort of make believe.

Jesus teaches us that there is joy in heaven over one sinner who repents. He does not say there is joy over one sinner who finally makes it to heaven. If justification were reversible, would not this rejoicing be premature? After all, it is not only the angels that rejoice but also God himself rejoices, as is indicated by the parable of the shepherd rejoicing over his lost sheep:

> What man of you, having a hundred sheep, if he has lost one of them, does not leave the ninety-nine in the open country, and go after the one that is lost, until he finds it? And when he has found it, he lays it on his shoulders, rejoicing. And when he comes home, he calls together his friends and his neighbors, saying to them, *"Rejoice with me,* for I have found my sheep that was lost." Just so, I tell you, there will be more joy in heaven over one sinner who repents than over ninety-nine righteous persons who need no repentance.
>
> (Luke 15:4–7)

The shepherd in the parable represents God. The lesson Jesus is teaching us is that God himself rejoices in the day that a sinner repents. The parable of the prodigal son shows this same joy in God. It is not reasonable to believe that God celebrates in this way when each sinner repents, knowing full well that it concerns someone who he will ultimately banish to hell.

People who wish to argue against the irreversible character of justification should heed the words of the puritan John Owen (1616–1683):

Neither is that parenthetical expression, of a change imagined in the persons concerning whom God's intentions are, any plea for his changeableness upon this supposal; for he either foresaw that change in them or he did not. If he did not, where is his prescience? yea, where is his deity? If he did, to what end did he really and verily intend and purpose to do so and so for a man, when at the same instant he knew the man would so behave himself as he should never accomplish any such intention towards him?...If one should really and verily intend or purpose to give a man bread to eat tomorrow, who he knows infallibly will be put to death tonight, such an one will not, perhaps, be counted changeable, but he will scarce escape being esteemed a changeling. Yet it seems it must be granted that God verily and really intends to do so and so for men, if they be in such and such a condition, which he verily and really knows they will not be in!...Either prove that God doth change, which he saith he doth not, or that the saints may perish though he change not, which he affirms they cannot, or you speak not to the business in hand.[74]

The Bible is consistent and conclusive. God does not change, and his gifts are irrevocable, which makes justification irrevocable. The promises of God to his people prove this and guard the truth from all sides. God's forgiveness cannot be repealed:

I, I am he who blots out your transgressions for my own sake, and *I will not remember your sins.* (Isaiah 43:25; emphasis added)

Who is a God like you, pardoning iniquity and passing over transgression for the remnant of his inheritance? He does not retain his anger forever, because he delights in steadfast love. He will again have compassion on us; he will tread our iniquities under foot. *You will cast all our sins into the depths of the sea.* (Mic. 7:18–19; emphasis added)

God forgives and forgets, in a manner of speaking. To cast something into the depths of the sea is a euphemism for casting it into a place from where it can never be retrieved and, therefore, will never again be seen!

---

74 John Owen, *The Doctrine of the Saints' Perseverance Explained and Confirmed*, vol. 11 of *The Works of John Owen* (Rio, WI: Ages Software Inc., 2000), 202.

For as high as the heavens are above the earth, so great is his steadfast love toward those who fear him; *as far as the east is from the west, so far does he remove our transgressions from us.*
(Ps. 103:11–12; emphasis added)

For I will be merciful toward their iniquities, and *I will remember their sins no more.* (Heb. 8:12; emphasis added)

"This is like the days of Noah to me: as I swore that the waters of Noah should no more go over the earth, so I have sworn that I will not be angry with you, and will not rebuke you. For the mountains may depart and the hills be removed, *but my steadfast love shall not depart from you, and my covenant of peace shall not be removed,*" says the LORD, who has compassion on you. (Isa. 54:9–10)

As this marvelous text goes on, it promises that God will keep his people until they are adorned with glory in the New Jerusalem described in Revelation 21 and 22. God even promises to sovereignly protect them in such a special way that no weapon or attack will be able to bring them harm and they will triumph over every accusation:

O afflicted one, storm-tossed and not comforted, behold, I will set your stones in antimony, and lay your foundations with sapphires. I will make your pinnacles of agate, your gates of carbuncles, and all your wall of precious stones. All your children shall be taught by the LORD, and great shall be the peace of your children. In righteousness you shall be established; you shall be far from oppression, for you shall not fear; and from terror, for it shall not come near you. If anyone stirs up strife, it is not from me; whoever stirs up strife with you shall fall because of you. Behold, I have created the smith who blows the fire of coals and produces a weapon for its purpose. I have also created the ravager to destroy; *no weapon that is fashioned against you shall succeed, and you shall confute every tongue that rises against you in judgment*. This is the heritage of the servants of the LORD and their vindication from me, declares the LORD.
(Isaiah 54:11–17; emphasis added)

The permanent nature of salvation finds one of its most beautiful witnesses in the book of Hebrews:

For by a single offering he has perfected for all time those who are being sanctified. And the Holy Spirit also bears witness to us; for after saying, "This is the covenant that I will make with them after those days, declares the Lord: I will put my laws on their hearts, and write them on their minds," then he adds, "I will remember their sins and their lawless deeds no more." Where there is forgiveness of these, there is no longer any offering for sin.   (Heb. 10:14–18)

Verse 14 affirms that those who are being sanctified by the blood of Jesus are perfected *for all time*, which means forever, once for all and in an unalterable way.

The next verse tells us that the Holy Spirit himself bears witness to this fact in the Old Testament. The quote comes from Jeremiah 31:33–34, where the New Covenant is prophesied. We are guided to focus our attention on the second part of the quote, where we read, "I will remember their sins and their lawless deeds no more."

According to the author of Hebrews, these words prove that the saved are perfected for all time. If God forgives a person and promises that he will never again remember their sins forever, what more needs to be said?

The words *no more* are the English translation of the strongest possible negative construction in biblical Greek (οὐ μὴ). It is reserved for things that absolutely cannot happen, no matter what, come what may. Their use in this frame emphasizes the finality of the matter. God will not remember our sins, period. If anyone rises and asks, "But what if this happens, or what if that comes to pass?" the answer is always, "No, God will not remember their sins at all!"

Does that amount to saying, "Once saved, always saved," no matter what happens? If justification is an act that can never be annulled, that seems to indicate that a believer can stop growing in Christ and abandon the way of sanctification, or even turn away from the faith completely and still continue to be saved.

Would that be the case? Are we now affirming what we rejected in the previous chapter? Absolutely not. Perseverance is necessary. It is not compatible with the character of God to promote sin. It is unthinkable that God's forgiveness could be made into a license for giving oneself over to sin with God's blessing.

Once again, it needs to be stated that what binds us to Christ is faith—a living and working faith. On the hypothesis of a justified believer abandoning the faith, we would be forced to admit that such a person would cease to be one of those to whom the biblical promises to "everyone who believes" apply.

This raises the issue of the second way in which a person could fall from a state of grace according to the Catholic position (i.e., by apostatizing from the faith). Some evangelicals have held that some saints do abandon the faith and that salvation is lost when this happens. This belief at least strives to line up with the vital principle of the Reformation that salvation is by faith alone, which cannot be said about the belief in losing salvation by committing sin. But this doctrine is only a half truth. It is true that perseverance is indispensable, but it is also true that, by God's grace, all saints persevere.

Saying that the saints would be condemned *if* they did not persevere does not contradict what has been stated about the definitive nature of justification. There are some things that are impossible. It is impossible for God to lie (Heb. 6:18), but that does not make it inappropriate for Jesus to say, "If I were to say that I do not know him, I would be a liar like you" (John 8:55). It is impossible for anything that God has spoken to fail or for any biblical prophecy to go unfulfilled (Matt. 5:18; John 10:35), but that doesn't keep Jesus from saying that the Scriptures would end up failing if he appealed to the Father to save him from the cross (Matt. 26:53–54).

The point is that it is not incompatible to affirm that it is absolutely impossible for a saint to fall to perdition and at the same time state that it is necessary for the saints to persevere, as long as there is a guarantee that is absolutely safe to the effect that all the saints will persevere in Christ until they are glorified. Such a guarantee does exist. It is not to be found in the saints themselves but in God. The immutable character of God allows us to join in with the apostle in stating, "I am sure of this, that he who began a good work in you will bring it to completion at the day of Jesus Christ" (Phil. 1:6).

The justification of the saints will never need to be reversed because the saints persevere; and the saints persevere because God, who is immutable, will not leave unfinished the work of salvation he began. This is the Reformed doctrine, as can be ascertained by its creeds and canons. To demonstrate this point, here are two quotes taken from important historic Baptist confessions of faith.

The *New Hampshire Baptist Confession* of 1833 declares the following:

11 Of the Perseverance of Saints

We believe that such only are real believers as endure unto the end; that their persevering attachment to Christ is the grand mark which distinguishes them from superficial professors; that a special Providence watches over their welfare; and they are kept by the power of God through faith unto salvation.

The *London Baptist Confession of 1689* supplies us what is perhaps the most beautiful statement on the perseverance of the saints to be found in all the historic creeds. Here is a portion of its text:

17:1 Those whom God hath accepted in the beloved, effectually called and sanctified by his Spirit, and given the precious faith of his elect unto, can neither totally nor finally fall from the state of grace, but shall certainly persevere therein to the end, and be eternally saved, seeing the gifts and callings of God are without repentance, whence he still begets and nourisheth in them faith, repentance, love, joy, hope, and all the graces of the Spirit unto immortality; and though many storms and floods arise and beat against them, yet they shall never be able to take them off that foundation and rock which by faith they are fastened upon; notwithstanding, through unbelief[75] and the temptations of Satan, the sensible sight of the light and love of God may for a time be clouded and obscured from them, yet he is still the same, and they shall be sure to be kept by the power of God unto salvation, where they shall enjoy their purchased possession, they being engraven upon the palm of his hands, and their names having been written in the book of life from all eternity.

It is important that we notice how in these confessions the perseverance of the saints is not attributed to man but to the faithfulness of God, safeguarding unto God all the glory. He himself is the One who keeps us by means of special providence, begetting and constantly nourishing in us faith, repentance, love, joy, hope, and all the graces of the Spirit, which are conducive unto eternal life.

If God is unconditionally committed to doing this—and he is—then there is no danger in blotting out all our sins *forever*. This truth is taught in the

---

75 The word *unbelief* in this context does not refer to apostasy from the faith or the absence of faith in Christ as Savior but to lapses in faith that befall believers when stricken with doubt.

same passage from Hebrews, where we read that God will put his laws on our hearts and write them on our minds. That is the reason why he can add that God will in no wise remember our sins.

It is a well-known fact that in the Catholic practice of canonizing saints a person can only become a saint after death, so the Catholic Church does not run the risk of embarrassment by canonizing someone who turns out to bring it shame. But we should not think of God as acting in this way. God knows all things. More than that, he sovereignly rules over all things.

God does not fear the future. He does not need to be cautious in granting eternal salvation to his own even while we are still in this world. There is no danger that he may lose us later on and come to regret having made his pronouncement that we are already justified.

It is evident that there are still conditions that need to be fulfilled so that we may be glorified, but God is quite able to keep us from stumbling and to present us blameless before the presence of his glory with great joy (Jude 1:24). The biblical teaching as to how God keeps us will be examined in the following chapters.

The Transforming Power of Regeneration

No man [truly] making a profession of faith sinneth; nor does he that possesses love hate any one. The tree is made manifest by its fruit; so those that profess themselves to be Christians shall be recognized by their conduct. For there is not now a demand for mere profession, but that a man be found continuing in the power of faith to the end.[76]   (Ignatius, AD 110)

The power of faith is such, that it exceeds every thing that is contrary to it and even the whole world itself that it stands in the way of it.... Divine instruction is a possession that abides forever....To him that has by exercise, proceeding from knowledge, got that virtue which cannot be lost, the habit of it becomes natural, and as heaviness to a stone, "so his knowledge cannot be lost," neither unwillingly nor willingly; by the power of reason, knowledge, and providence, it is so established that it cannot be lost; through a godly fear it becomes so as that it cannot be lost. The greatest thing therefore is the knowledge of God, because this is so preserved that virtue cannot be lost....We shall not fall into corruption, who pass through into incorruption, "because he sustains us"; for he hath said, and he will do it.[77]   (Clement of Alexandria, AD 190)

In the previous chapters, two aspects of Reformed doctrine were considered: (1) the truth that every believer in Christ must persevere unto the end in faith and sanctification to enter eternal glory, and (2) the fact that justification is a one-time irrevocable pronouncement made by God at the moment an individual is brought to genuine faith in Christ. Some biblical reasons for these conclusions were also set forth.

---

76 Ignatius: *Epistle of Ignatius to the Ephesians*, ed. A. Roberts and J. Donaldson, Volume 1 of *The Ante-Nicene Fathers*, The Master Christian Library (Rio, Wisconsin: AGES Software, 2000) 110–111.

77 Clemens Alexandrinus, quoted by John Gill, *The Cause of God and of Truth*, Part 4, Chapter 5, Section 6, The Ultimate Christian Library (Rio, Wisconsin: AGES Software, 2000), 814–815.

At first glance, one might judge these two propositions to be at odds with each other. All it would take is for one saved person to fall away from the Lord and not persevere to reveal a contradiction. The person would either be lost as a result of not persevering, proving justification to be reversible, or remain justified, proving perseverance to be unnecessary.

The paradox is resolved when we understand that we have secure reasons to believe that all the saved do, in fact, persevere. The perseverance of the saints is certain because God Almighty, who is unchanging, takes measures to infallibly keep all those whom he saves so that none are ever lost to him.

Jude reminds us that it is God who keeps us, for he is perfectly able to do so:

> Jude, a servant of Jesus Christ and brother of James, To those who are called, beloved in God the Father and *kept* for Jesus Christ.
> (Jude 1:1; emphasis added)

> Now to him who *is able to keep you from stumbling and to present you blameless before the presence of his glory* with great joy, to the only God, our Savior, through Jesus Christ our Lord, be glory, majesty, dominion, and authority, before all time and now and forever. Amen.   (Jude 1:24–25; emphasis added)

Similarly, Peter remarks the following:

> Blessed be the God and Father of our Lord Jesus Christ! According to his great mercy, he has caused us to be born again to a living hope through the resurrection of Jesus Christ from the dead, to an inheritance that is imperishable, undefiled, and unfading, kept in heaven for you, *who by God's power are being guarded through faith* for a salvation ready to be revealed in the last time.
> (1 Peter 1:3–5; emphasis added)

These passages are not speaking of God keeping us from accidents or sicknesses, nor from physical harm that people may inflict. Jude is talking about God keeping us from stumbling to present us blameless before the presence of his glory. What Peter has in mind is that we are kept by God unto an inheritance in heaven that is imperishable, undefiled, and unfading. That is to say that in this world we are kept by God until we reach the eternal glory of his presence in heaven.

PERSEVERANCE RESULTS FROM PRESERVATION

Some have framed their reasoning concerning the security of the believer and the possibility of losing salvation as if it were a choice between believing in perseverance or preservation. They ask, "Do we remain saved because we persevere or because God keeps us?"

That is actually a false dilemma. Both of these concepts are taught in the Bible, so we cannot choose one and throw out the other. In the same context, Jude wrote that we are kept by God and that we are to keep ourselves in the love of God:

> But you, beloved, build yourselves up in your most holy faith; pray in the Holy Spirit; *keep yourselves* in the love of God, waiting for the mercy of our Lord Jesus Christ that leads to eternal life.
>
> (Jude 1:20–21; emphasis added)

The same two truths are also set side by side in Paul's epistle to the Philippians:

> Therefore, my beloved, as you have always obeyed, so now, not only as in my presence but much more in my absence, *work out your own salvation* with fear and trembling, for *it is God who works in you, both to will and to work for his good pleasure*.
>
> (Phil. 2:12–13; emphasis added)

Since these two realities go hand in hand, what we need to understand is how these two truths harmonize and how they relate to each other. The question we ought to ask is this: "Does the Bible teach that God keeps us *as long as we persevere*, or does it teach that we persevere *as long as God keeps us*?" That is the real issue. In other words, is our perseverance the reason God keeps us, or is it the result of God actively keeping us?

The biblical passages cited above indicate that it is God's preserving work that results in our perseverance rather than the other way around. In the first place, consider the words of Peter, "who by God's power are being guarded through faith," for final salvation. Just like Jude, Peter tells us that we are kept (passive voice). Of course, we are pictured as active when the Bible speaks about our persevering, but we are not said to have any participation in God's activity of keeping us.

By way of contrast, when we are exhorted to work out your own salvation (the area in which we are active), God is still portrayed as being involved, acting in an imperceptible way to guarantee that we persevere since it is God who works in us, both to will and to work for his good pleasure (Phil. 2:12–13).

It should be pointed out that God does not work in us depending on our willingness. He works in us "to will," which means that he is the One who makes us willing, so he is not dependent on our willingness.

How, then, does God go about keeping us? Peter says that he does so "through faith." Once more we find διά with the genitive (διὰ πίστεως), which means "through faith" or "by means of faith," as by means of an instrument and not with the accusative, which would mean "because of faith." The message is that God keeps us through our faith, not on according to our faith.

This is significant because it tells us that it is God who sustains our faith and that in doing so he keeps us. That is exactly the opposite of saying that God only keeps us if we persevere in the faith. If we had to sustain our own faith in order to be kept by God, we would certainly fall. "And it is significant that it is Peter who writes these words—that same Peter who had learned an unforgettable lesson about the weakness of unaided human nature when he denied that he had ever known Jesus."[78]

Moreover, Jude tells us that God is able to keep us from stumbling to present us blameless before the presence of his glory with great joy. What does it mean to keep us from stumbling? Certainly it does not mean that God will only keep us as long as we don't stumble. To claim that God will only keep believers if they persevere is to reduce God's activity to something superfluous. What, then, would God keep us from? If God's activity did not keep us from stumbling, God would only keep those who have no need of being kept. It would be absurd to say that only those who do not stumble qualify to be kept from stumbling.

Evangelicals who believe it possible for Christians to lose their salvation are ready to admit that it would be impossible for believers to persevere without receiving help from God. However, they consider that what God does on their behalf is not enough to make their perseverance certain, because they believe that it is still possible for believers to lose themselves, despite all that God does for them. Therefore, in the final analysis, staying saved depends on what each Christian does for oneself.

---

78 Anthony A. Hoekema, *Saved by Grace* (Grand Rapids: William B. Eermans Publishing Company, 1994), 244.

The right perspective is that the perseverance of all the saints is the infallible result of what God does to keep us. It is important to maintain this order of things so that we do not start to think of continuing saved as a reward for good performance. We do not stay saved as a prize for fulfilling certain requirements but as a gift from God. When we consider this life as a probation period in which we have to prove ourselves before God in order to obtain his ongoing protection, we are still reflecting our persistent tendency to believe that salvation is in some measure our own achievement. But when we understand that the cause of our perseverance is God's actively keeping us from falling, salvation is understood to be a gift of grace from beginning to end.

Thus, we need to turn our attention back to what the Bible itself declares to be the measures God takes to keep his saved people while in this world. As we do so, it will become abundantly clear that they are sufficient to guarantee that the saints will never turn away from him. Beginning in this chapter, we will examine three specific things that God does to keep those he has saved from losing their salvation: he regenerates, he seals with the guarantee of the indwelling Holy Spirit, and he preserves us through his providence.

WHAT IS REGENERATION?

We will begin by focusing on the biblical teaching about regeneration. What exactly does the term *regeneration* refer to? Peter mentions it twice in his first epistle:

> Blessed be the God and Father of our Lord Jesus Christ! According to his great mercy, he has caused us to be born again to a living hope through the resurrection of Jesus Christ from the dead.
>
> (1 Pet. 1:3)

> Since you have been born again, not of perishable seed but of imperishable, through the living and abiding word of God.
>
> (1 Pet. 1:23)

A literal rendering of the Greek word here translated as "born again" would be *regenerated*. Peter's choice of words shows that the reality he is speaking of is the beginning of new spiritual life. Other passages in the Bible speak of regeneration as a spiritual birth (John 1:13; 3:3–8) and as a spiritual resurrection (John 5:24–25; Eph. 2:1–6).

Some Christians have not grasped the specific meaning of regeneration and end up equating it with justification or associating it with baptism in their minds. In reality, regeneration is something completely different from

80

justification. While justification refers to being forgiven and receiving the righteousness of Christ by imputation, regeneration has to do with the internal transformation of the person.

The apostle Paul distinguishes between the two terms, explaining that we were regenerated *so that* we would be justified:

> He saved us, not on the basis of deeds which we have done in righteousness, but according to His mercy, by the washing of regeneration and renewing by the Holy Spirit, whom He poured out upon us richly through Jesus Christ our Savior, that being justified by His grace we might be made heirs according to the hope of eternal life.
>
> (Titus 3:5–7, NASB)

Regeneration is *not* the same as conversion either. We can say that it is God who converts us, in the sense that it is God who works in us to bring us to conversion; but the term *conversion* properly refers to our act of abandoning error and turning to God. That is why the Bible treats conversion as something that we do (Acts 3:19; 1 Thess. 1:9; 1 Pet. 2:25).

But regeneration is not something that we do; it is something that the Holy Spirit does in us that triggers our conversion. In the words of Jesus, to be regenerated, or born again, is to be born from the Spirit (John 3:6–8). Paul describes it as the washing of regeneration and renewing by the Holy Spirit (Titus 3:5). All this is to say that it is a work of the Spirit of God that cleanses and renews us so that we are no longer the same.

Essentially, regeneration is a transformation in the character and disposition of the heart, which leads the once-hardened and resistant sinner to love and obey God. Martyn Lloyd-Jones proposes that:

> It is the act of God by which a principle of new life is implanted in a man or woman with the result that the governing disposition of the soul is made holy.[79]

> In regeneration, a real change takes place and that within us. It is more than a mere change in our relationship to truth or to a person. A change takes place in us and not outside us only.[80]

Why is it necessary for there to be this type of change in us? The answer is that sin has corrupted the human race so profoundly that without this

---

79 D. Martyn Lloyd-Jones, *Great Doctrines of the Bible, Volume II, God the Holy Spirit* (Wheaton, IL: Crossway, 2012), 77–78.

80 Ibid., 86.

transformation people are voluntary slaves to sin (John 8:34), people who love darkness more than light (John 3:19) and who uniformly fail to do good or seek for God (Rom. 3:10–12).

In his epistle to Titus, Paul describes the state in which Christians were before being regenerated:

> For we ourselves were once foolish, disobedient, led astray, slaves to various passions and pleasures, passing our days in malice and envy, hated by others and hating one another. (Titus 3:3)

That is the exact context into which the washing of regeneration and renewing by the Holy Spirit comes in and changes everything. This biblical contrast is useful in pointing out the meaning of the term *regeneration*. Just as the meaning of the term *justification* can be perceived by the contrast biblical authors make between *justify* and *condemn*, here too we can comprehend that *regenerate* means to transform a person so as to no longer be foolish, disobedient, led astray, a slave to various passions and pleasures, etc.

Similarly, Paul reminds us in his epistle to the Ephesians that we were dead in the trespasses and sins in which we once walked, following the course of this world, following the devil, living in the passions of our flesh, carrying out the desires of the body and the mind, and being by nature children of wrath, like the rest of mankind (Eph. 2:1–3). Here too all this changed because God, being rich in mercy, because of the great love with which he loved us, while we were still in such a spiritually dead condition, made us alive—that is, he regenerated us.

In Romans, we once again find this same contrast between regenerate and unregenerate people:

> For those who live according to the flesh set their minds on the things of the flesh, but those who live according to the Spirit set their minds on the things of the Spirit. To set the mind on the flesh is death, but to set the mind on the Spirit is life and peace. For the mind that is set on the flesh is hostile to God, for it does not submit to God's law; indeed, it cannot. Those who are in the flesh cannot please God. You, however, are not in the flesh but in the Spirit, if in fact the Spirit of God dwells in you. Anyone who does not have the Spirit of Christ does not belong to him. (Rom. 8:5–9)

There are several things that should be noted in this passage. First of all, what is most obvious in this passage is that there are two types of

82

people: those who set their minds on the things of the flesh and those who set their minds on the things of the Spirit. The first group is made up of the unregenerate, here described as those who are in the flesh. In the second group are the regenerate, described as those who are in the Spirit.

The second thing that should stand out in our minds is the clear-cut difference in nature and disposition of these two different types of people. Those who are in the flesh set their minds on the things of the flesh and are hostile to God, for they do not submit to God's law; indeed, they cannot. They find themselves unable to please God. It is beyond their capacity because they are enslaved by their inward inclination toward sin, which, in turn, is the basis for all their decisions.

In 1 Corinthians 2:14 Paul goes so far as to say that the natural man does not accept the things of the Spirit of God, because they are folly to him, and he is not able to understand them because they are spiritually discerned. People in this condition are spiritually blind, having been made captive by the devil to do his will (2 Tim. 2:26).

But what a contrast is found in those who are in the Spirit. These set their minds on the things of the Spirit, submit to God's law, and walk not according to the flesh but according to the Spirit of God (v. 4). This is the change that is brought about by the washing of regeneration and renewing by the Holy Spirit. This is the kind of transformation that must take place inside a person and without which one cannot enter the kingdom of God (John 3:5).

What the Bible is saying here is very profound. It is showing us that a person does not become a true Christian the same way someone becomes part of any other religion. Conversions to a false religion happen apart from a transforming work of the Spirit of God. An alcoholic and a thief who doesn't believe in God may become a Mormon and quit drinking and stealing. All this can happen without regeneration.

Someone involved in idolatry, witchcraft, and immorality may be outwardly changed by becoming a Jehovah's Witness. The conversion may even be followed by great enthusiasm to propagate the new religion. Changes of this type are actually commonplace in non-Christian religions. But we know from the Bible that people who are following false religions are not saved, nor are they regenerate, even if they manifest changes on the outside. Conversions of this kind are nothing more than human decisions that happen without God removing the heart of stone and replacing it with a heart of flesh.

There is a difference when a genuine conversion to God occurs. The difference is much greater than a mere matter of religious creed. We should not imagine that what goes on in the heart of someone who adheres to a cult would be a real conversion if only it happened in a church that is doctrinally orthodox. A real salvation has a whole dimension that is absent in conversions to false religions.

In order to be saved, a devout follower of a false religion needs more than to be intellectually persuaded of the truth. He needs a transformation of his whole being that only the Holy Spirit can produce. A decisional conversion without regeneration may change one's religious affiliation, but unless the heart is regenerated, it will still love the world and be hostile toward God.

Becoming religious is not the same as experiencing regeneration. It is possible to do many good things for purely fleshly motives. Religious devotion itself can be motivated by pride and a desire to be respectable in the eyes of others. The Pharisees, who were zealous of the law, received a severe rebuke from Jesus:

> "Woe to you, scribes and Pharisees, hypocrites! For you clean the outside of the cup and the plate, but inside they are full of greed and self-indulgence. You blind Pharisee! First clean the inside of the cup and the plate, that the outside also may be clean. Woe to you, scribes and Pharisees, hypocrites! For you are like whitewashed tombs, which outwardly appear beautiful, but within are full of dead people's bones and all uncleanness. So you also outwardly appear righteous to others, but within you are full of hypocrisy and lawlessness."
>
> (Matt. 23:25–28)

> And he said to them, "You are those who justify yourselves before men, but God knows your hearts. For what is exalted among men is an abomination in the sight of God." (Luke 16:15)

Just as the Ethiopian cannot change his skin or the leopard his spots, so are we not able to change our nature or our inward bent toward sin. We can decide to become religious, but only the Holy Spirit's work of regeneration can change us on the inside so that we stop loving sin and truly love God.

We need to recognize that conversions without regeneration can also happen where the authentic Gospel is preached. The conversion of Simon Magus is a biblical example of this (Acts 8:13–23). The parable of the sower (Matt. 13:18–23) tells us of people who receive the message of the Gospel and later turn away from it. Some lack real roots and therefore fall away as soon as they are faced with tribulation or persecution. Others, still attached to sin in their hearts, are eventually drawn away by the cares of this world, the deceitfulness of riches, and the pleasures of life. But "the ones who have heard the word in an honest and good heart," Jesus assures us, "hold it fast, and bear fruit with perseverance" (Luke 8:15, NASB).

People who make a profession of faith without ever having been born again may fool others in the church and may even deceive themselves, but they will only last until they are exposed to trials that reveal the true condition of their hearts. We sometimes discover things that we never imagined about people when we see them confronted with adverse circumstances, persecution, or new temptations. Many young people who were active in their small town churches were "lost" to this world when they moved to the big city. The occasion only reveals what was on the inside all along. True Christianity is more than the lack of a good opportunity to sin. A regenerate person possesses a new nature.

> When the redemptive work of Christ is applied to the heart of the elect by the Spirit of God, the transformation is so great, so radical and profound, that it is described in the Bible as regeneration. The man is born again; he is made a new creature. It is not a superficial transformation, but a transformation of the essence of the person... It is not a mere human decision, or submission, but a radical transformation. A spiritual heart transplant is performed: the Holy Spirit removes the corrupted heart of stone and implants a totally new kind of heart.[81]

THE EFFECT OF REGENERATION IN A PERSON'S LIFE

What is the effect of regeneration? Paul answers that question in Romans 6:17:

> But thanks be to God, that you who were once slaves of sin have become obedient from the heart to the standard of teaching to which you were committed.

When God regenerates someone, it will change the person's life forever. That is why we find the Bible categorically stating that regeneration prevents a person from ever abandoning the way of God.

Hebrews 8:7 reminds us that there was something lacking in the Old Covenant. It promised many things to the people of Israel, but it did not

---

81 Paulo Anglada, *Calvinismo—As Antigas Doutrinas da Graça* (São Paulo, Brazil: Editora Os Puritanos, 2000), 87.

promise that God would change the hearts of all those who were included in the covenant in such a way that they would never cease to love and obey him. The history of Israel in the Old Testament is one of a people who broke God's covenant with them and turned their backs to him over and over. The Old Covenant was external in its nature. Not all the people of the covenant were converted. An eight-day-old boy was circumcised and included in the Covenant, but we know that many of them remained unbelievers their whole lives. That is why they ended up breaking their covenant with God.

When the prophet Jeremiah announces the New Covenant, however, he reveals that this second Covenant would be of a different order. God would write his laws on the minds and hearts of all those who were comprised in the New Covenant, changing the source of their thoughts and affections. In other words, the New Covenant would be made up exclusively of regenerate people.

For this reason, Scripture says it is a covenant that will never be broken because the change God works on the inside of all its members guarantees that they will all continue to fear God and that none of them will depart from him:

> Behold, the days are coming, declares the LORD, when I will make a new covenant with the house of Israel and the house of Judah, not like the covenant that I made with their fathers on the day when I took them by the hand to bring them out of the land of Egypt, my covenant that they broke, though I was their husband, declares the LORD. But this is the covenant that I will make with the house of Israel after those days, declares the LORD: I will put my law within them, and I will write it on their hearts. And I will be their God, and they shall be my people. And no longer shall each one teach his neighbor and each his brother, saying, "Know the LORD," for they shall all know me, from the least of them to the greatest, declares the LORD. For I will forgive their iniquity, and I will remember their sin no more. (Jere. 31:31–34)

The difference between the two covenants is not that in the New Covenant God would prove to be faithful. God had been faithful in the Old Covenant. The problem was unfaithfulness on the part of the people, and that is exactly what will be avoided in the New Covenant. God promises to work an internal change in all those included as members in the New Covenant so that it will never be necessary for one of its members to be instructed to know the Lord.

86

The effect of this divine working is described in words that explicitly contradict the possibility of any New Covenant members ever turning away from the Lord:

> I will give them one heart and one way, that they may fear me forever, for their own good and the good of their children after them. I will make with them an everlasting covenant, that I will not turn away from doing good to them. And I will put the fear of me in their hearts, that they may not turn from me. (Jer. 32:39–40)

We would do well to pay close attention to all that God does for his people according to this text. God himself imprints his laws on their minds and hearts, he gives them one heart and one way, he puts the fear of God in their hearts, and he takes it upon himself to never cease to do good to them. Now if God does all this for someone, it becomes inconceivable for such a person to turn away from God, because the new internal disposition will compel the believer to follow Christ faithfully. And that is precisely the intended result.

As God speaks through the prophet, twice he uses the words "that they may" to point out what he has in mind with all this. He says that it is "that they may fear me forever, for their own good and the good of their children," and "that they may not turn from me." Since God has this as his aim, we can be sure that he knows how to achieve it, for no purpose of his can be thwarted (Job 42:2).

Spurgeon, preaching on this text in Jeremiah 32, shared in this bold assurance:

> How, then, are they preserved? Well, not as some falsely talk, as though we preached, "that the man who is converted may live as he likes." We have never said so; we have never even thought so. The man who is converted cannot live as he likes; or, rather, he is so changed by the Holy Spirit, that if he could live as he likes, he would never sin, but live an absolutely perfect life. Oh, how deeply do we long to be kept clear of every sin! We preach not that men may depart from God and yet live; but that they shall not depart from him.[82]

The prophet Ezekiel brings us another text which shows how regeneration affects a person:

---

82 Charles Spurgeon, *Perseverance In Holiness*, Sermon Number 2108, *The Metropolitan Tabernacle Pulpit Vol. 35*, The Master Christian Library (Rio, WI: Ages Software Inc., 2000), 695.

And I will give you a new heart, and a new spirit I will put within you. And I will remove the heart of stone from your flesh and give you a heart of flesh. And I will put my Spirit within you, and *cause you* to walk in my statutes and be careful to obey my rules....Then you will remember your evil ways, and your deeds that were not good, and you will loathe yourselves for your iniquities and your abominations. (Ezekiel 36:26–31; emphasis added)

Once more, the Bible is teaching that it is God who changes the nature and internal disposition of those whom he saves, removing the heart of stone and replacing it with a sensitive heart. In addition, God also puts his Spirit in us. By taking these measures, God causes us to walk in his statutes and be careful to obey his rules. This result is not just a possibility or even a probability. God's people will most certainly observe God commandments, because God says he will make it happen. "I will put my Spirit within you, and cause you to walk in my statutes," he says. No words could be clearer to prove that it is what God does that causes this behavior in us and that it is not our own doing.

According to the words of verse 31, after this renewal of the person there is no risk of the Christian going back to a life of deliberate sin, because what has taken place is not merely an external reformation. The regenerated person still has weaknesses, but the new heart cries out for holiness and detests sin. Now there is a profound aversion to sin. When the regenerate remember their past evil ways and deeds, they don't look back in fondness, as if saying, "Ah, those were the days! It's too bad they're gone." On the contrary, there is a sense of shame and of loathing the time that was wasted in rebellion against the Lord.

It is fundamental to recognize that a change of behavior can occur on the surface while the inmost of one's being is still bound by love for sin. Such a change is not the biblical concept of the new birth. Every person who is in a Christian church but who loves this world and refuses to renounce it is a false Christian.

The apostle John wrote that whoever loves the world does not love the Father (1 John 2:15). We cannot lower the biblical standard here. Nothing should be considered a true conversion that comes short of the God-wrought transformation of the heart, which conforms the person to the inspired words: "Then you will remember your evil ways, and your deeds that were not good, and you will loathe yourselves for your iniquities and your abominations." No one whose heart has so been renewed is inclined to go back to a lifestyle of sin.

But someone may wonder if this sensibility cannot be lost. Are we to believe that when a person is born again he or she will never become hardened again? There is no room for speculation on this matter, for the Bible provides us with the answer. The words of the prophet Ezekiel give us a strong indication. Sayings like "Give a new heart and a new spirit" and "Remove the heart of stone" describe an overhaul of the soul, not a passing influence of the Holy Spirit.

But the fact that the effects of regeneration are permanent becomes explicit in John's first epistle. There we find John laboring to differentiate between people who have truly experienced regeneration (born of God) and those who profess to be Christians but never knew God:

> And by this we know that we have come to know him, if we keep his commandments. Whoever says "I know him" but does not keep his commandments is a liar, and the truth is not in him.　(1 John 2:3–4)

In his concern to make this vital matter understood, he tells us that we can know whether or not *we have come to know* God (in the past) by whether or not we *keep his commandments* (in the present). That is saying more than that whoever does not keep his commandments does not have an ongoing relationship with God. The message is that the way we currently respond to God's commandments serves as a test to prove or disprove our profession of having come to know God at any time.

John returns to this matter in chapter 3. In verse 6, he makes an even clearer statement of this same truth:

> No one who abides in him keeps on sinning; no one who keeps on sinning has either seen him or known him.　　(1 John 3:6)

First, John states that there is not one single person who abides in Christ who "keeps on sinning." The Greek verb tense employed in this construction denotes linear action and points to a lifestyle. This is not denying that true Christians fall into sin (1 John 1:8–2:1); what John denies is that a person can go on living in sin while being a Christian.

In the second part of the verse, he goes even further and says, "No one who keeps on sinning has either seen him or known him." It is important to pay close attention to the verb tenses here. "No one who keeps on sinning" describes the present condition of a person, while "has either seen him or known him" encompasses the person's entire past.

There are certainly many who were once active members in evangelical churches but who now are turned aside and are living in sin. What should we conclude about them? That they used to be true believers? Perhaps someone would suggest that only some of them were true believers while others among them have never truly known Christ.

But what the Bible says is that "*no one* who keeps on sinning *has either seen him or known him.*" The apostle John emphatically rejects the notion that there can be any person now living in sin who was once saved.

This same message comes up again in John's third epistle:

Whoever does good is from God; whoever does evil has not seen God. (3 John 1:11)

"Has not!" says the Bible. Has the person who today does evil seen or known God? The answer is that such a person "has not."

As he proceeds, John explains why he can assert this truth so boldly:

Little children, let no one deceive you. Whoever practices righteousness is righteous, as he is righteous. Whoever makes a practice of sinning is of the devil, for the devil has been sinning from the beginning. The reason the Son of God appeared was to destroy the works of the devil. No one born of God makes a practice of sinning, for God's seed abides in him, and he cannot keep on sinning because he has been born of God. By this it is evident who are the children of God, and who are the children of the devil: whoever does not practice righteousness is not of God, nor is the one who does not love his brother. (1 John 3:7–10)

First of all, John reminds us that not every professed believer is actually converted. In order not to be deceived, we must bear in mind that all who are saved practice righteousness (v. 7). Those who make a practice of sinning (linear action) are of the devil (v. 8). He then comes to a crucial point: "*No one born of God makes a practice of sinning*" (v. 9), he says. People who have been born of God (regenerated), not only in general but in every case without exception, are so transformed that they do not make a practice of sinning.

Why is this so? "For God's seed abides in him, and he cannot keep on sinning because he has been born of God" (v. 9). The new nature implanted by the divine working along with the indwelling Holy Spirit makes it impossible to keep on sinning. "He cannot"—that is, he is unable to keep on sinning (habitual action in the present), "because he has been born of God" (ὅτι ἐκ τοῦ θεοῦ γεγέννηται—perfect passive indicative, which denotes *concluded* past action, with remaining results in the present).

By applying this test, we can discern who is and who is not a true child of God, for "this is how we know who the children of God are and who the children of the devil are" (v. 10, NIV).

What John is telling us is that if a person has ever really been born again, nothing will reverse the effect this has on the person's life. This is a concept that is reinforced throughout the epistle. There is no such thing as a saved person who does not make progress in personal sanctification because "everyone who thus hopes in him purifies himself as he is pure" (1 John 3:3).

For the true Christian, it is not burdensome to live according to God's commandments, "for everyone who has been born of God overcomes the world" (1 John 5:4).

> We know that everyone who has been born of God does not keep on sinning, but he who was born of God [a reference to Christ] protects him, and the evil one does not touch him.   (1 John 5:18)

These verses totally debunk the popular concept that it is possible to leave the path of sanctification and revert to a life of sin after having experienced the new birth. Since this would necessarily have to happen for a true Christian to fall away from the Lord, there is simply no way to harmonize 1 John with the idea that Christians can lose their salvation.

> To talk of a child of God falling in love again with sin is tantamount to suggesting that there is no real difference between one who has passed from death unto life, who has had the principle of holiness communicated to him, who is indwelt by the Spirit of God, and those who are unregenerate. That one who has been merely intellectually impressed and emotionally stirred to temporarily reform his outward conduct may indeed return to his former manner of life, is readily conceded; but that one who has experienced a supernatural work of grace within, who has been made "*a new creature in Christ Jesus,*" can or will lose all relish for spiritual things and become satisfied with the husks which the swine feed on, we emphatically deny.[83]

---

83   A. W. Pink, *Eternal Security* (Grand Rapids: Baker Book House, 1979), 99 (emphasis in original).

REGENERATION PRECLUDES TURNING SECURITY INTO LICENSE

We often hear dire concerns expressed to the effect that if Christians are taught that salvation cannot be lost they will abuse their security and turn it into a license to sin. We are told that it is a doctrine that will lead believers to become lax in their conduct and encourage neglect of Christian service.

In reality, such worries only demonstrate that there is a lack of understanding of what it means to be regenerated. Are we to believe that the character of true saints is to dive headlong into sin as soon as they have obtained a guarantee from God that they will remain saved forever? Instead, would they not respond with even more gratitude in light of receiving such a comforting promise? Do the saved have no interest in serving God other than to secure their own blessedness? Could that even be considered real love for God?

We find the answer to this type of objection in the Bible. The apostle Paul knew that his teaching that salvation is by grace, apart from works, would raise objections. He knew people would claim that his teaching would detract from holiness. In anticipation of such objections, he asked, "What shall we say then? Are we to continue in sin that grace may abound?" (Rom. 6:1).

If Paul believed it were possible for Christians to lose their salvation, he could have simply responded, as many today do, that to remain in sin after justification would cause a Christian to fall back into condemnation. But how did he actually respond? "By no means! How can we who died to sin still live in it?" (Rom. 6:2).

By no means, he says, will we remain in sin. And why not? Because for those of us who have died to sin, it is impossible to continue to live in sin. By asking how such a thing could ever happen, he shows that it cannot. As he moves forward, he focuses our attention on the implications of regeneration: "We know that our old self was crucified with him in order that the body of sin might be brought to nothing, so that we would no longer be enslaved to sin" (Rom. 6:6).

In verse 15, he returns to the type of objection he foresees rising up against his teaching. "What then? Are we to sin because we are not under law but under grace?" (v. 15) Once more, however, his response is not to resort to threats but rather to demonstrate that questions of this nature simply do not take into account what it means to have experienced a true conversion:

By no means! Do you not know that if you present yourselves to anyone as obedient slaves, you are slaves of the one whom you obey, either of sin, which leads to death, or of obedience, which leads to righteousness? But thanks be to God, that you who were once slaves of sin have become obedient from the heart to the standard of teaching to which you were committed, and, having been set free from sin, have become slaves of righteousness.   (Rom. 6:15–18)

As a person is the servant of the one whom he or she obeys, true conversion puts a halt to the obedience to sin and offers oneself up as a servant to righteousness. It is already a consummate fact that all who are saved are no longer servile to sin. It is true that in the past we were slaves to sin. However, thanks be to God, we have come to obey from the heart (internal change) the standard of teaching to which we were committed. And having been set free from sin, we have become slaves of righteousness (v. 17). Where this transformation has taken place, is there a danger of God's grace being twisted into an excuse for more sinning? By no means! The one who fears that it may needs to come to a better understanding of the nature of regeneration.

There is no justification whatsoever for claiming that the saints will become indolent and careless or that they will not remain faithful until death, unless they believe that salvation can be lost. This sort of fearmongering is simply false. Does anyone seriously contend that the Christians who believe that salvation can be lost are the only ones who mortify the flesh? What ought we to say of the Puritans? They held to the doctrine defended in this book, yet their devotion to piety is unmatched by any other evangelical movement we know of from history! It is simply an irrefutable fact that the doctrine of the perseverance of the saints has gone hand in hand with the highest levels of holy living that can be found among God's people in any age, nor has any other doctrine been sealed with the blood of so many steadfast martyrs.

What often goes unsaid, however, is that the real peril for people's souls lies in ignoring the biblical teaching about regeneration. This has been responsible for many superficial presentations of the Gospel. Many have led sinners to believe that to be saved nothing more is involved than making a profession of faith and attending a Christian church. When the internal dimension of salvation is not adequately presented, even the unregenerate become convinced that they are saved.

On this basis a man may make a profession without ever having his confidence in his own ability shattered; he has been told absolutely nothing of his need of a change of nature which is not within his own power, and consequently, if he does not experience such a radical change, he is not dismayed. He was never told it was essential, so he sees no reason to doubt whether he is a Christian. Indeed the teaching he has come under consistently militates against such doubts arising. It is frequently said that a man who has made a decision with little evidence of a change of life may be a 'carnal' Christian who needs instruction in holiness, or if the same individual should gradually lose his new-found interests, the fault is frequently attributed to a lack of 'follow-up', or prayer, or some other deficiency on the part of the Church. The possibility that these marks of worldliness and falling away are due to the absence of a saving experience at the outset is rarely considered.[84]

We can observe this danger in the message that is transmitted to those who made a profession of faith that looked good externally but who later went back to a life of sin. What is being said to someone in that condition? Only those who understand the return to a life of sin as proof positive that that person has never been born again will tell the person that he or she has certainly never been saved. Those who work on the presupposition that it is possible that real salvation was experienced will be giving the person a different message.

Depending on their doctrinal views, it may sound something like this:

1. "As long as you stay that way, you are missing out on a deeper dimension in your spiritual life. You remain saved, of course, but you would be happier if you were more consecrated and your life would not be wasted on things that have no eternal value."

2. "You are still saved, but if you keep on living like you are now, you run the risk of losing your salvation. Before that happens, you need to come back to church and become *the way you used to be*."

3. "As long as you live like that, you are lost. You need to come back to church and become *the way you used to be* again."

None of these approaches are adequate. They simply do not say what the person needs to hear. What is needed is not an exhortation to rededicate one's life to the Lord. Instead, what the person needs is to understand that he or she was never saved. As long as the idea prevails that a genuine

---

84 Iain H. Murray, *The Forgotten Spurgeon* (Carlisle, PA: The Banner of Truth Trust, 2012), 111–112.

salvation experience has already taken place, the person will believe that all that is needed is to return to the same condition which existed previously for everything to be right with God.

But what took place in the past was not an authentic conversion. The fact that it was possible to fall away and go back to a life of sin proves this. It is not enough to repeat the process and resume the previous religious stance, whatever it may have been. There needs to be a deeper sort of change. Otherwise, the person can resume church attendance and behave a little better without ever receiving a new heart from God, and the exhortation to change can end up being a recipe for disaster even while it appears to be accomplishing its goal.

If this happens, the person will be assured that he or she is ready to leave this world, when in fact this is not the case, for there still needs to be a new birth, a divine work that changes the heart forever.

However, it should be stressed that this message is for those who give themselves over to a lifestyle of sin and rebellion. According to the guidelines laid out by the apostle John, in order to identify who has been born of God and who is a child of the devil, we must differentiate between committing sins and living in sin, or abandoning oneself to sin.

The saints can fall into serious sins, even of the type that would call for ecclesiastical discipline. The Bible never denies this. On the contrary, it supplies us with examples of this reality, as in the cases of David and Peter. Even so, we should not overlook the fact that they were unable to persist in sin. Having been transformed in their hearts, they were not capable of going on in a life that contradicted the principle of life that God had planted in them, so when they were confronted with their error, they were both overwhelmed with brokenness and repentance. It could not have been otherwise.

David confessed as much when he wrote the following:

For when I kept silent, my bones wasted away through my groaning all day long. For day and night your hand was heavy upon me; my strength was dried up as by the heat of summer.   (Ps. 32:3–4)

This is in perfect accord with what the Bible teaches about the impossibility of a person who has been born again falling away. Regeneration makes it impossible for a believer to go back to the old life of sin. A saint will be in anguish and torment of soul over unresolved sin, making repentance inevitable.

The Reformed doctrine recognizes that true believers can experience a serious fall, but not a total and final falling away from the Lord.[85] "Using the figure of a boat at high sea, we may say that the believer can fall on the deck, but never out of the boat so as to perish."[86]

David and Peter are today in heaven with the Lord. They serve as models of the fact that the saints get up when they fall and persevere until they reach their eternal inheritance.

---

85 The *Westminster Confession of Faith* (WCF 17.3) states this truth in the following terms: Nevertheless, they may, through the temptations of Satan and of the world, the prevalency of corruption remaining in them, and the neglect of the means of their preservation, fall into grievous sins; and, for a time, continue therein: whereby they incur God's displeasure, and grieve His Holy Spirit, come to be deprived of some measure of their graces and comforts; have their hearts hardened, and their consciences wounded; hurt and scandalize others, and bring temporal judgments upon themselves.

86 In keeping with this principle, we should not jump to conclusions regarding the salvation of those who experience a notorious fall. In such cases we should be cautious, neither affirming nor denying their salvation. However, if even after confrontation and church discipline a person deliberately persists in a course of sin, it becomes an entirely different matter. Under such circumstances we have reasons to conclude that we are dealing with a person who has not been born of God. Jesus recognized this in His teaching about excommunication, saying, "If he refuses to listen to them, tell it to the church. And if he refuses to listen even to the church, let him be to you as a Gentile and a tax collector" (Matt. 18:17). In essence Jesus instructs us to consider as an unbeliever someone who prefers to remain in sin, even at the cost of being put out of the church. A true Christian will not despise reproof and display such indifference toward the privilege of being in fellowship with Christ's church. The rebuke will help bring about repentance. But in the case of an unsaved person the reproof may be the occasion of a true conversion or it may serve to expose and remove an unbeliever from the church. Paulo Anglada, *Calvinismo—As Antigas Doutrinas da Graça* (São Paulo, Brazil: Editora Os Puritanos, 2000), 93.

The Guarantee of the Holy Spirit

Therefore to say, that the temple of God, in which the Spirit of the Father dwells, and the members of Christ, shall not partake of salvation, but be brought down to destruction, is it not the highest blasphemy?[87]
(Irenaeus [AD 180] commenting on 1 Corinthians 3:17, "If anyone destroys God's temple, God will destroy him.")

But now to the saints predestinated to the kingdom of God by God's grace, the aid of perseverance that is given is not such as the former [given to Adam], but such that to them perseverance itself is bestowed; not only so that without that gift they cannot persevere, but, moreover, so that by means of this gift they cannot help persevering.[88]   (Augustine, AD 430)

The apostle Peter wrote that the saved are kept by the power of God through faith (1 Pet. 1:5) and that by his divine power we have been granted all things that pertain to life and godliness (2 Pet. 1:3). One of the things granted by God that leads to life and godliness is the "new heart," effected by regeneration, when God takes away the heart of stone and replaces it with a heart of flesh (Ezek. 36:26), which is a God-fearing heart that will never depart from him (Jer. 32:40). Another is the gift of the Holy Spirit, as is taught in Ezekiel 36:27:

And I will put my Spirit within you, and cause you to walk in my statutes and be careful to obey my rules.   (Ezek. 36:27)

The Holy Spirit is very much at work in the salvation of a soul. It is he who convicts of sin, righteousness, and judgment (John 16:8). Regeneration is the washing of renewing wrought by the Holy Spirit (Titus 3:5). But God goes even further as he puts his Holy Spirit within us to dwell in us, to be with us forever (John 14:6), which also becomes a guarantee that once saved we will remain saved forever.

---

87 Irenaeus, quoted by John Gill, *The Cause of God and of Truth*, Part 4, Chapter 5, Section 4, The Ultimate Christian Library (Rio, Wisconsin: AGES Software, 2000), 810.

88 Augustine, *Augustin: Anti-Pelagian Writings, Treatise on Rebuke and Grace*, ed. Philip Schaff, Volume 5 of *The Nicene and Post-Nicene Fathers, Series 1*, The Master Christian Library (Rio, WI: Ages Software Inc., 2000), 1156.

On several occasions, the apostle Paul compares the indwelling Holy Spirit to a seal and a guarantee:

> In him you also, when you heard the word of truth, the gospel of your salvation, and believed in him, were *sealed* with the promised Holy Spirit, who is *the guarantee of our inheritance* until we acquire possession of it, to the praise of his glory. (Eph. 1:13–14; emphasis added)

> And do not grieve the Holy Spirit of God, by whom you were sealed for the day of redemption. (Eph. 4:30)

> And it is God who establishes us with you in Christ, and has anointed us, and who has also put his seal on us and given us his Spirit in our hearts as a guarantee. (2 Cor. 1:21–22)

> For while we are still in this tent, we groan, being burdened—not that we would be unclothed, but that we would be further clothed, so that what is mortal may be swallowed up by life. He who has prepared us for this very thing is God, who *has given us the Spirit as a guarantee*. (2 Cor. 5:4–5; emphasis added)

What are these comparisons meant to convey? When the Holy Spirit is called a guarantee (the guarantee of our inheritance), the point is that the Holy Spirit is given to us by God as a pledge, or a deposit, which serves as a guarantee that we will infallibly enter our glorious inheritance.

The word translated as "guarantee" carries the idea of a deposit of value that a buyer would give a seller at the beginning of a business transaction as a security, serving as a guarantee that the transaction would definitely be completed. In terms of our salvation, what this means is that although we did not enter our inheritance immediately upon believing, there can be no doubt that we ultimately will, for God has already given us the Holy Spirit as a guarantee, in order to remove any insecurity from our hearts regarding our final salvation. The fulfillment is so sure that a safety deposit has already been made in advance.

Paul likewise means for us to understand that the future of those who receive the Holy Spirit is secure when he uses the metaphor of a seal to portray the significance of having the Spirit of God placed within. In the ancient world, the two main purposes for which seals were employed were to protect and to authenticate:

The word used here (from σφραγιζω) means to seal up; to close and make fast with a seal, or signet; as, e.g., books, letters, etc. that they may not be read. It is also used in the sense of setting a mark on anything, or a seal, to denote that it is genuine, authentic, confirmed, or approved, as when a deed, compact, or agreement is sealed. It is thus made sure; and is confirmed or established.[89]

There is a legitimate application of the second meaning of sealing in the fact that receiving the Holy Spirit authenticates the individual as a genuine Christian. The presence of the Holy Spirit brings about sanctification, mortification of the flesh, the fruit of the Spirit (Gal. 5:22–23), and discernment of the truth (1 Cor. 2:10–12). These things are marks of an authentic Christian, for all who are led by the Spirit of God are sons of God (Rom. 8:13–14).

However, the first meaning associated with sealing is clearly intended by Paul when he ties it to the day of redemption ("The Holy Spirit of God, by whom you were sealed for the day of redemption" [Eph. 4:30]). To seal for the day of redemption bears the idea that what has been sealed is thus protected so that it cannot be violated until that day.

The connection between the seal and things that are still future is also made clear when Paul says that as Christians we "were sealed in Him with the Holy Spirit of promise" (Eph. 1:13, NASB). Therefore, the primary application of being sealed with the Holy Spirit is that he is given us to "lock" us or protect us against any violation until the redemption of our body (Rom. 8:23).

The Bible contains an illustration of how this type of sealing worked. When Daniel was thrown into the lion's den, the entrance of the den was sealed by the king. This gesture meant that the den was under royal protection and anyone who dared break the seal would be executed.

And a stone was brought and laid on the mouth of the den, and the king sealed it with his own signet and with the signet of his lords, that nothing might be changed concerning Daniel.   (Dan. 6:17)

In like fashion, God seals us with the Holy Spirit when he saves us so that we are kept safe in this world of spiritual dangers. The manner in which the Spirit of God dwelling in us guarantees our future salvation shines forth

---

89 Albert Barnes, *Barnes' Notes on the Bible, Volume 14–1 Corinthians–Galatians*, The Master Christian Library (Rio, WI: Ages Software Inc., 2000), 583.

when we look into the wonder of his operation within us. The Bible teaches that his mission is to guide us, advancing our sanctification, producing the fruit of the Spirit in our lives, and keeping us from apostatizing into doctrinal error.

THE HOLY SPIRIT'S PROTECTION AGAINST HERESY

According to apostolic teaching, a Christian's progressive sanctification is a byproduct of the ongoing work of the Holy Spirit. Those who fulfill the righteous requirement of the law do so by the Spirit (Rom. 8:4). We are involved in this process, but it is the Spirit who enables us to overcoming the flesh, as we are led by him. As it is written, "For if you live according to the flesh you will die, but if by the Spirit you put to death the deeds of the body, you will live. For all who are led by the Spirit of God are sons of God" (Rom. 8:13–14).

Those who truly belong to God are the ones who are led by the Spirit of God to put to death the deeds of the flesh. To walk in the Spirit means to not gratify the desires of flesh (Gal. 5:16). The leading of the Spirit is not something mystical that reveals what direction to go while we are walking down the street; it is a moral guidance that prevails upon us to mortify the desires of the sinful nature.

Where this is lacking, there is no indication that God's Spirit is present. To live according to the flesh is to be heading for eternal death; it is evidence of the absence of the Holy Spirit. But wherever the Spirit of the Lord dwells, he opposes the flesh bringing forth the fruit of the Spirit (love, joy, peace, patience, kindness, goodness, faithfulness, gentleness, and self-control). Thus, the Holy Spirit causes us to walk in God's statutes (Ezek. 36:27) and progressively transforms us into his likeness, in ever-increasing glory.

> Now the Lord is the Spirit, and where the Spirit of the Lord is, there is freedom. And we all, with unveiled face, beholding the glory of the Lord, are being transformed into the same image from one degree of glory to another. For this comes from the Lord who is the Spirit.
>
> (2 Cor. 3:17–18)

The context of this passage indicates that the freedom brought about by the Spirit of the Lord is freedom from religious deception, which blinds people so as not to believe in Christ. Paul had just been describing the bondage of those who have, as it were, a veil over their hearts when they read the Scriptures so that they do not understand to the point of being saved through faith in Christ. But when one turns to the Lord, the veil is removed (2 Co. 3:15–16).

There is a plethora of false doctrines in the world. They all come from the deception that the devil, father of lies, has spread over all the earth. Some wrong doctrinal concepts are of the kind that can confuse the people of God and disrupt the unity of the body of Christ without being an impediment to possessing saving faith in Christ. It is plain to all that the new convert does not fully understand all that God has revealed to us in his Word. On becoming a believer, the basic truths of the Gospel have been understood and salvation has taken place, but there is certainly still a lot to be learned in terms of biblical doctrine. From that point on, the whole Christian life will be a process of growing in the knowledge of God and of the Scriptures.

Believers do not all experience the same progress. Even among churches that stand united on the essential doctrines of Christianity, there are many divergent doctrines on secondary matters, and we realize that faithful Christians arrive at different conclusions on a variety of issues. This is not owing to some fault in the divine revelation entrusted unto us, for God is not the author of confusion. Every error proceeds from our own imperfection and from the subtlety of Satan, who sows confusion and discord, even among the people of God. That is why every believer must strive to understand the Scriptures and interpret them correctly.

Although Timothy was already an ordained minister of the Gospel, Paul did not refrain from instructing him in this regard:

> Do your best to present yourself to God as one approved, a worker
> who has no need to be ashamed, rightly handling the word of truth.
> (2 Tim. 2:15)

Handling the Word of truth rightly does not happen automatically, and we cannot neglect the means God has ordained for our growth, or we will end up being ashamed. Along with the Bible, God places people in the church who are gifted and qualified to teach, and we do well to make the most of the ministry they afford us so that we may all attain to the unity of the faith and no longer be spiritual children, tossed to and fro and carried about by every wind of doctrine (Eph. 4:11–14).

It is evident that one can be saved without having a grasp on all the doctrines of the Bible, but that is no reason to aspire to believe wrongly about things. If we as a church faithfully made use of the resources God has made available unto us, we could correct many errors that exist in Christian circles, despite the fact that we will never attain perfect knowledge in this world.

But there are also false teachings that contradict the essentials of the Christian faith. I'm now referring to heretical beliefs that a person can never hold to and at the same time be saved. For instance, Peter spoke of false teachers who "secretly bring in destructive heresies, even denying the Master who bought them, bringing upon themselves swift destruction" (2 Pet. 2:1).

Jude, referring to the same heretics, says that "certain people have crept in unnoticed who long ago were designated for this condemnation, ungodly people, who pervert the grace of our God into sensuality and deny our only Master and Lord, Jesus Christ" (Jude 1:4).

There are many cults, like the Jehovah's Witnesses and the Mormons, which deny that the Lord Jesus Christ is the only Master and Lord. This is heresy that is destructive of the soul. As the apostle John put it, "No one who denies the Son has the Father" (1 John 2:23).

Salvation by works is another such heresy (see chapter 2). To embrace a doctrine of this sort is to apostatize from the faith. Remaining in Christ necessarily means keeping the faith. Paul made it clear that some would apostatize from the faith by following doctrines spun out by demons:

> But the Spirit expressly says that in later times some will fall away from the faith, paying attention to deceitful spirits and teachings of demons. (1 Tim. 4:1)

As opposed to what some have assumed, a person can fall away from the faith without ever having been a believer. To fall away from the faith, in this context, does not refer to abandoning the act of believing (losing one's personal faith in Christ), but has to do with repudiating the content of the Christian message which we refer to as our "faith".

What the text is saying is that individuals will turn their backs on the "Christian faith," which is the truth, to wander off following other doctrines. This happens every time a person who has been instructed in the truth comes to reject it, and says nothing as to whether or not there was personal saving faith in Christ.

102

What is nonetheless clear is that turning away from the true faith and following doctrines of demons is a sure path to eternal perdition. Therefore, if the saved are to remain saved, they must not fall into the deceit of deadly heresies. Yet once more the Bible assures us that the saved will not become ensnared unto their perdition, for the Bible testifies that the Holy Spirit keeps us from this spiritual danger, not allowing us to be deceived by heresies that would destroy us.

Right from the beginning of our Christian experience, the Holy Spirit is directly involved with our understanding and accepting of the truth. It is the Spirit of God that opens our minds and enlightens our understanding for us to comprehend and believe the Gospel. It is noteworthy how Paul attributes our conversion to the operation of the Spirit:

> But we impart a secret and hidden wisdom of God, which God decreed before the ages for our glory. None of the rulers of this age understood this, for if they had, they would not have crucified the Lord of glory. But, as it is written, "What no eye has seen, nor ear heard, nor the heart of man imagined, what God has prepared for those who love him"—*these things God has revealed to us through the Spirit....*Now we have received not the spirit of the world, but the Spirit who is from God, that we might understand the things freely given us by God. And we impart this in words not taught by human wisdom but taught by the Spirit, interpreting spiritual truths to those who are spiritual. *The natural person does not accept the things of the Spirit of God, for they are folly to him,* and he is not able to understand them because they are spiritually discerned.
>
> (1 Cor. 2:7–14; emphasis added)

Since people in their natural state do not accept the things of the Spirit of God, only a work of the Holy Spirit can open people's minds and hearts to believe the Gospel. That is why we have received the Spirit who is from God, that we might understand the things freely given us by God (v. 12).

When Peter demonstrated a correct understanding of the person of Christ, he was told, "Blessed are you, Simon Bar-Jonah! For flesh and blood has not revealed this to you, but my Father who is in heaven" (Matt. 16:17).

Paul was saying the same to the Corinthians. Acknowledgment of the truth can only take place when God reveals it to us by his Spirit. At the same time, Paul recognizes that this is a privilege that is not given to all people. It is the "wisdom which none of the rulers of this age has understood; for if they had understood it, they would not have crucified the Lord of glory" (v. 8 NASB).

Jesus expressed this truth in his prayer, "I thank you, Father, Lord of heaven and earth, that you have hidden these things from the wise and understanding and revealed them to little children" (Matt. 11:25). So a supernatural operation is needed if a person is to believe the truth and be converted.

But the illuminating work of the Spirit does not end at that point. He takes up residence in us as believers to safeguard us against any corruption of our faith by which we are justified in Christ. This is taught unequivocally in John's first epistle:

> Children, it is the last hour, and as you have heard that antichrist is coming, so now many antichrists have come. Therefore we know that it is the last hour. They went out from us, but they were not of us; for if they had been of us, they would have continued with us. But they went out, that it might become plain that they all are not of us. But you have been anointed by the Holy One, and you all have knowledge. I write to you, not because you do not know the truth, but because you know it, and because no lie is of the truth. Who is the liar but he who denies that Jesus is the Christ? This is the antichrist, he who denies the Father and the Son. No one who denies the Son has the Father. Whoever confesses the Son has the Father also. Let what you heard from the beginning abide in you. If what you heard from the beginning abides in you, then you too will abide in the Son and in the Father. And this is the promise that he made to us—eternal life. I write these things to you about those who are trying to deceive you. *But the anointing that you received from him abides in you, and you have no need that anyone should teach you.* But as his anointing teaches you about everything—and is true and is no lie, just as it has taught you—abide in him.   (1 John 2:18–27; emphasis added)

At this point in John's epistle, he is dealing with false teachers and their heretical doctrines. He says that many "antichrists" have appeared—that is, many who had been in Christian churches had departed, falling prey to false teachings, deceiving, and being deceived. This is a mark of the "last hour" in which we already find ourselves since Christ's first coming.

Every generation of Christians has observed the same reality. Ignorant and unstable people reject the exclusive authority of the Scriptures or despise the instruction of those who could help them understand what the Bible really means, isolate themselves from good teaching under a delusion of self-sufficiency, and end up ascribing to the Sacred Text novel and twisted interpretations to their own destruction (2 Pet. 3:16). False teachings appear and reappear, deceiving people who had previously been in Christian congregations. Some rise up in orthodox churches teaching heresy and carry off disciples to integrate their cults. Paul warned that this would happen:

> I know that after my departure fierce wolves will come in among you, not sparing the flock; and from among your own selves will arise men speaking twisted things, to draw away the disciples after them. Therefore be alert, remembering that for three years I did not cease night or day to admonish everyone with tears.   (Acts 20:29–31)

False teachers never tire of seeking new proselytes for their movements among those who are under sound teaching in biblical churches. By their influence, some go astray from the truth. As Jesus predicted, "many false prophets will arise and lead many astray" (Matt. 24:11).

Doctrines of demons have many faces. Paul cautioned Timothy to guard the deposit entrusted to him, avoiding the irreverent babble and contradictions of what is falsely called "knowledge," because by professing it some have gone astray from the faith (1 Tim. 6:20–21). We should recognize that all who wage war on biblical truth are false religious teachers, even if they present their dogmas under the guise of science or philosophy.

There are many who seek to undermine faith in the central truths of Christianity in classrooms or in secular publications, propagating ideas like secular humanism, evolution, or atheism, which are nothing more than doctrines of demons. The attacks of theological liberalism have led many to disbelieve in the inspiration of the Bible, eternal punishment, justification through faith in Christ, his resurrection, his second coming, and the Day of Judgment. We may discern the deception of Satan in all such opposition to the saving message of Christ.

False teachers do lead many astray, but in light of this grim reality, the apostle John maintains that there are two things of which we can be absolutely certain: (1) true believers never become the victims of their false teaching, and (2) those who have gone out from us had never been saved. These two points merit our consideration.

TRUE CHRISTIANS CANNOT BE LURED AWAY FROM CHRIST BY FALSE TEACHING

Just as John is sounding the alarm against false prophets, so does he express his confidence that the saints—*all* the saints—possess an anointing and have knowledge that effectively protects them. He writes, "But you have been anointed by the Holy One, and *you all* have knowledge. I write to you, not because you do not know the truth, but because you know it, and because no lie is of the truth" (1 John 2:20–21).

The anointing mentioned is the Holy Spirit, whom God poured out on the church (Acts 2:16–18; 10:45). All believers have this anointing (Rom. 8:9; 1 Cor. 12:13), and it proves sufficient to teach Christians to identify and reject the heresies of deceivers. In fact, John is so confident of this that he goes so far as stating that there is no need for anyone to instruct believers to keep them from being deceived:

> These things I have written to you concerning those who try to deceive you. But the anointing which you have received from Him abides in you, and you do not need that anyone teach you; but as the same anointing teaches you concerning all things, and is true, and is not a lie, and *just as it has taught you, you will abide in Him*.
>
> (1 John 2:26–27, NKJV; emphasis added)

It is true that the teaching from other Christians is essential for believers to grow in the knowledge of the truth and reach spiritual maturity. However, at this point, we are dealing with false teachings that corrupt the essentials of the Christian faith. In matters of this nature, the indwelling Holy Spirit teaches us "all things." That being the case, whenever a false teacher seeks to lead a saved person astray, the Holy Spirit in that person does not allow the believer to be deceived, even if no one is present to point out the error. The anointing of the Holy Spirit simply will not permit it to happen. Deep in the soul, the Christian will know that it is not the voice of his or her Master and will reject it. This is what was promised in the prophecy of Isaiah:

> And though the Lord give you the bread of adversity and the water of affliction, yet your Teacher will not hide himself anymore, but your eyes shall see your Teacher. And your ears shall hear a word behind you, saying, "This is the way, walk in it," when you turn to the right or when you turn to the left. Then you will defile your carved idols overlaid with silver and your gold-plated metal images. You will scatter them as unclean things. You will say to them, "Be gone!"   (Isa. 30:20–22)

John returns to this theme in chapter 4, declaring our victory over the false teachers with all confidence and attributing it to the fact that there is One in us who is greater than the devil and all his instruments for deception. The One who is in us, of course, is God, the Holy Spirit:

> Little children, you are from God and have overcome them [the false teachers], for he who is in you is greater than he who is in the world. They are from the world; therefore they speak from the world, and the world listens to them. We are from God. Whoever knows God listens to us; whoever is not from God does not listen to us. By this we know the Spirit of truth and the spirit of error.   (1 John 4:4–6)

The false teachers make many proselytes indeed, but only from those who are of the world. If the Holy Spirit were in them, they never could be taken in by heretical teachings. There is good reason for Jude to say, "It is these who cause divisions, worldly people, devoid of the Spirit" (Jude 1:19). Those who belong to God, John asserts, give heed to the apostolic message. The manner in which a person responds to the teachings of heretics reveals whether they are really of God or not.

THOSE WHO DEPART HAVE NEVER BEEN SAVED

Fully persuaded that true Christians do not fall prey to false teaching, the apostle is bold enough to make an all-encompassing judgment of those who had departed. The idea that they were Christians but had lost their salvation is not the right explanation. On the contrary,

> They went out from us, but they were not of us; for if they had been of us, they would have continued with us. But they went out, that it might become plain that they all are not of us.   (1 John 2:19)

The truth is that they had been in the visible church for a while and appeared to have been believers during that time. However, even back then, "they *were not* of us."

Those who think it is possible for a believer to lose his salvation have no way of harmonizing this text with their doctrine. While they may be ready to concede that some people who have gone out of the church were not saved, acknowledging that all the deserters were unsaved destroys their position. Yet there is no escaping it. If they argue that this text does not prove that all genuine believers necessarily remain in the truth, they will not be dealing objectively with the text.

John did not merely say that some of those who went out from us "were not of us." He goes much further and completely shuts the door on speculation about the possibility of any true saints having so gone astray when he states, "For if they had been of us, they would have continued with us."

Do we grasp the weight of those words? John does not allow for any other possibility! He doesn't say that if they had been of us they *might* have remained with us, nor that they *probably* would have remained. The statement is not qualified in the least. According to this passage of Scripture, none of those who had left the church would have departed had they been authentic Christians. Such a strong statement can only be justified if true Christians *never* apostatize from the faith.

Particular notice should be paid to the word *for* in this verse. Its function is to introduce the reason why John reaches his conclusion that those who went out from us were not of us. After all, someone could question his assertion asking, "Why is that so? How can we be so sure that they were not of us?"

So before any objection can be voiced, John anticipates it and tells us why we can be sure: "They went out from us, but they were not of us; *for* if they had been of us, they would have continued with us. But they went out, that it might become plain that they all are not of us." John is basing his conclusion that they had never been saved on that which he knows for sure, namely that if they had been of us they never would have gone out from us.

Fully persuaded of this premise, he does not hesitate in making such a blanket statement concerning all the apostates. Bearing in mind that John is writing a general epistle that is not directed to a single local church, we can surmise that there are not just a few specific people from one specific location in mind when he says that "many" have gone out following false doctrines.

It is fair to conclude that John wouldn't have personally known all those who had left the churches or even been familiar with all the specific cases that could come to mind as his intended audience read his letter. Even so, he had no need of knowing the specifics about each case in order to speak in absolutes. He did not base his evaluation on a personal knowledge of each individual. It was enough to know that they had become apostates. By taking nothing more into consideration to reach his verdict, John teaches us that we can categorically affirm that all such people have never been true Christians. It suffices to know that "if they had been of us, they would have continued with us."

Having said that, he adds, "But they went out, that it might become plain that they all are not of us."[90] These words reinforce in even plainer language that for John the problem was not that they had gone, for when this happens, it merely reveals a problem that was already present, though ignored. Before their defection, they were believed to be Christians in the churches where they had been accepted as brothers and sisters. Now, however, "their going showed that none of them belonged to us" (NIV), not even a single one.

It is not only in 1 John that the Bible teaches that it is impossible for a false teacher to lead real disciples of Jesus astray from the true Gospel. When Jesus prophesied that false prophets would multiply, he said, "For false Christs and false prophets will appear and perform great signs and miracles to deceive even the elect—if that were possible" (Matt. 24:24, NIV).

To disclose how persuasive these masters of deception can be, Jesus uses "the elect" as the embodiment of that which is the hardest to deceive and says that even the elect would be deceived, "if that were possible." His underlying assumption is that deceiving the elect is actually impossible.

The teaching of Jesus in this regard finds full expression in John chapter 10:

> Most assuredly, I say to you, he who does not enter the sheepfold by the door, but climbs up some other way, the same is a thief and a robber. But he who enters by the door is the shepherd of the sheep. To him the doorkeeper opens, and the sheep hear his voice; and he calls his own sheep by name and leads them out. And when he brings out his own sheep, he goes before them; and the sheep follow him, for they know his voice. Yet they will by no means follow a stranger, but will flee from him, for they do not know the voice of strangers.

---

90   The rendition of this last part of the verse in the King James Version is misleading: "that they might be made manifest that they were not all of us" (KJV). In fact, the New King James Version was careful to correct this sentence so that it would plainly transmit the meaning of the original Greek into English.

By building upon the imperfect translation in the King James Version and without going to the trouble of checking the original, some have maintained that among those who left the church, there were some who were believers and some who were not.

For example, the Methodist commentator Adam Clark wrote, "These false teachers probably drew many sincere souls away with them; and to this it is probable the apostle alludes when he says, they were not ALL of us. Some were; others were not." Adam Clarke, Clarke's Commentary of the New Testament, Vol. 8, The Master Christian Library (Rio, WI: Ages Software Inc., 2000) 892 (emphasis in original).

In reality, that is the exact opposite of the meaning of the text. The original construction literally says that they departed so that it would become manifest that all of them were not of us. That is an emphatic way of stating that none of them were of us.

Jesus used this illustration, but they did not understand the things which He spoke to them. Then Jesus said to them again, "Most assuredly, I say to you, I am the door of the sheep. All who ever came before Me are thieves and robbers, but the sheep did not hear them. I am the door. If anyone enters by Me, he will be saved, and will go in and out and find pasture."   (John 10:1–9, NKJV)

In this passage, Jesus calls "sheep" those whom he called "the elect" in Matthew 24. When Jesus "has brought out all his own, he goes before them, and the sheep follow him, for they know his voice" (v. 4).

But besides Jesus, the Good Shepherd, there are thieves and robbers in this world, which is to say false teachers. Is there a possibility that they may lead Christ's sheep astray? Is it possible for any of Christ's sheep to be misled by strangers so as to no longer follow the Good Shepherd? No, it is not possible.

Using the experience of pastors who lead their herds by their voice, Jesus illustrates the manner in which those who belong to him will never be beguiled by those who falsify the Gospel: "Yet they will by no means follow a stranger, but will flee from him, for they do not know the voice of strangers" (v. 5, NKJV).

The words of Jesus are very strong in verse 5 and are variously translated: "And a stranger they simply will not follow, but will flee from him" (NASB) and "But they will never follow a stranger; in fact, they will run away from him" (NIV). What each version labors to get across is that Jesus clearly stated that it is impossible for his sheep to wander off following a stranger; they simply will not do it—never, by no means!

Even prior to the Lord's coming into the world, many false teachers had come, "but the sheep did not listen to them" (v. 8). Jesus had a perfect track record up to that time. Never had any of his sheep been lost, victimized by a false teacher, and Jesus assures us that things will stay that way.

Arthur Pink's comments on John 10:5 are most helpful:

This is very important, for it describes a mark found on all of Christ's sheep. A strange shepherd they will not heed....Instead, speaking characteristically, they will *flee* from such. It is not possible to deceive the elect (Matt. 24:24). Let a man of the world hear two preachers, one giving out the truth and the other error, and he can discern no difference between them. But it is far otherwise with a child of God. He may be but a babe in Christ, unskilled in theological controversies, but instinctively he will detect vital heresy as soon as he hears it. And why is this? Because he is indwelt by the Holy Spirit, and has received an "unction" from the Holy One (1 John 2:20). How thankful we should be for this. How gracious of the Lord to have given us this capacity to separate the precious from the vile![91]

It needs to be clearly stated that it is apostasy that proves that a person was never saved, not merely a momentary confusion. As a pastor in a local church, Christians occasionally come to me full of questions after having heard a false teacher. A heresy may be presented in such a convincing way that it can create confusion in the mind of a child of God. The Christian may run into doubts feeling compelled to seek out fellow Christians or good books for adequate answers.

Nevertheless, if the person is truly saved, he or she will not become persuaded by the heresy or join up with it. Inside, there will be the discernment that it is not a message from God, even if no help can be found providing satisfactory answers. An illustration of this principle can be seen in the many Christians who have rejected the theory of evolution, even though they lacked scientific resources or arguments that could refute it. The same takes place with a myriad of false teachings. A believer may not have all the answers or the wherewithal to outdebate the heretic, but Christ's sheep will have enough light to know better and not be deceived.

GUARDING AGAINST HERESY

In light of this biblical teaching, how should we deal with the threat of false doctrine? The fact that those who have the Holy Spirit overcome the false prophets does not mean that we should be lax in teaching and warning against heresies. On the contrary, following his prediction that some will depart from the faith, Paul instructs Timothy to labor intensely in combating false doctrine:

> If you put these things before the brothers, you will be a good servant of Christ Jesus...Until I come, devote yourself to the public reading of Scripture, to exhortation, to teaching. Do not neglect the gift you have...Keep a close watch on yourself and on the teaching. Persist in this, for by so doing you will save both yourself and your hearers. (1 Tim. 4:6–16)

---

91 Arthur W. Pink, *Exposition of the Gospel of John* (Grand Rapids: Zondervan, 1975), 517; (emphasis in original).

In his epistles to churches, Paul went to great lengths to oppose the errors of deceivers.

Although it is true that the saints cannot be led away unto their perdition by false teaching, it should be realized that there are always people under the teaching of the truth who have not truly come to a personal conviction. It is those who are "just escaping from those who live in error" (2 Pet. 2:18, NIV) that the false teachers can entice and carry away.

Since people like this are an ever-present reality in the church, it behooves us to counteract false teaching just as surely as we must preach the Gospel itself. Faith comes by hearing, and hearing through the Word of Christ. As long as we have opportunity, we should strive to teach the truth and warn against apostasy, for that is the means which God uses to bring people to genuine unshakable faith.

If a church or a church member comes under the influence of false teachers, we should employ every resource at our disposal to withstand the error immediately. That is how Paul reacted to the incursion of the Judaizers among the Galatians. As soon as news of what was happening reached him, he dispatched a passionate letter to the churches they were affecting. He is shocked at how quickly churches he had planted were opening themselves to another gospel (Gal. 1:6). He preferred to believe that the Judaizers were only being tolerated because many had not perceived the real implications of their doctrine, and that once they were exposed by means of his letter they would no longer enjoy freedom to operate among the Galatian churches.

He expresses this expectation when he writes, "I have confidence in the Lord that you will take no other view than mine, and the one who is troubling you will bear the penalty, whoever he is" (Gal. 5:10). But at the same time, he does not discount the possibility that his missionary labor in that region might have resulted in far fewer true conversions than at first he had thought.

This concern comes across as he admits, "I am afraid I may have labored over you in vain....my little children, for whom I am again in the anguish of childbirth until Christ is formed in you! I wish I could be present with you now and change my tone, for I am perplexed about you" (Gal. 4:11; 19–20).

Paul handles the situation in a very cautious manner, refraining from any hasty conclusions as to the spiritual condition of the Galatians. The whole situation had left him perplexed. Being away from them, he lacked full knowledge of how the Galatians were reacting to the false teaching. At any rate, he now seeks to refute the error and keep all of them on the side of the truth. He wars against the false teaching with all at his disposal, unwilling to relinquish a single soul to our adversary.

In case anyone was still wavering, short of the internal conviction that the Holy Spirit brings about, Paul demonstrates clearly that his intention is to win them over now, once for all. If need be, he will go through "the anguish of childbirth" all over again, until Christ is formed in them.

Paul should serve as our model. If at any time we find those who we have accepted as brothers in a similar situation, we should warn them not to apostatize, being confident all along that the truly converted will certainly heed us, and being hopeful that any who may have been superficial will now come to full faith by the Word of Christ. This is also in keeping with the instruction of Jude: "And have mercy on those who doubt; save others by snatching them out of the fire" (Jude 1:22–23).

The Care of Providence

Charity never falls; so, the possession and house of the saints never falls, is never taken away, is never separated from their right; for how can that house be separated from the priest, which is built upon the foundation of the apostles and prophets, in which Jesus Christ is the chief corner stone?...The church, as the building of Christ, who builds his own house wisely upon the rock, cannot admit of the gates of hell; which indeed prevail against every man without the rock and church, but can do nothing against it....He that is now a little one, can neither be offended nor perish, for great peace have they which love the name of God, and nothing shall offend them. Even he that is the least of all the disciples of Christ, cannot perish, and therefore he is great, and may say this, Who shall separate us from the love?[92]

(Origen of Alexandria, AD 230)

Those whom God foreknew would be devoted to him, them he chose to enjoy the promised rewards; that those who seem to believe and do not continue in the faith begun, may be denied to be God's elect; for whom God hath chosen, they continue with him....Whom God foreknew to be fit for himself, these continue believers, for it cannot be otherwise, but that whom God foreknows, them he also justifies, and so hereby glorifies them, that they may be like the Son of God. As to the rest, whom God has not foreknown, he takes no care of them in this grace, because he has not foreknown them...they do not continue that they may be glorified; as Judas Iscariot...who, being chosen, afterwards were offended, and departed from the Savior.... Whom God is said to call, they persevere in faith; these are they whom he has chosen in Christ before the world began, that they be unblameable before God in love.[93]   (Hilary Deacon, AD 380)

---

92 Origines Alexandrinus, quoted by John Gill, *The Cause of God and of Truth*, Part 4, Chapter 5, Section 8, The Ultimate Christian Library (Rio, Wisconsin: AGES Software, 2000), 819–820.

93 Origines Alexandrinus, quoted by John Gill, *The Cause of God and of Truth*, Part 4, Chapter 5, Section 8, The Ultimate Christian Library (Rio, Wisconsin: AGES Software, 2000), 819–820.

We have already considered how regeneration and the guarantee of the Spirit are granted by God to his own to keep them from ever departing from him. In addition to these internal protections that God implants in each believer at conversion, the Bible teaches that God sovereignly conducts all his creation in such way as to ensure the security of his people and render their perseverance certain.

In John 6:35–40 and in Romans 8:28–39, the Scriptures explicitly rule out the idea that Christ could ever lose anyone that belongs to him. Both passages teach that there is no possibility of such a thing ever happening due to God's providential care for his own.

God is no mere observer of human history. He rules over all events as they unfold, guiding them according to his eternal plan so that nothing escapes his control:

> God is not…allowing things to happen on their own. On the contrary, in his infinite wisdom and in his absolute might, God exerts his power…to sustain, direct, provide, and govern all creatures and circumstances, causing all things to work together for the fulfillment of his eternal purposes. This is what we call the doctrine of divine providence.[94]

CHRIST'S MISSION INVOLVES NEVER LOSING ANY OF HIS OWN

The reality of God's providence has much to do with the doctrine under consideration. If God is sovereign and nothing is beyond his control, then it is in his hands to sustain the faith of a believer, so long as he desires to do so. As we shall see ahead, it is God's own determination in never losing any that belong to him (instead of any determination on our part), which appears in Scripture as the reason why we can be sure that all the saints will persevere:

> Jesus said to them, "I am the bread of life; whoever comes to me shall not hunger, and whoever believes in me shall never thirst. But I said to you that you have seen me and yet do not believe. All that the Father gives me will come to me, and whoever comes to me I will never cast out. For I have come down from heaven, not to do my own will but the will of him who sent me. And this is the will of him who sent me, that I should lose nothing of all that he has given

---

94 Heber Carlos de Campos, *A Providência e a sua realização histórica* (São Paulo: Editora Cultura Cristã, 2001), 13–14.

me, but raise it up on the last day. For this is the will of my Father, that everyone who looks on the Son and believes in him should have eternal life, and I will raise him up on the last day."   (John 6:35–40)

Jesus here speaks of conversion as coming to him, "Whoever comes to me," a reference to believing unto salvation, "I will never cast out" (v. 37), Jesus promises. But what is it exactly that Jesus promises? This has nothing to do with an assurance that nobody will be rejected by Christ at the entrance door. His words are very clearly a guarantee that nobody who is ever converted can become lost again subsequently. Jesus is not speaking of turning people away from coming in but of casting people out. As A.W. Pink noted,

> The last clause "I will in no wise cast out" assures the eternal preservation of everyone that truly cometh to Christ. Those words of the Saviour do not signify (as generally supposed) that He promises to reject *none* who really come to Him, *though that is true*; but they declare that under no imaginable circumstances will He ever expel any one that *has* come.[95]

The meaning Jesus intended to communicate is that whoever is converted to him will not be rejected at any later point in time:

> The second part of the verse moves from the collective whole to the individual, and from the actual coming (consequent on being part of the gift) to preservation. This interpretation is suggested by the verb *ekballō*, "drive away" or "cast out." In almost all of its parallel occurrences, it is presupposed that what is driven out or cast out is already "in." "I will never drive away" therefore means "I will certainly keep in." This interpretation, however strongly supported by the verb, is required by the context, the next three verses.[96]

It does become perfectly clear from the context (verses 38–40) that this is the intended meaning of the words of Christ. Verse 38 begins with the word *for*. Jesus will now explain why he will not cast out any of those who come to him. And what is his reason? It is because it is his Father's will that he should *lose none* of all those who were given to him, which are precisely those who come to him. For this reason, Jesus will perfectly preserve all those who are ever converted unto him.

---

95 Arthur W. Pink, *Exposition of the Gospel of John* (Grand Rapids: Zondervan, 1975), 330–331 (emphasis in original).

96 D. A. Carson, *The Gospel According to John* (William B. Eerdmans Publishing Company, 1991), 290 (emphasis in original).

The shift from the collective whole to the individual, noted by Don Carson, is also significant. The mission Jesus claims for himself is not that of saving people who make up a group that is subject to increase or decrease in number. His mission is to see to it that no one (i.e., not even one individual) who comes to him ends up being lost but makes it safe and sound until the day of the resurrection, for that is the will of the Father.

So what is the possibility of anyone who comes to Christ today becoming a reject at a later point in time? Jesus said, "Whoever comes to me I will *never* cast out" (v. 37; emphasis added). The original Greek makes use of the most emphatic form of negation (οὐ μὴ), which means under no circumstances. We need not speculate if Jesus would or would not be moved to cast anyone out depending on what might happen, because Jesus has said that he will "certainly not" (NASB) do it.

Of course, such a statement presupposes that there are some things that are impossible and, therefore, simply will not happen. Jesus is not saying that a believer is secure even in the event of apostasy. Christ's declaration is undergirded by the understanding that Jesus will not fail in his mission of keeping all those who come to him so that apostasy on their part is not to be postulated as something that *could* actually happen. But in view of all the things that can actually happen, come what may, Jesus will never cast out a single person that comes to him in true conversion.

> The entire purpose of the incarnation, of his coming *down from heaven*, was not to do his own will, but the will of the Father who sent him (v. 38), and that will was that the Son should lose none (i.e. no individual) of all that the Father had given him...In other words, if any of them failed to achieve this goal, it would be the Son's everlasting shame: it would mean either that he was incapable of performing what the Father willed him to do, or that he was flagrantly disobedient to his Father.[97]

When we consider the subject at hand, our tendency is to think of it from our perspective, in terms of what implications there are for us if a justified believer could lose his or her salvation. But when we read the words of Jesus, we begin to realize that from his point of view the real issue is whether *God will lose any of his own*. If this happened, he would see his plans of saving them frustrated.

---

97 Ibid., 290–291 (emphasis in original).

What does this do to his honor and sovereignty? Although things that displease God do happen, we know that even these things fit in with his eternal purposes, for no purpose of his can be thwarted (Job 42:2). If God began by saving a person, intending for that person to never be lost again, but then saw his plan thwarted and intention frustrated by man or the devil, he could no longer say, "I am God, and there is none like me, declaring the end from the beginning and from ancient times things not yet done, saying, *'My counsel shall stand, and I will accomplish all my purpose'*" (Isa. 46:10; emphasis added).

The opponents of the doctrine of the perseverance of the saints are forced to defend that God can be thwarted in his purpose to keep his people unto their final salvation. For instance, Robert Shank dismisses John 6:39 as indicating nothing more than willingness on God's part for something that may or may not come to pass:

> It is not the Father's will that any who come to Jesus should subsequently be lost. But neither is it His will that any should perish (2 Pet. 3:9) or fail to come to the knowledge of the truth and be saved (2 Tim. 2:4). But there is a vast difference between God's perfect will and His permissive will.[98]

His whole argument runs into difficulties that are beyond the scope of this book, yet it should be noted how it is entirely inadequate. Shank seems to ignore that the Son is given the task of not losing any of those who come to him. This means that if the will of the Father is not accomplished on this matter, it would mean a failure on the part of the Lord Jesus himself. He would fail to accomplish that which he himself assumes to be his own mission.

Besides that, Shank's argument deals only with the first part of verse 39 and doesn't take everything that Jesus said into account. Once Jesus said that it is the Father's will that he "should lose" [aorist subjunctive active] none, Jesus concludes with a prophecy in verse 40, where he predicts, "And I will raise him up [future indicative active] on the last day."

This goes far beyond saying that God would like for this to happen. Jesus prophesies that he will certainly accomplish the Father's will on this matter. The grammatical change from the subjunctive to the indicative mood reveals that at the end of our Lord's statement he does more than continue explaining what the will of the Father is. Instead, it is a prophecy of what

---

98 Robert Shank, *Life in the Son* (Bloomington: Bethany House Publishers, 1989), 360.

will come to pass on the last day, namely that each individual that comes to Christ will be raised up to enjoy eternal life.

As a whole, the impetus of what Jesus says is that there is no possibility that any individual who comes to Christ could end up being lost, for that would be contrary to the will of the Father. Instead of that, what will infallibly come to pass is that each one of them will be raised up at the last day. But if even one single individual came to Christ and ended up being cast out later, then this prophecy of Jesus would go unfulfilled. But we know that the words of Jesus never fail. Heaven and earth shall pass away, but his words will not pass away (Matt. 24:35).

We will not see humans causing the words of Christ to go unfulfilled. God has made hundreds of prophecies that involved human decisions and actions, yet not a single one of them failed to come to pass as predicted, despite the fact that people are invested with free agency. This never has and never will keep the Most High, whose dominion is an everlasting dominion and whose kingdom endures from generation to generation, from doing according to his will among the host of heaven and among the inhabitants of the earth. There is no one who can stay his hand or say to him, "What have you done?" (Dan. 4:34–35). Is there anything that is too hard for the Lord? (Gen. 18:14)

CHRIST'S PROVIDENCE PROTECTS HIS OWN

So how does Jesus keep his own so as to not lose any of them? Other passages in the fourth gospel shed light on this question. Further along in the book, we read the following:

> Then Jesus, knowing all that would happen to him, came forward and said to them, "Whom do you seek?" They answered him, "Jesus of Nazareth." Jesus said to them, "I am he." Judas, who betrayed him, was standing with them. When Jesus said to them, "I am he," they drew back and fell to the ground. So he asked them again, "Whom do you seek?" And they said, "Jesus of Nazareth." Jesus answered, "I told you that I am he. So, if you seek me, let these men go." *This was to fulfill the word that he had spoken: "Of those whom you gave me I have lost not one."* (John 18:4–9; emphasis added)

When Jesus was arrested, he knew his disciples were still unprepared for the kind of trial they would undergo if they were arrested along with him. Jesus had already predicted that that night they would all fall away and that Peter would deny him three times—all this without any of them even being arrested.

Later on, the apostles would become martyrs for Christ, but Jesus knew just how much pressure they were able to bear at that time, and he knew what the consequences would be for their faith if they were tested so severely that early on, before having understood his death and witnessed his resurrection. Therefore, he interfered sparing them, in order to fulfill the word he had spoken: "Of those whom you gave me I have lost not one."

This text shows us that, among other things, Jesus's providential care for his people is one of the ways he fulfills his mission of not losing a single one of us. He controls the circumstances in which we find ourselves to prevent us from being subjected to any trials that would overwhelm us. He carefully adjusts the intensity of our temptations so that even when we sin we never fall totally and finally away but rise up again, renewed in our commitment.

The case of Peter in particular is very instructive. He denied three times that he was a follower of Christ, going as far as cursing and swearing. But God, in his grace, transformed even this failure on his part into a growing experience, making Peter come out of it more grateful and more committed than ever.

Things didn't just turn out this way by chance. The hand of Jesus was at work in everything that transpired. In fact, Jesus had even confided to Peter that he would remain faithful, but not because of his own efforts. In our Lord's own words, he was told the following:

> "Simon, Simon, behold, Satan demanded to have you, that he might sift you like wheat, *but I have prayed for you that your faith may not fail*. And when you have turned again, strengthen your brothers."
>
> (Luke 22:31–32; emphasis added)

Jesus told Peter that Satan, desirous of sifting Peter like wheat, had asked God to allow him to crush his faith. The devil wanted more than to see Peter fall into a temptation. He wanted to cause him to fall completely. But this demand was not granted. This spiritual insight that Jesus shares should cause us to realize two things.

First, Jesus shows Peter how fragile he is and how dependent he is upon the grace of God. He wouldn't stand a chance if Satan assaulted him with all his malice and astuteness. It would actually be easy for the devil to demolish Peter's faith. Jesus said that Satan had tried to get permission to sift him like wheat. Sifting wheat is not a hard thing to do. Causing Peter to lose his faith would have been an extremely easy task for Satan, like the kind of job that even a child can do in a wheat field to help out the adults.

However, the second thing we should realize is that to do so, the devil needed to get authorization from God. Jesus here pictures the devil having to deal with God before he can set up any trap or temptation. This truth is quite shocking for many today who have come to think of the spiritual conflict going on in this world in almost dualistic terms. But the clear teaching of the Scriptures is that the devil and the demons cannot act as they well please in the world. All their doings in this world—whether in the area of temptation, deceit, false doctrines, or anything else—are circumscribed by God, who delineates what may and may not be done.

The account of Job's trials teaches us this truth. Satan was not able to bring a single trial upon Job without first receiving authorization from God. Thus, all the trials that Job underwent were being regulated by God who, knowing in advance how much Job would handle well, stipulated the precise limits of what the enemy could put him through. In the end, the result of all his affliction was that Job emerged stronger, closer to God and heading on toward a heavenly reward, eternal weight of glory that is beyond all comparison. Likewise, in the case of Peter, Satan had desired to make full use of his tricks in order to destroy Peter, but such a thing was not granted because Jesus prayed to the Father on his behalf. It was God who determined the intensity of Peter's testing. As a result, in his weakness, Peter did, in fact, deny Christ, but his faith did not fail, and he turned again to strengthen his brothers.

Combined, the implications of these two truths are enormous. We are no better than Peter. If the devil were free to do as he pleased, taking away our salvation would be a pushover. No matter how determined, how valiant, or how vigilant we might strive to be, we could not overcome Satan unless it was granted to us from on high. This truly does not depend on human will or exertion but on God showing mercy.

CHRIST'S INTERCESSION ON BEHALF OF HIS OWN

For those who are converted, this understanding should be a great encouragement. If not even a sparrow will fall to the ground apart from God's consent, certainly no Christian will fall to eternal perdition in violation of the express will of God. Even so, there is no doubt that many sincere Christians suffer, fearing what may overtake them in the future.

Are you such a Christian? Do you have biblical warrant to be sure that you are saved but still fear that your faith may someday fail? Perhaps this insecurity has often led you to pray and ask your Christian brothers and sisters to pray for you as well, though never finding peace. Perhaps it would be a great comfort if the Lord Jesus personally prayed for you, just as he did for Peter.

Wouldn't it be marvelous if Jesus himself prayed for you that your faith may not fail? Be of good cheer! He has prayed for you! He has prayed for all who would come to faith in him. Indeed, he continues to intercede for us before the Father. This is the testimony of Scripture:

> I am praying for them. I am not praying for the world but for those whom you have given me, for they are yours. All mine are yours, and yours are mine, and I am glorified in them. And I am no longer in the world, but they are in the world, and I am coming to you. Holy Father, keep them in your name, which you have given me, that they may be one, even as we are one. While I was with them, I kept them in your name, which you have given me. I have guarded them, and not one of them has been lost except the son of destruction, that the Scripture might be fulfilled. But now I am coming to you, and these things I speak in the world, that they may have my joy fulfilled in themselves. I have given them your word, and the world has hated them because they are not of the world, just as I am not of the world. I do not ask that you take them out of the world, but that you keep them from the evil one. They are not of the world, just as I am not of the world. Sanctify them in the truth; your word is truth. As you sent me into the world, so I have sent them into the world. And for their sake I consecrate myself, that they also may be sanctified in truth. I do not ask for these only, but also for those who will believe in me through their word, that they may all be one, just as you, Father, are in me, and I in you, that they also may be in us, so that the world may believe that you have sent me. (John 17:9–21)

Christ's high priestly prayer is profoundly moving. Jesus is just hours away from the cross. As his mission on earth draws to an end, he entreats the Father on behalf of his disciples who would continue in this spiritually dangerous world and beseeches him to protect them so that not even one of them might be lost. His prayer is not for all people in general but for a select group of people specifically: "I am praying for them. I am not praying for the world but for those whom you have given me, for they are yours" (v. 9).

In light of the fact that they are still to remain for some time in this world of sin and spiritual dangers, Jesus asks the Father that they be kept and protected:

And I am no longer in the world, *but they are in the world*, and I am coming to you. *Holy Father, keep them in your name*, which you have given me, that they may be one, even as we are one.

(v. 11; emphasis added).

Exactly what is meant by Jesus's request to the Father that they be kept is revealed in the words "That they may be one" and in the following verse, where he adds, "While I was with them, I kept them...I have guarded them, and not one of them has been lost."

Very plainly, Jesus is asking the Father to protect them against being lost. It is through Christ that Christians are "one." United to Christ by faith, all true Christians form one spiritual body. But Jesus does not ask that they be kept *as long as* they remain in Christ and thus united. His request is for the Father to "keep them...*that they may be one*." Jesus is confident that they will remain "one" as long as the Father answers his prayer and keeps them.

Through his teaching, his warnings against sin, and by means of his protective actions (like those recorded in John 18:4–9 and Luke 22:31–32), Jesus personally had protected them while he was with them. The result of his protection was that none of them had been lost except Judas, and that does not properly count as an exception since Judas had never actually been a believer and was never under the protection of Jesus.[99]

Just as Jesus had a perfect record in his guarding of them, so was he sure that by leaving them in the Father's care the result would be no different. So much so that he could say, "I do not ask that you take them out of the world, but that you keep them from the evil one" (v. 15). If Jesus were not certain that none of them would be lost under these conditions, he might very well have asked that they be taken out of the world.

But that would not be necessary in order for them to be safe. Remaining in this world would not constitute a risk of any being lost, so long as the Father kept them from the evil one (v. 15) and sanctified them in the truth (v. 17). This way, they could remain safely in the world until their mission here had been accomplished, as indicated in verse 18: "As you sent me into the world, so I have sent them into the world."

---

99 The phrase in verse 12 about Judas, "Except the son of destruction, that the Scripture might be fulfilled," will be examined in detail in the next chapter along with proofs that Judas was never saved.

All this did not apply exclusively to the disciples of Christ from that generation, because Jesus did not ask these things for them alone. In verse 20, he proceeds, praying, "I do not ask for these only, but also for those who will believe in me through their word." We find that on that day Jesus actually prayed for each person who throughout the years would come to believe in him through the apostolic testimony.

Now that is to us something precious and personal. On that day, right before going to the cross, Jesus prayed for me! He included even me as he prayed to the Father to keep his people so that none of them should be lost! He prayed for me that my faith may not fail!

That is what the Gospel of John seeks to impress upon the minds of all who come to faith in the Lord Jesus: Christ himself has prayed for us. Not only so, but the Scriptures further inform us that he *continues* to pray for us:

> Who is to condemn? Christ Jesus is the one who died—more than that, who was raised—who is at the right hand of God, who indeed is interceding for us. (Rom. 8:34)

Does this truth not fill our souls with new life? How many times have we been comforted just to know that a brother or a sister in Christ was praying for us? How much more to think that *Jesus* is interceding for us? How often may the devil have desired to shipwreck our faith, ensnaring us and dragging us down with him to the abyss where he will face his own fate?

But just as Jesus prayed for Peter, so has he interceded on our behalf as well. If there be any who have overcome the evil one, it is because Jesus mercifully does not allow the devil to lay hands upon his or her soul:

> We know that everyone who has been born of God does not keep on sinning, but he who was born of God protects him, and the evil one does not touch him. (1 John 5:18)

Our security owes itself to this wonderful protection, which is worthy of all our trust that we may rest assured in him. Sarah Kalley expressed this profound truth most beautifully in the words of a hymn:

> Your hands, oh Lord, direct my life and future,
>> The hands that for me were nailed to the cross.
> To purge my sins they were pierced through and suffered.
>> In them I truly find that can trust!

Raised up in heaven ever interceding,
    Your holy hands will not entreat in vain.
Into their care, I place my soul's safekeeping.
    Upheld by them eternal life I'll gain![100]

We find this same assurance of protection in the early church, which lived under intense persecution and trials. Among the many witnesses on this matter, we find the following words from Tertullian, written around AD 200:

Satan cannot do anything against the servants of the living God, unless he permits, either that he may destroy him through the faith of the elect, which overcomes in temptation, or that he may openly show that the men were his, who fell off to him. You have an example in Job. So he desired power to tempt the apostles, not having it but by permission; since the Lord in the Gospel says to Peter, *Satan hath desired that he might sift thee as wheat; but I have prayed for thee, that thy faith fail not* lest only it should be permitted to the devil, as that faith should be in danger;' whereby it showed, that both are with God, and shaking of faith, and the protection of it; since both are desired of him, shaking by the devil, protection by the Son; and seeing the Son of God has the protection of faith in his own power, which he requested of the Father, from whom he receives all power in heaven and in earth; how can the devil have the shaking of faith in his own hand?

What if, therefore, a bishop, a deacon, a widow, a virgin, a doctor, yea, even a martyr, should fall from the rule, shall heresies on that account seem to obtain truth? Do we prove faith by persons, or persons by faith? No man is wise, but a believer; no man of great name, but a Christian; no man a Christian, but he who shall persevere to the end.[101]

GOD MAKES ALL THINGS WORK TOGETHER FOR OUR GOOD

It is not without cause that the intercessory work of Christ should inspire such confidence. In his epistle to the Romans, even the apostle Paul refers to this same truth as he elaborates on the impossibility of our being separated from Christ. In the eighth chapter of Romans, Paul focuses on our glorification, which is the future aspect of our salvation experience. It is the destiny of

---

100 Sarah Poulton Kalley, second stanza of hymn number 163 in *Novo Cântico Hinário Presbiteriano*, ed. Cláudio Antônio Batista Marra (São Paulo, Brazil: Editora Cultura Cristã, 2003), 254–255.

101 Tertullian, quoted by John Gill, *The Cause of God and of Truth*, Part 4, Chapter 5, Section 7, The Ultimate Christian Library (Rio, Wisconsin: AGES Software, 2000), 816–817.

those who have been justified, for "if children, then heirs—heirs of God and fellow heirs with Christ, provided we suffer with him in order that we may also *be glorified with him*" (Rom. 8:17; emphasis added).

Although the path to glory is a way of suffering, Paul is sure that "the sufferings of this present time are not worth comparing with the glory that is to be revealed to us" (v. 18). History is marching on toward that day when this destiny will become a reality. Seeing that since the fall and its consequent curse "the creation was subjected to futility" (v. 20), Paul treats the arrival of that glorious day as something that is anxiously anticipated by all of creation.

Because of the wondrous transformation that this day will bring about, the revealing of the sons of God is something that the creation itself is awaiting with eager longing to "be set free from its bondage to decay and obtain the freedom of the glory of the children of God" (v. 21).

At this point, Paul makes a transition back to us as Christians and the fact that our longing is also to make it into eternal glory. So much is this the case that we groan inwardly as we wait eagerly for the day when our hope will be fulfilled:

> For we know that the whole creation has been groaning together in the pains of childbirth until now. And not only the creation, but we ourselves, who have the firstfruits of the Spirit, *groan inwardly as we wait eagerly for adoption as sons, the redemption of our bodies.* For in this hope we were saved. Now hope that is seen is not hope. For who hopes for what he sees? But *if we hope for what we do not see, we wait for it with patience.*　　　(Rom. 8:22–25; emphasis added)

It is in this context that Paul recalls how we are laden with weakness and don't even know how to pray as we should. But undaunted in his confidence, he immediately redirects our focus from our weakness to the assistance we are afforded from God, the Holy Spirit:

> Likewise the Spirit helps us in our weakness. For we do not know what to pray for as we ought, but the Spirit himself intercedes for us with groanings too deep for words. And he who searches hearts knows what is the mind of the Spirit, because the Spirit intercedes for the saints according to the will of God.　　　(Rom. 8:26–27)

So we find both the Son and the Holy Spirit interceding in favor of the saints, that we may finish the race having kept the faith and making it all the way to our glorification. And we can be sure that the Father grants what is being requested because it is according to the will of God that the Spirit intercedes for the saints (v. 27). All this leads up to Paul's most beautiful pronouncement: "And we know that God causes all things to work together for good to those who love God, to those who are called according to His purpose" (v. 28, NASB).

This verse is often quoted out of context, causing a lot of confusion. Paul is saying much more than what is conveyed in the popular saying that "every cloud has a silver lining." It is true that we often go through unpleasant experiences that in hindsight are perceived to have been blessings in disguise, delivering us from accidents, financial loss, or other such things of this life. This happens to the saints as well as to those who do not love God.

But it is evident that God also subjects his children to tribulation, distress, persecution, famine, nakedness, danger, or sword—things that clearly do not advance their overall wellbeing in this world. All things do not work together for the temporal good of those who love God. However, the "good" that Paul has in mind is not our health, long life, economic progress, or a happy life. The "good" of which he is speaking is the eternal good, which is synonymous with our final salvation. The "good" toward which God causes all things to work together is the glorification of those who love God, as can be ascertained from the immediate context.

What Paul is teaching is that in answer to the intercession of the Spirit on behalf of the saints, God makes all things work for their eternal good— that is, for those who truly love God, having been called according to his unchangeable purpose. This all means that nothing can ever happen that will ultimately turn out to be bad for those who love God, because God runs the whole universe, never allowing for anything to exist or happen except those things that, in the final analysis, will be seen to have promoted the glorification of those who love him:

> The ruling thought is that in the sovereign love and wisdom of God they are all made to converge upon and contribute to that goal. Many of the things comprised are evil in themselves and it is the marvel of God's wisdom and grace that they, when taken in concert with the whole, are made to work for good. Not one detail works ultimately for evil to the people of God; in the end only good will be their lot.[102]

---

102 John Murray, *The Epistle to the Romans, Volume I* (Grand Rapids, MI: William B. Eerdmans Publishing Company, 1997), 314.

WILL I MAKE IT TO HEAVEN?

Now that is a thought to be pondered! If God makes all things work together for the good of those who love him, can anything happen that would result in the saints losing their health or their property? Yes, if it results in their good. Can the saints face persecution and martyrdom for their faith? Yes, indeed, but only if it turns out to be for their good. Can the devil assail them with grievous temptations? Once more, the answer is yes, but only if in the end this too ends up contributing to their eternal good.

But now we come to the inevitable question: can it come to pass that a Christian should lose his or her salvation? Absolutely not! That obviously could never be made to work together for his or her good. That would be the exact opposite of that toward which God causes all things to work together.

Some have resisted this conclusion, arguing that the promise is only for those who love God so that it would cease to apply to a believer who quits loving God. But such a rationale is futile. All that does is lead us right back to the same question: Could it come to pass for a believer to grow cold spiritually until all love for God has been lost? Of course not, because in no way could *that* be made to work for his or her ultimate good. Therefore, if we are to believe that God causes *all things* to work together for the good of those who love God, we must necessarily believe that God never allows the love of any of the saints to dwindle and die.

> **All things** is utterly comprehensive, having no qualification or limits. Neither this verse nor its context allows for restrictions or conditions. **All things** is inclusive in the fullest possible sense. Nothing existing or occurring in heaven or on earth "shall be able to separate us from the love of God, which is in Christ Jesus" (8:39).
>
> Paul is not saying that God prevents His children from experiencing things that can harm them. He is rather attesting that the Lord takes all that He allows to happen to His beloved children, even the worst things, and turns those things ultimately into blessings...
>
> No matter what our situation, our suffering, our persecution, our sinful failure, our pain, our lack of faith—in those things, as well as in **all** other **things**, our heavenly Father will work to produce our ultimate victory and blessing.[103]

---

103 John MacArthur, *The MacArthur New Testament Commentary Romans 1–8* (Chicago: Moody Press, 1991), 472–473.

Paul identifies those who love God as "those who are called according to his purpose." This reminds us that God has a purpose or an objective for human history. It is in accordance to this eternal plan that God calls (converts) people. We should not suppose that anything could hinder God from fulfilling his plan. After all, there is nothing that could catch God by surprise or derail the execution of his eternal plan.

God alone is self-existent and eternal; thus all things that came into being were created by him (John 1:3), as proclaimed by the twenty-four elders in Revelation, "Worthy are you, our Lord and God, to receive glory and honor and power, for you created all things, and by your will they existed and were created" (Rev. 4:11). If God created all that there is by his will and if he knew all the long-term consequences and ramifications of bringing each created thing into being, we are forced to conclude that there is not a single thing in existence that will not perfectly fit in with God's overall plan, and that includes each angel and each reprobate individual.

As Proverbs 16:4 says, "The LORD has made everything for its purpose, even the wicked for the day of trouble." It may make us uncomfortable to grapple with this truth, but we cannot escape it.

God foresees all of history and in his providence has placed all things in their proper places so that his goals would be achieved, without any shortcomings or leftovers. This understanding permeates the whole Bible.

By divine providence, there was a ram caught in a thicket by his horns so that Abraham could sacrifice it instead of Isaac (Gen. 22:13). When Haman determined to execute the Jews, Mordecai surmised correctly that it was no coincidence that Esther had been raised to the position of queen at such a time (Esther. 4:14). By that same providence, in the days when Jesus was about to be born, a decree went out from Caesar Augustus that all the world should be registered (Luke 2:1), fulfilling the Scripture that the Messiah would be born in Bethlehem.

According to the Bible, even the angels are restrained from having any influence other than that for which they have been designed so that they can only come on the scene at the exact moment of God's choice and in order to fulfill God's purposes. "So the four angels, who had been prepared for the hour, the day, the month, and the year, were released to kill a third of mankind" (Rev. 9:15).

Because of this, no purpose of God is ever thwarted. Saul was never able to kill David, notwithstanding his being the king and surrounded by all the advantages from a human point of view. He was always impeded by divine providence, whether through the appeals of Jonathan, by the embarrassment of falling into the hands of David and being spared, or by the Philistine army choosing to invade Israel at the precise moment when David would have finally been captured.

As it is written, "No wisdom, no understanding, no counsel can avail against the LORD" (Prov. 21:30). If God planned for David to become king in Israel, who could stand in his way? Saul knew he was fighting against God (1 Sam. 24:20). Even so, he wearied himself uselessly to kill David. Just as surely, if God has called someone according to his purpose, will any be able to stand in his way? Or to put it in the words of the apostle Paul, "If God is for us, who can be against us?" (Rom. 8:31).

God actively intervenes in the course of human history, ruling over all his creation, moving all things along in a manner pleasing to himself in order that all events unfold according to his predetermined council. "He changes times and seasons; he removes kings and sets up kings; he gives wisdom to the wise and knowledge to those who have understanding" (Dan. 2:21).

There is no human authority but that which has been instituted by God (Rom. 13:1). "The LORD kills and brings to life... The LORD makes poor and makes rich; he brings low and he exalts" (1 Sam. 2:6–7). It is he who occasions prosperity and he who brings about calamity (Isa. 45:7).

In recognition of his sovereignty, the prophet Amos asks, "Does disaster come to a city, unless the LORD has done it?" (Amos 3:6). For this same reason, Job also responded to disaster that beset him saying, "The LORD gave, and the LORD has taken away; blessed be the name of the LORD" (Job 1:21).

The hand of God is at work in everything that transpires to ensure our good, and only our good, as God's elect. This is something we can know for sure. "*We know* that for those who love God all things work together for good, for those who are called according to his purpose" (Rom. 8:28; emphasis added).

Our Lord provides us one illustration of how this works in his prophetic words: "And unless those days had been cut short, no life would be saved, but for the sake of the elect those days shall be cut short" (Matt . 24:22, NASB).

It is marvelous to recognize that God sovereignly conducts all that happens to secure the good of those whom he saves This gives us a whole new perspective on history, from the grand scheme down to the events in our own personal lives.

There are moments when each believer would fall away if the forces of error and temptation were allowed to intensify, but God sets their limits for the simple reason that he loves us and is committed to our protection. He suffers Satan to go so far, but no further.

Along with each trial, God gives a dispensation of his grace in sufficient measure so as to never lose any who have been called according to his purpose. God prevents that which would lead to the perdition of any of the saints. Since God is sovereign, we need not fear the future. Meditating upon these things will enrich our appreciation of Paul's triumphant words, "What then shall we say to these things? If God is for us, who can be against us?" (v. 31).

But Paul has more to say before he comes to verse 31. He still has an important point to clarify. Verse 29 begins with the word *for*, establishing a logical connection with the previous verse. The sentence that constitutes verses 29 and 30 is meant to explain the reason why "God causes all things to work together for good to those who love God, to those who are called according to His purpose" (v. 28, NASB). And here is the reason:

> For those whom he foreknew he also predestined to be conformed to the image of his Son, in order that he might be the firstborn among many brothers. And those whom he predestined he also called, and those whom he called he also justified, and those whom he justified he also glorified.   (Rom. 8:29–30)

Although a detailed consideration of the biblical teaching on election is beyond the scope of this book, we can note in passing that it is on the doctrine of predestination that the divinely inspired text anchors the fact that nothing can ever work against the eternal good of those who have been saved.

Consequently, we can be sure that any attempt to explain the meaning of predestination in the Bible that does not require a belief in the infallible perseverance of the saints as a corollary must be wrong. According to Paul, those who are justified are the same as those who are glorified, because they are the same who had previously been predestinated to be conformed to the image of Christ.

We find in verses 29 and 30 what Cambridge theologian William Perkins (1558–1602) called "the golden chain" of salvation in his book of the same name. There are in these verses, as if it were, five links in a chain (God foreknew, predestined, called, justified, and glorified his people). And those who experience all these blessing are the same people from beginning to end. In other words, those whom God foreknew are the same as those who were predestinated—no more, no less. Likewise, those who were predestinated are the same as those who were then called, the same who were justified, and then finally glorified. Nobody is lost along the way.

This clear biblical statement "Those whom he justified he also glorified" will never make peace with the idea that there are some who experience justification but fail to make it all the way to glory. That would necessarily mean that there is a difference between those whom God justifies and those whom he glorifies in the end.

Such a concept could be harmonized with statements like "For the most part, he glorified those whom he justified" or "Most of those he justified he also glorified," but never with the inspired words of God as they stand in the Bible. If one—no more than one—of those whom he justified is not also glorified, it will forever become inappropriate to say, "Those whom he justified he also glorified." But as Scripture cannot fail (John 10:35), these verses are enough to prove that no one who was justified will miss out on being glorified.

NOTHING CAN EVER SEPARATE US FROM THE LOVE OF CHRIST

The thought of such an unbreakable chain lifts the apostle Paul to the heights of victorious exultation:

> What then shall we say to these things? If God is for us, who can be against us? He who did not spare his own Son but gave him up for us all, how will he not also with him graciously give us all things? Who shall bring any charge against God's elect? It is God who justifies. Who is to condemn? Christ Jesus is the one who died—more than that, who was raised—who is at the right hand of God, who indeed is interceding for us. Who shall separate us from the love of Christ?

Shall tribulation, or distress, or persecution, or famine, or nakedness, or danger, or sword? As it is written, "For your sake we are being killed all the day long; we are regarded as sheep to be slaughtered." No, in all these things we are more than conquerors through him who loved us. For I am sure that neither death nor life, nor angels nor rulers, nor things present nor things to come, nor powers, nor height nor depth, nor anything else in all creation, will be able to separate us from the love of God in Christ Jesus our Lord. (Rom. 8:31–39)

The text speaks for itself to any impartial reader. Since it is true that God also glorifies those whom he justifies, and since all things work together for the good of those who love God, Paul now celebrates what all this means for us as Christians. It means that we can never be condemned (v. 34) or separated from the love of Christ (v. 35):

In this context, the love of Christ represents salvation. Paul is therefore asking rhetorically if any circumstance is powerful enough to cause a true believer to turn against Christ in a way that would cause Christ to turn His back on the believer.[104]

"What then shall we say to these things?" (v. 31) Paul asks. Since there are none who are called except those who were beforehand predestined to be conformed to the image of Christ, we can know already that the final condition of all who are truly converted is that glorious state unto which they have been predestined. If God has predestined it to be so, who can keep it from coming to pass? What opposition could there possibly be that would stand in the way of God and debar him from carrying out his decrees? "If God is for us, who can be against us?" (v. 31).

If God's determination to save us was such that he "did not spare his own Son but gave him up for us all, how will he not also with him graciously give us all things?" (v. 32) God has already paid the supreme price for our salvation. It is reasonable to imagine that now he would be unwilling to do less costly things in order to secure our eternal bliss.

Not only so, but we can no longer be condemned for our sins anyway, because having been justified there are no longer any sins on our "accounts." "Who shall bring any charge against God's elect? It is God who justifies. Who is to condemn?" (v. 33–34a). There is no higher court than God to

104 MacArthur, *The MacArthur New Testament Commentary Romans* 1–8, 510.

overrule his pronouncement of our justification. No one can ever condemn us because "Christ Jesus is the one who died—more than that, who was raised—who is at the right hand of God, who indeed is interceding for us" (v. 34b). Christ's vicarious death in our place has expiated our sins, a fact that is confirmed by his resurrection. Our sins are, therefore, paid in full, and a second punishment will not be required for them.

The continual intercession of Christ on our behalf also assures us that we will ever be granted grace to prevail, no matter what trials we may go through. And finally, nothing will ever cause any Christian to succumb and be separated from Christ. Persecutions or adversities most certainly cannot precipitate our spiritual downfall, for whether we undergo tribulation, or distress, or persecution, or famine, or nakedness, or danger, or sword, true Christians are more than conquerors in all these things (v. 35–37).

Nothing—absolutely nothing—can cause someone who was called according to the purpose of God to be cut off from Christ. That is the conviction of the apostle Paul as he launches into his concluding doxology:

> For I am sure that neither death nor life, nor angels nor rulers, nor things present nor things to come, nor powers, nor height nor depth, nor anything else in all creation, will be able to separate us from the love of God in Christ Jesus our Lord.　　　　　(Rom. 8:38–39)

The list of what can never separate us from the electing love of God is worthy of our consideration. In first place, "neither death nor life" can be instrumental in separating a believer from the Lord. There is no need to be fearful of what may happen at death, as if the kind of death or the occasion of our death could shake our faith and drive a wedge between us and Christ. Not so! Our death too is subject to the decree of God, who, in his providence, assigns a dispensation of sustaining grace unto each believer, according to the vale that must be trod.

Neither should it be feared that life will turn out to be a fatal trap for our souls. As it is, some live longer than others. Some are called from this world to be joined with the Church Triumphant in heaven soon after they are converted (as was the case of the criminal in Luke 23:39–43 who repented while on the cross), while the lives of others are prolonged to serve Christ in this wicked world.

Here below, some members of the church militant go through frightful persecutions while others drink from a much milder cup. Some are exposed to pressures and temptations that are of a greater severity and longer duration than others, certainly few as grievous as the trials of Job.

Yet none of this happens by chance or randomly but always according to divine providence. Such was the belief of the psalmist when he wrote, "Your eyes saw my unformed substance; in your book were written, every one of them, the days that were formed for me, when as yet there were none of them" (Ps. 139:16). Therefore, neither death nor life can present a threat to those whom God is determined to save.

The angelic beings, whether elect or fallen angels, mysteriously exert their influence in the world. When people apostatize embracing false teachings, they are led astray by human cunning (Eph. 4:14), through the insincerity of liars whose consciences are seared (1 Tim. 4:2). Still we know that behind the human instrument there is the operation of deceitful spirits (1 Tim. 4:1).

Paul teaches us elsewhere that "if our gospel is veiled, it is veiled to those who are perishing, in whose case the god of this world has blinded the minds of the unbelieving, that they might not see the light of the gospel of the glory of Christ, who is the image of God" (2 Cor. 4:3–4). The devil is at work in temptations too. Those in whom the Word of God does not abide have not overcome the wicked one (1 John 2:14) and are said to have strayed after Satan (1 Tim. 5:15).

Could the ploys of Satan and the demons succeed in ensnaring any of the saints? Paul is adamant that they could not, for "nor angels nor rulers" will be able to separate us from Christ.

In fact, nor can "things present nor things to come" do so. Nothing that is presently taking place, nor anything that may take place in the future will be able to uproot a child of God from the Everlasting Rock. There is not the slightest chance that it may happen, not now, not ever. Pulling off such a feat against the purposes of God will not be achieved by anything in existence, nor yet by anything that may someday come to exist.

Nor do "powers, nor height nor depth" constitute a threat. With these words, Paul seeks to extend his list to include every possible sphere, upward or downward, in any dimension of creation. And finally, lest it be alleged that his list has left out a particular something and that it is that which was omitted that could separate us from Christ, Paul adds, "Nor anything else in all creation, will be able to separate us from the love of God."

The words "anything else in all creation" or "any other created thing" (NASB) are not referring to anything else other than ourselves, as some have postulated. Interpreted in light of its context, "any other created thing" can only mean anything other than the things that Paul had just enumerated (death, life, angels, rulers, things present, things to come, powers, height, and depth).

Therefore, Paul's pronouncement is all encompassing and is designed to preclude any argument to the effect that anything or anybody at all could separate us from Christ, and we, as part of the created order, are necessarily included. So not even we ourselves would be able to frustrate God's plan and open a rift between ourselves and Christ.

That is the extent of our security! Therefore, the inspired words of the apostle are absolutely unequivocal: *nothing* can separate those who are saved from Christ. On the contrary, "God causes *all things* to work together for good to those who love God, to those who are called according to His purpose" (v. 28, NASB; emphasis added). This Pauline conviction, resulting from his doctrine of predestination, should be ours as well.

UNDERSTANDING OUR SECURITY INSPIRES CONFIDENCE AND SERVICE

In his book *Remarkable Work of Grace*, Jonathan Edwards recounts a curious episode involving a Native American who was converted under the preaching of David Brainerd. This lady had been under a profound conviction of sin for a long time. In a penitent spirit, she had been crying out to God for forgiveness. Even so, inconsolable, she often burst into tears, believing that she was beyond being saved, doubting that she would be able to love Christ sincerely. After describing how she wrestled with doubt and anguish, Edwards writes the following:

> Although this has been the habitual frame of her mind for several weeks together, so that the exercise of grace appeared evident to others, yet she seemed wholly insensible of it herself, and never had any remarkable comfort and sensible satisfaction till this evening.[105]

This prolonged struggle went on until, at last, the assurance of salvation dawned in her soul. She felt such joy that right there, in the middle of the service, she had a very unusual reaction:

---

105 Jonathan Edwards, *Remarkable Work of Grace, The Works of Jonathan Edwards, Volume 5*, The Master Christian Library (Rio, WI: Ages Software Inc., 2000), 439.

[She] could not but burst forth in prayer and praises to God before us all, with many tears, crying sometimes in English and sometimes in Indian, "O blessed Lord, do come, do come! O do take me away, do let me die and go to Jesus Christ! I am afraid if I live I shall sin again! O do let me die now! O dear Jesus, do come! I cannot stay, I cannot stay! O how can I live in this world! do take my soul away from this sinful place! O let me never sin any more! O what shall I do, what shall I do! dear Jesus, O dear Jesus," etc.—In this ecstasy she continued some time, uttering these and such like expressions incessantly. And the grand argument she used with God to take her away immediately, was, that if she lived, she should sin against him.[106]

How can we help someone that is going through this kind of agony in their spirit? Is there any legitimacy to such fear? If it were true that some who experience salvation do later fall away, we would be obliged to agree that her request is most reasonable. It would definitely be preferable to die today and die saved than to live one more day and run the risk of being lost eternally.

If everything that God does for us is still not enough to guarantee our perseverance, if it depends on our own constancy too, what person with any sense at all would be desirous to stay in this world serving Christ? If that is our way of thinking, perhaps the most sensible thing to do would be to sit down with this anguishing person and start crying out to die as well.

But if we are enlightened as to the guarantees the Bible affords us concerning our security in God's hands, we will be relieved of all such fears. When our trust is in God and God alone, when we learn to rest in his promises instead of focusing on ourselves, we become bold and fearless, ready to face decades of labor in the midst of temptation, opposition, and persecution, confident that everyone who has been born of God overcomes the world.

Believing in this way, we can take Paul's words as our personal motto and join him in saying, "For to me to live is Christ, and to die is gain" (Phil. 1:21), assured that remaining in the flesh can only mean more fruitful labor for us. This optimistic outlook will not allow us to think of immediate death as the more desirable prospect but will put us in the same dilemma that the Paul felt:

---

106 Ibid., 437–438.

Yet which I shall choose I cannot tell. I am hard pressed between the two. My desire is to depart and be with Christ, for that is far better. But to remain in the flesh is more necessary on your account.

(Phil. 1:22b–24)

The doctrine of the perseverance of the saints has given many the courage to forego the safety and spiritual benefits found in the fellowship of a well-structured local church and venture off into the mission field where everything around them seemed to militate against their spiritual progress. The assurance that our final salvation by God's keeping enables us to look beyond ourselves and joyfully work to win others for the kingdom of God for his glory. That, after all, is our calling in this world, and God will keep us safe throughout our time of service here.

We should not doubt God's resolve nor his power to bring to fruition the final salvation of all those whom he converts. To claim that the future is unknown to God is unbiblical and unorthodox. At the same time, it borders on blasphemy to suggest that God is dismayed in heaven, impotently lamenting that there is nothing he can do, even though he knows in advance that a certain day and time one of his redeemed people will renounce faith in Christ.

It is just as unacceptable to maintain that God does have the power to intervene but refuses to because he leaves it up to people to prove themselves worthy if they wish to inherit eternal life. Not only does this portray God as uncommitted and indifferent toward the final state of those whom he one day lovingly justified, but also this kind of logic reduces salvation to a sort of reward for the deserving.

Salvation is a gift of God. We must rid our minds from any vestiges of the carnal reasoning that salvation is an achievement of human merit. We must reject the notion that God does nothing more than make salvation *possible* for all while leaving it up to individual Christians to prove themselves worthy, thus making eternal life a reward to those who earn it. Such a perspective is profoundly unevangelical. May we escape from such misguided reasoning and return to a biblical way of thinking.

Salvation is certainly a "prize" that is won by those who believe and persevere in faith. Nevertheless, salvation is all of grace. Whether it be our initial faith or our perseverance in faith, we have nothing that we have not received. We owe everything to God's grace. All who actually inherit eternal life are obliged to acknowledge that it was due to the grace of God that they were delivered from unbelief and persevered unto the end. The grace of God is the only thing that makes any of us turn out different from Judas or the inhabitants of Sodom.

Once this has been grasped, instead of fixing a fearful gaze upon our own weaknesses, we are able to turn our eyes unto the One who is our Savior, knowing that if he has drawn us with loving kindness unto himself, it is because he has loved us with an everlasting love (Jer. 31:3). Let us trust in him who has called and justified us, for he will get us home safely. His providence will not falter. Oh, that our hearts may learn to rest in the Lord and say confidently with the psalmist, "Hold me up, that I may be safe and have regard for your statutes continually!" (Ps. 119:117).

6

What about Apostates?

The Lord, the protector and defender of his people, will not suffer, the wheat to be taken from off his floor, but the chaff only can be separated from the church...He that is not planted in the precepts and admonitions of God the Father, he only can depart from the church...The church which believes in Christ, and which holds that which it has once known, never departs from him at all; and they are the church who remain in the house of God; but there is a plantation which is not planted by God the Father, whom we see are not made firm and solid with the stability of wheat, but are winnowed like chaff with the breath of the scattering enemy; of whom John in his epistle says, They went out from us.[107]   (Cyprian, AD 250)

This great and good man (Cyprian), who not only held the doctrine, but had the grace of perseverance unto the end; for when the proconsul [offering a last chance to recant before execution] put the question to him, "Dost thou then persevere in this mind, that thou wilt not sacrifice?" he answered, "A good mind which knows God cannot be changed."... [His deacon, Pontius, recorded the event and concluded:] "Let no man think, that good men can depart from the church. The wind does not take away the wheat, nor does a storm root up the tree that is founded with a solid root; empty chaff is carried away with a tempest; weak trees are overturned at meeting a whirlwind."[108]

Up to this point, this book has sought to present positive reasons to believe in the doctrine of the certain perseverance of the saints. But the treatment of the matter would be incomplete without an examination of the biblical passages that some regard as teaching contrary to the position here taken.

107 Cyprian, quoted by John Gill, *The Cause of God and of Truth*, Part 4, Chapter 5, Section 9, The Ultimate Christian Library (Rio, Wisconsin: AGES Software, 2000), 822.
108 John Gill, *The Cause of God and of Truth*, Part 4, Chapter 5, Section 9, The Ultimate Christian Library (Rio, Wisconsin: AGES Software, 2000), 823.

The main reason why there are Christians who reject the doctrine of the perseverance of the saints is because they are convinced that there are texts in the Bible that are incompatible with it. Of course a doctrine is only satisfactory if it is in harmony with the Bible as a whole. We cannot preach one message in Romans and then undo it when we preach through Hebrews, or vice versa.

The real proof that a doctrine is biblical is its capacity to withstand a cross-examination from each part of the Holy Scriptures and come out unscathed, for there are no contradictions or inconsistencies in the inspired Word. This has been my thesis in rejecting the doctrines that assume it is possible for true Christians to go back to a life of sin or lose their faith, by seeking to demonstrate that such concepts are in conflict with various biblical texts.

But could there also be biblical texts that weigh against the doctrine of the perseverance of the saints, as some claim? We will now move on to examine texts that many Christians consider as obstacles to believing that the perseverance and final salvation is certain for all who experience justification. This is a welcome challenge.

By no means is it problematic to demonstrate that the perseverance of the saints is consistently taught throughout the whole Bible. There are certainly passages of Scripture that seem to pose a difficulty at first. That happens with other biblical truths too, even with the most incontrovertible doctrines of the Bible, such as the omniscience of God, the deity of Christ, and the immortality of the soul. Nevertheless, when a doctrine is accurate, a careful examination can show that there is no reason to call its veracity into question.

The exegetical arguments raised against the doctrine of the perseverance of the saints can be grouped into two categories: (1) attempts to prove that it is possible for salvation to be lost as a necessary deduction from passages that warn against apostasy, and (2) attempts to present concrete cases of individuals who experienced salvation and subsequently perished.

WHY ARE WARNINGS AGAINST APOSTASY NECESSARY?

When passages that warn against apostasy are utilized, the argument is that their presence in the Bible proves that there must be a possibility of apostasy for real Christians, for otherwise it wouldn't make any sense to warn Christians of the danger. This kind of argument is rather precarious. There can be no doubt that the doctrine of the perseverance of the saints would be refuted if the Scriptures contained clear statements to the effect that some people who were saved went on to lose their salvation.

However, one must keep in mind that the need to persevere unto the end is not in opposition to the doctrine here maintained; it is part and parcel of it. So nothing would be more unreasonable than to insist that a doctrine cannot be true because we find in the Bible elements that are essential to it.

The simple fact that believers are warned to persevere does not constitute a proof that some of them do not persevere. That is nothing more than an inference but not a necessary inference, unless it can be demonstrated as well that some of the saints actually despise the divine warnings.

If, on the other hand, the sheep of Christ hear the voice of the Good Shepherd and follow him, we have reason to believe that all the saints heed the warnings, which never fail to achieve their intended purpose of spurring the saints onward in their faith.

The matter can be summarized as follows: It is a fact that only those who persevere to the end inherit eternal life. It is also a fact that God is determined to infallibly conduct each one of his children all the way to glory. Therefore, it can be expected that God will do whatever is necessary to ensure that end. He transforms them internally so that they cling to him; he grants them the Holy Spirit and surrounds them with protection through his marvelous providence.

Among the many operations of his providence, he employs solemn warnings to make them understand that they will be eternally lost if they fail to persevere. All those who have received ears to hear—that is, as many as have been regenerated—are moved by this message to become properly determined to persevere unto the end. Thus, God reaches his objective. The question is not whether or not the warnings are meaningful or if discounting them ensues in real danger. The real question is whether the Word of God will accomplish that which he intends it to and whether it will succeed in the purpose for which it was sent forth (Is. 55:11).

Take, for instance, the words of the apostle Paul: "If we endure, we will also reign with him; if we deny him, he also will deny us" (2 Tim. 2:12).[109] Another example is the exhortation in Hebrews:

---

109 See also Acts 11:23; 13:43; 14:22.

> Therefore do not throw away your confidence, which has a great reward. For you have need of endurance, so that when you have done the will of God you may receive what is promised.
>
> (Heb. 10:35–36)

Are such words utterly useless? Not at all. The Bible never promised salvation to people who do not persevere. But how do the saved persevere? Do they do so mechanically or rationally? Do they persevere apart from any knowledge of the will of God or through an understanding that comes through the Word of God?

Obviously, God uses his Word to instruct us in the way of holiness. Should God therefore command us not to worship other gods and to stay away from idols? Should he teach us not to live in dishonesty and immorality? Of course! We find such lessons in the Bible directed toward us as God's people because they are the means by which God communicates his will to us and brings about our conformity to his law.

In the same way, if it truly is necessary for believers to persevere unto the end, it is to be expected that the sacred text would contain exhortations to that end as well. They reiterate and reinforce the message that was preached from the beginning, that salvation is for those who follow Christ unto the end. They are useful precisely because they ensure the perseverance of those whom he has given ears to hear.

There are several biblical parallels that illustrate how an urgent warning is not incompatible with an infallible promise. Perhaps the best example is found in the account of the shipwreck during Paul's journey to Rome. After having prophesied that everyone on the ship would survive, Paul warned that the sailors absolutely had to remain on board for otherwise lives would be lost:

> Since they had been without food for a long time, Paul stood up among them and said, "Men, you should have listened to me and not have set sail from Crete and incurred this injury and loss. Yet now I urge you to take heart, for there will be no loss of life among you, but only of the ship. For this very night there stood before me an angel of the God to whom I belong and whom I worship, and he said, 'Do not be afraid, Paul; you must stand before Caesar. And behold, God has granted you all those who sail with you.' So take heart, men, for I have faith in God that it will be exactly as I have been told. But we must run aground on some island."

143

When the fourteenth night had come, as we were being driven across the Adriatic Sea, about midnight the sailors suspected that they were nearing land. So they took a sounding and found twenty fathoms. A little farther on they took a sounding again and found fifteen fathoms. And fearing that we might run on the rocks, they let down four anchors from the stern and prayed for day to come. And as the sailors were seeking to escape from the ship, and had lowered the ship's boat into the sea under pretense of laying out anchors from the bow, Paul said to the centurion and the soldiers, "Unless these men stay in the ship, you cannot be saved." Then the soldiers cut away the ropes of the ship's boat and let it go.

As day was about to dawn, Paul urged them all to take some food, saying, "Today is the fourteenth day that you have continued in suspense and without food, having taken nothing. Therefore I urge you to take some food. It will give you strength, for not a hair is to perish from the head of any of you." And when he had said these things, he took bread, and giving thanks to God in the presence of all he broke it and began to eat. Then they all were encouraged and ate some food themselves. (We were in all 276 persons in the ship.) And when they had eaten enough, they lightened the ship, throwing out the wheat into the sea.

Now when it was day, they did not recognize the land, but they noticed a bay with a beach, on which they planned if possible to run the ship ashore. So they cast off the anchors and left them in the sea, at the same time loosening the ropes that tied the rudders. Then hoisting the foresail to the wind they made for the beach. But striking a reef, they ran the vessel aground. The bow stuck and remained immovable, and the stern was being broken up by the surf.

The soldiers' plan was to kill the prisoners, lest any should swim away and escape. But the centurion, wishing to save Paul, kept them from carrying out their plan. He ordered those who could swim to jump overboard first and make for the land, and the rest on planks or on pieces of the ship. And so it was that all were brought safely to land. (Acts 27:21–44)

There is an exact correlation in the way Paul's urgent warning was in keeping with his infallible prophecy in this story and how the biblical promises of our final salvation are compatible with the biblical admonitions to persevere. Luke's narrative leaves no doubt that Paul prophesied that all on board would survive. Paul's exact words were the following: "There will be no loss of life among you" (v. 22).

His prophecy rested on a divine revelation, given by an angel who stated, "God has granted you all those who sail with you" (v. 24). Testimony is given to the fulfillment of the prophecy in the conclusion, "So it was that all were brought safely to land" (v. 44). At the same time, we cannot deny that Paul spoke frankly and urgently when he warned, "Unless these men stay in the ship, you cannot be saved" (v. 31).

Since it had been infallibly predicted that all would survive, could anyone object that Paul's warnings were inappropriate? Could they be deemed useless? Could they just as well have been disregarded? Absolutely not! We truly cannot come to any other conclusion than that lives actually would have been lost had the sailors abandoned the ship.

Of what use then was the warning? The answer is that they played a vital role in the fulfillment of the divine prophecy. It was used by God in his providence at the right moment to safeguard the accurate fulfillment of what had been predicted. Even the fact that Paul noticed the sailors' intent to flee was providential, as was the apostle Paul's having gained the respect and trust of the centurion. Things could not have gone differently, for this is how God had purposed to realize his promise.

This text exemplifies the fallacy of trying to use warnings to persevere as proof that other passages cannot mean that the perseverance of the saints is infallibly guaranteed by God. That would be like pointing to Paul's warning to the centurion as proof that the survival of everyone on that trip had not really been predicted. The reality is that the promise of divine protection does not eliminate the responsibility to act prudently, just as the responsibility to be prudent cannot be construed as an argument against the plain meaning of the prophecy.

We have our difficulties in understanding how God uses means to fulfill his decrees. We tend to think that if something is predetermined by God it follows that the ends will be achieved regardless of any means. Nothing illustrates this better than the objection often raised against the concept of predestination that if certain people are predestined to life then there is no need for them to hear and believe the Gospel because they are bound to be saved anyway.

Of course, that is not how things work. That manner of thinking ignores that predestination is inseparably linked to the means by which God carries out his decrees. The Bible says that God chose people from the beginning to be saved, through sanctification by the Spirit and belief in the truth (2 Thess. 2:13–14).

The same applies to the messianic prophecies. They were infallible, and indeed, not a single one of them failed to come to pass as predicted. Yet it was Jesus who stated that they would fail if he avoided the cross:

> "Do you think that I cannot appeal to my Father, and he will at once send me more than twelve legions of angels? But how then should the Scriptures be fulfilled, that it must be so?"   (Matt. 26:53–54)

We run into many other such cases in the life of Christ when God employed warnings as means to ensure a predetermined result. We know that nothing could kill Christ before his hour had come (cf. John 7:30; 8:20). Even so, God used warnings to move Joseph to protect the infant Jesus, thus keeping him alive:

> Now when they had departed, behold, an angel of the Lord appeared to Joseph in a dream and said, "Rise, take the child and his mother, and flee to Egypt, and remain there until I tell you, for Herod is about to search for the child, to destroy him."   (Matt. 2:13)

> But when he heard that Archelaus was reigning over Judea in place of his father Herod, he was afraid to go there, and being warned in a dream he withdrew to the district of Galilee.   (Matt. 2:22)

What would have occurred if Joseph had ignored the heavenly warning? Would God simply have saved Jesus's life by some other means? Did God have a plan B, just in case? Or can we confidently maintain that he used the dream to warn Joseph knowing that it would suffice? After all, in God's providence, Joseph had already been shaped into the kind of man who would heed his instructions.

A point that needs to be stressed is that the fulfillment of God's decrees is always through his providence. This understanding has been consistently taught in the Reformed tradition, as can be substantiated by many witnesses of which a few may be cited as particularly useful.

The *Second Helvetic Confession* (put together in 1562 by Heinrich Bullinger and adopted by reformed churches in Switzerland, France, Scotland,

Hungary, and Poland) contains a very clear assessment in chapter 6, "Of the Providence of God":

> ALL THINGS ARE GOVERNED BY THE PROVIDENCE OF GOD. We believe that all things in heaven and on earth, and in all creatures, are preserved and governed by the providence of this wise, eternal and almighty God...Wherefore we disapprove of the rash statements of those who say that if all things are managed by the providence of God, then our efforts and endeavors are in vain. It will be sufficient if we leave everything to the governance of divine providence, and we will not have to worry about anything or do anything... For God, who has appointed to everything its end, has ordained the beginning and the means by which it reaches its goal.

Similarly, Charles Spurgeon censures the folly of ignoring the means by which God fulfills his decrees:

> God's decrees shall be fulfilled. There are, however, persons who argue from this, that therefore we may sit down and do nothing as to the salvation of others. Such persons are very foolish, because they must be aware that the same logic which would drive them to do nothing spiritually would require them to do nothing in other matters, so that they would neither eat, nor drink, nor think, nor breathe,—do nothing, in fact, but lie like logs, passive under fate's iron sway. This is too absurd to need an answer.[110]

As Arthur Pink indicates, the way in which God's providence attends to the fulfillment of his Word can be perceived in how the prophecy of David becoming king of Israel was brought to pass:

> God promised the kingdom of Israel to David and while yet a youth he was anointed to it (1 Sam. 16:13). What! notwithstanding all interveniences? Yes, for the Lord had said it and shall He not do it! Therefore if Saul cast a javelin at him, unsuspected, to nail him to the wall, a sharpness of eye and agility of body shall be given him to discern and avoid it (18:11). If he determined evil against him, Jonathan is moved to inform him (19:7). If he send messengers to Naioth to arrest him, they shall forget their errand and fall a

---

110 Charles H. Spurgeon, *The Light of the World*, Sermon No. 1109, *The Metropolitan Tabernacle Pulpit Vol. 19*, The Master Christian Library (Rio, WI: Ages Software Inc., 2000), 303–304.

prophesying (20:24). If he be in a city that will betray him, and no friend there to acquaint him of his peril, the Lord Himself is the intelligencer and sends him out (23:12). If Saul's army encompasses him about and no way to escape is left, the Philistines invade his land and the king turns away to meet them (vv. 26–27). Though there were not on earth to deliver *"He* (said David) *shall send from heaven and save me"* (Psa. 57:3). Shortly after Saul was slain and David came to the throne![111]

The case of David also furnishes us yet another example of how God makes use of warnings as a means of accomplishing what he has settled must come to pass. In 1 Samuel 23:7–13, we read an account of how David was divinely forewarned to get out of Keilah to avoid capture. It is fair to assume that if he had despised God's prompting he would have died at the hands of Saul. God kept this from happening by enjoining him to flee precisely because it was an adequate means to secure his safety.

This same principle plays itself out in the warnings against apostasy:

> Yet this is one of the silly inferences which Arminians are fond of drawing. They say, "If it is absolutely certain that God will preserve His people from total apostasy, then there is no real need why they must persevere"—as well might we argue that it is unnecessary for us to breathe because God gives us breath, or that Hezekiah needed no longer to eat and drink because God had promised he should live another fifteen years.[112]

There is no justification for contending that the biblical warnings addressed to believers would be pointless if believers most certainly do not fall away. The proper use of such warnings has been painstakingly clarified by reformed theologians:

> They prompt self-examination, and are instrumental in keeping believers in the way of perseverance. They do not prove that any of those addressed will apostatize, but simply that the use of means is necessary to prevent them from committing this sin… They do not prove that any of the believers exhorted will not persevere, but only that God uses moral means for the accomplishment of moral ends.[113]

111 A. W. Pink, *Eternal Security* (Grand Rapids: Baker Book House, 1979), 19.
112 Ibid., 25.
113 Louis Berkhof, *Systematic Theology* (Lexington: 2015), 529.

The reason for these passages is that we need warnings from God in order to persevere. Or, to put it in other language, it is by means of such warnings that God ensures our perseverance. The proof of this is seen in the different ways in which unbelievers and believers react to such warnings. Do the verses...trouble unbelievers? Not at all. Either they regard them as mere foolishness, something hardly to be considered, or they take them in a straightforward manner but assume that their lives are all right and that the verses therefore do not concern them. It is only believers who are troubled, because they are concerned about their relationship with God and do not want to presume that all is well with their souls when it may not be.[114]

What then is the purpose of the biblical warnings against apostasy if the saved cannot apostatize from the faith? On the one hand, they are the means that God uses to get the saved to persevere... Just as repentance and faith are means by which salvation is applied to the heart of the elect by the Holy Spirit (from whence there are exhortations to repent and believe), so also the exhortations warning to not depart from God (or fall away) are the means (the grace, the deliverance) that the Holy Spirit powerfully uses to mobilize the elect to persevere in salvation... Of course the non-elect that have somehow mingled with the elect, being deceived by the devil, do not avail themselves of the deliverance that has been provided and fall away (from a profession of faith; not from salvation). Unto them the biblical warnings serve the purpose of leaving them without any excuse.[115]

The quotes cited above do sufficiently express the reason for the warning passages in the Bible. When we say that we are safe in the grace of God, we are not saying that God's grace guarantees our final salvation regardless of any perseverance on our part. What we mean is that God's grace guarantees our final salvation *through* our perseverance. After all, God does not grant us his grace in order for our efforts to be rendered unnecessary but to establish their success.

ANALYSIS OF THE WARNINGS AGAINST APOSTASY

With this in mind, we may now consider the texts that warn against abandoning the faith. It is somewhat surprising that when we begin to

---

114 James Montgomery Boice and Philip Graham Ryken, *The Doctrines of Grace* (Wheaton, Illinois: Crossway Books, 2002), 173–174.

115 Paulo Anglada, *Calvinismo—As Antigas Doutrinas da Graça* (São Paulo, Brazil: Editora Os Puritanos, 2000), 98–99.

149

examine the proof texts presented by those who seek biblical evidence that salvation can be lost we find that they invariably cite texts that teach exactly the opposite. All the standard works that teach the reversibility of salvation naively appeal to texts that state that a person is only a true Christian today if he or she perseveres until the end.

But what is that if not an affirmation of the doctrine of the perseverance of the saints? Those who believe they have an arsenal of proofs that genuine believers do sometimes commit apostasy need to take another look at the passages they are claiming as their own.

> But Christ was faithful as a Son over His house—whose house we are, if we hold fast our confidence and the boast of our hope firm until the end. (Heb. 3:6, NASB)

> For we have become partakers of Christ, if we hold fast the beginning of our assurance firm until the end. (Heb. 3:14, NASB)

Only reading these two verses carelessly would anyone conclude that they teach the possibility of losing one's salvation. In his book *Exegetical Fallacies* D. A. Carson exposes I. Howard Marshall's mistake of appealing to the verses in Hebrews 3 as evidence that salvation can be lost. He points out how that is a classic example of misunderstanding the text by failing to give proper attention to how the verb tenses employed bear upon its meaning:

> Exegetical and theological fallacies arise in this area when conclusions are drawn without adequate attention being paid to the relationships between clause and clause, established (usually) by the verbal forms. For instance, I. Howard Marshall interprets Hebrews 3:6b ("And we are his house, if we hold on to our courage and the hope of which we boast," NIV) and Hebrews 3:14 ("We have come to share in Christ if we hold firmly till the end the confidence we had at first," NIV) as if they say exactly the same thing, that "membership of God's household is conditional upon perseverance." In one sense, of course, that is correct, but close attention to the tenses in their context in Hebrews 3:14 reveals an extra ingredient in this verse. We have become (γεγόναμεν [*gegonamen*])—past reference, I would argue—partakers of Christ if we now, in the present, hold firmly to the confidence we had at first. It follows from this verse that although perseverance is mandated, it is also the evidence of what has taken place in the past. Put another way, perseverance becomes one

of the essential ingredients of what it means to be a Christian, of what a partaker of Christ is and does. If persevering shows we have (already) come to share in Christ, it can only be because sharing in Christ has perseverance for its inevitable fruit.[116]

What Carson is underscoring is that a proper attention to verb tenses in texts of this nature will reveal that there can never be any loss of salvation. According to Hebrews 3:6, it is only true that we *are* (in the present) the house of God *if* we hold fast to the end (in the future). Inversely, this means that it will become evident that we actually are not the house of God today if at any point in the future we fail to hold fast to the hope we now profess.

Hebrews 3:14 applies this same concept to the past when it says that it is only true that *we have become*[117] (in the past) partakers of Christ if we continue to hold our original confidence firm to the end. Such a statement forces us to conclude that those who do not keep the faith to the end are people who have never become partakers of Christ to begin with. But what is the doctrine that salvation can be forfeited if not the belief that some who have become partakers of Christ do not hold firm to the end? That happens to be precisely what the text under consideration refutes.

The message the author of Hebrews wishes to impress upon his reader's minds is that apostates perish. But the way in which he goes about delivering his message makes it clear that those who are true Christians will not commit apostasy. His outlook is that those who will end up abandoning their profession of faith are those who have not truly become partakers of Christ at all. Therefore, even at present, they do not constitute the house of God.

We use such language when we speak of tests that reveal whether something is genuine or not. For instance, someone who goes to a jeweler to find out if an object is of any real value might hear something along the lines of "What you have there is a diamond if it cuts this glass." Obviously, what is meant is not that a failure to cut the glass would make a genuine diamond suddenly become something else.

Another illustration would be a statement to the effect that, "Those earrings are gold if they never rust." Again, this does not mean that the earrings would cease to be gold the moment they rusted. Such a development would only prove that they were not really made of gold all along.

---

116 D. A. Carson, *Exegetical Fallacies* (Grand Rapids: Baker Academic, 2004), 84–85.
117 In the original Greek, verb tense is Perfect Indicative Active, denoting completed past action.

The same observation applies to some other passages that are also used inappropriately as proof texts for the idea that salvation can be lost.

> And you, who once were alienated and hostile in mind, doing evil deeds, he has now reconciled in his body of flesh by his death, in order to present you holy and blameless and above reproach before him, if indeed you continue in the faith, stable and steadfast, not shifting from the hope of the gospel that you heard, which has been proclaimed in all creation under heaven, and of which I, Paul, became a minister. (Col. 1:21–23)

Again, it should be noted that Paul qualifies his assertion that the Colossians have in fact been reconciled (in the past) for the purpose of being glorified if indeed they presently continue in the faith, not shifting from the hope of the Gospel. The laws of logic, when applied to this verse, oblige us to conclude that God has not reconciled (in the past) those who do not (in the present) continue in the faith.

> Now I would remind you, brothers, of the gospel I preached to you, which you received, in which you stand, and by which you are being saved, if you hold fast[118] to the word I preached to you—unless you believed in vain. (1 Cor. 15:1–2)

Once more, the attentive reader will pick up on the fact that the grammar Paul uses does not say anything at all about Christians losing their salvation. What Paul says is that the ones who are now being saved are those who hold fast to the Word. If that is how things are, it follows inevitably that all who have abandoned the faith are not being saved, but it says nothing to prove that any who have abandoned the faith were saved at anytime in the past. Such people are said to have "believed in vain"—that is, when they believed (in the past), it was with no real effect.

> So Jesus said to the Jews who had believed in him, "If you abide in my word, you are truly my disciples." (John 8:31)

In this passage, Jesus is not calling into question whether or not his hearers *will continue* to be his disciples but whether or not they *truly are* his disciples (in the present). The test that Jesus announces will prove whether a person is truly converted is abiding in his words henceforth. Anything short of this reveals, according to our Lord, that a person is not truly one of his

---

118 This is a first-class condition in the Greek with the verb in the indicative mood, suggesting the protasis is assumed to be a fact.

disciples. One more time, we find the Bible teaching that a failure to persevere in the future will manifest that there is no authentic faith in the present.

Nothing in these texts indicates that a true Christian can lose his or her salvation. On the contrary, they all militate against such a doctrine. The reason people get confused is because the typical approach when handling these texts is to raise a false dilemma, as if there were only two possibilities: (1) either the Bible teaches that Christians can apostatize from the faith without losing their salvation, or (2) the Bible teaches that Christians can lose their salvation.

When only these two options are contemplated, which view do these texts line up with? It's obvious that what leaps out from the texts is that apostates perish. So when those are the only two alternatives considered, it is understandable why people favor the second proposition.

But we are not forced to choose between believing in unconditional security for those who abandon Christ and believing in the possibility of losing one's salvation. In reality, both options above cited fall short, as neither one of them truly harmonizes with what is actually said in the verses we are examining. They certainly teach that one cannot commit apostasy and continue saved; but at the same time, they signify that those who are really saved will never commit apostasy, which completely rules out the doctrine that salvation can be lost.

ANALYSIS OF THE CASES OF APOSTASY IN SCRIPTURE

We now come to the second argument raised against the doctrine of the perseverance of the saints. This second argument claims that the Bible contains real accounts of people who experienced genuine salvation but became apostates and ended up lost forever. These cases begin with the recurrent episodes in Israel's history when "the sons of Israel did what was evil in the sight of the LORD and forgot the LORD their God" (Judg. 3:7, NASB).

Was there loss of salvation in these cases of apostasy? Actually, there was not, because the individuals who turned away from the Lord were those who had never known him. The book of Judges bears clear witness as to how this kind of apostasy took place in Israel:

> And the people served the LORD all the days of Joshua, and all the
> days of the elders who outlived Joshua, who had seen all the great

work that the LORD had done for Israel. And Joshua the son of Nun, the servant of the LORD, died at the age of 110 years. And they buried him within the boundaries of his inheritance in Timnath-heres, in the hill country of Ephraim, north of the mountain of Gaash. And all that generation also were gathered to their fathers. And there arose another generation after them who did not know the LORD or the work that he had done for Israel. And the people of Israel did what was evil in the sight of the LORD and served the Baals. (Judg. 2:7–10)

The biblical narratives of apostasy in Israel are of this sort. We never find the faithful departing from God. Instead, those who had truly been converted served the Lord all their days. It was those who had never been circumcised in their hearts who forgot the Lord.

That is precisely what is taught in the book of Jeremiah, where God denounced the sins of that generation declaring that his people had abandoned him, the One who had been their husband, and worshipped other gods:

For my people have committed two evils: they have forsaken me, the fountain of living waters, and hewed out cisterns for themselves, broken cisterns that can hold no water. (Jer. 2:13)

But this happened on account of the fact that all the house of Israel was "uncircumcised in heart" (Jer. 9:26). We should bear in mind that the Old Covenant was external in nature and included people who had never been personally converted. That is the reason why they broke the Covenant (Jer. 31:32).

Paul reasons that the failures of the people of Israel should serve as a lesson to the church:

Now these things happened to them as an example, but they were written down for our instruction, on whom the end of the ages has come. (1 Cor. 10:11)

In Romans chapter 11, he applies what we learn from Israel's apostasy to the church:

But if some of the branches were broken off, and you, although a wild olive shoot, were grafted in among the others and now share in the nourishing root of the olive tree, do not be arrogant toward the branches. If you are, remember it is not you who support the root, but the root that supports you. Then you will say, "Branches were broken off so that I might be grafted in." That is true. They were broken off because of their unbelief, but you stand fast through faith. So do not become proud, but stand in awe. For if God did not spare the natural branches, neither will he spare you. Note then the kindness and the severity of God: severity toward those who have fallen, but God's kindness to you, provided you continue in his kindness. Otherwise you too will be cut off. (Rom. 11:17–22)

What does this text teach us about apostasy? Indeed, Paul is alerting Christians that there is a real danger of apostasy. But to understand his word of caution, we must identify whom Paul is referring to as the natural branches that got cut off. It is an incontrovertible fact that when Paul says "natural branches" and tells us that some of them were cut off, he is referring to the Jews who rejected Christ. Among them are Caiaphas and Annas, along with the whole multitude of Israel that rejected the Gospel.

Now could it be that Paul is declaring that the totality of Jews had been converted up to the time when they lost their salvation by rejecting the Messiah? Not at all. We know that the vast majority of the Jews in the time of Christ had never been born again. In that generation, as was the case throughout its history, only a remnant of Israel was saved, according to the election of grace (Rom. 11:5).

Consequently, those who were "cut off," or "broken off," are those of Israel who had never been truly converted. They were in the midst of the people of the Covenant; they read the Scriptures and sang the psalms. Yet they were broken off on account of their unbelief. We should not suppose, therefore, that the words "share in the nourishing root of the olive tree" (v. 17) are intended to denote partaking in individual spiritual salvation. The fall described by Paul is not that of saved individuals. If it were, we would have to admit the doctrine of repeated regeneration, in as much as Paul states that it is possible for those who were broken off to be grafted in again, if only they come to faith (Rom. 11:23).

How, then, does Paul's admonishment apply? He is warning us that the same thing that happened to the unbelieving Jews can happen among professing Christians. He is *not* saying that something *different* can happen in the church community than what happened in Israel but the *same* thing. A whole generation can rise up in the church that does not know the Lord.

People can be present among the faithful community and still end up getting cut off due to unbelief. In fact, this has happened countless times and is a real concern. Churches need to be warned. Many churches down through history have apostatized, but it happened without a single regenerate and justified individual losing his salvation.

It typically takes place when the Gospel ceases to be central in the church, bolstering an increase in the proportion of unbelievers in a church. Eventually, the church is overwhelmed by a generation that does not know the Lord, and there is no longer an authentic church. Just as Jews who never knew salvation were broken off, so it will be with professing Christians who do not retain the Gospel. That is how the warning found in Romans 11 properly applies to the church, but that lends no support to the concept that personal salvation can be lost.

But what about those individuals who were part of the church for some time and then departed? Many of us know people personally who we believed to be converted but who abandoned the faith. Not only so, the Bible itself contains examples of people who seemed to have started out well, but who did not finish well. Paul wrote to Timothy that "in later times some will depart from the faith" (1 Tim. 4:1). What about them?

As was noted in previous chapters, the biblical response is that such people had never been saved. They were false conversions. On the outside, they appeared to be authentic, but they had no real life within. For instance, Jesus opened his remarks to the church in Sardis with the rebuke: "I know your deeds, that you have a name that you are alive, but you are dead" (Rev. 3:1, NASB). Despite its reputation, there were only a few people in that church who had not "soiled their garments" and would get to walk with Jesus in white (Rev. 3:4).

The Lord Jesus also predicted the following:

> On that day many will say to me, "Lord, Lord, did we not prophesy in your name, and cast out demons in your name, and do many mighty works in your name?" And then will I declare to them, "I never knew you; depart from me, you workers of lawlessness."
>
> (Matthew 7:22–23)

The Lord here speaks to us about people who were active in church, even being in visible positions and in leadership. They were Christians in the eyes of onlookers and in their own estimation. But on the Day of Judgment, the Lord Jesus will send them off to eternal punishment. It is of utter significance for our purpose that Jesus did not leave any margin for us to believe that those who will be found in this condition on that day are ex-believers who lost their salvation, for he will not say unto them, "I no longer know you." Instead, his words will be, "I never knew you." It is crystal clear that we are dealing with people who were never saved at all.

The case of Simon Magus is unquestionably a biblical example of a false conversion. The Bible describes his response to the Gospel in what seems to indicate an authentic conversion, but we soon learn it was not:

> Even Simon himself believed, and after being baptized he continued with Philip. And seeing signs and great miracles performed, he was amazed… Now when Simon saw that the Spirit was given through the laying on of the apostles' hands, he offered them money, saying, "Give me this power also, so that anyone on whom I lay my hands may receive the Holy Spirit." But Peter said to him, "May your silver perish with you, because you thought you could obtain the gift of God with money! You have neither part nor lot in this matter, for your heart is not right before God. Repent, therefore, of this wickedness of yours, and pray to the Lord that, if possible, the intent of your heart may be forgiven you. For I see that you are in the gall of bitterness and in the bond of iniquity." (Acts 8:13–23)

In light of the circumstances, Philip did the right thing in baptizing Simon without calling into question his profession of faith. We should treat someone who professes to be a believer as a fellow Christian, unless there is reasonable motive for doubting his or her faith. It is not for us to presume to know other people's hearts.

We can learn this from the very way in which Jesus kept the hypocrisy of Judas unnoticed. Although he knew that Judas was a traitor, Jesus acted in a way that led the other apostles to treat him as an equal. All this goes to show that God does not prevent there being people in our midst that we will wrongly assume to be converted.

Just as in Acts 8, the Bible sometimes describes false conversions in language that appears to be a description of a real conversion. Simon "believed" (Acts 8:13). The Gospel of John recounts how many "believed" in Jesus, but not in the sense of having saving faith:

> Now when he was in Jerusalem at the Passover Feast, *many believed in his name* when they saw the signs that he was doing. But Jesus on his part did not entrust himself to them, because he knew all people. (John 2:23–24; emphasis added)

So Jesus said to the Jews *who had believed in him*, "If you abide in my word, you are truly my disciples." (John 8:31; emphasis added)

Nevertheless, many even of the authorities *believed in him*, but for fear of the Pharisees they did not confess it, so that they would not be put out of the synagogue; for they loved the glory that comes from man more than the glory that comes from God.
(John 12:42–43; emphasis added)

We should not conclude that these people necessarily experienced salvation just because they are said to have "believed," because in each case the assertion is somehow qualified. In the first passage, John informs us that Jesus did not put any faith in those who believed in him. And by the way in which the Gospel of John proceeds, it may very well be that Nicodemus is presented as an example of one of those who "believed" but had never been born again.

In the context of the second passage, Jesus establishes the criterion of permanence to distinguish those who were truly his disciples from the rest of those who had "believed," in some sense of the word. In the third passage, John qualifies the faith of the people he mentions as a secret faith and explains that they valued the approval of other people more than the approval of God. So it is quite evident that there is a kind of faith that is not saving faith, because it is not willing to suffer hardship for the sake of Christ, nor does it make a true disciple of Christ out of a person because it is not enduring in nature.

THE PARABLE OF THE SOWER

An important lesson to remember when we read the parable of the sower is that there are those who "have no root; they believe for a while, and in time of testing fall away" (Luke 8:13).

It is a mistake to view the parable as portraying such people as experiencing an authentic conversion and later falling away. Many who preach that salvation can be lost fall into this error, resorting to this parable to sustain their doctrine. It is curious how they prefer to make use of Luke's rendering of the parable as it is better suited to their purpose, since only in Luke do we find any expression that can be wielded to give the impression that true salvation took place among those who never went so far as bearing any fruit. The single word on which they build their whole argument is the word *believe* as it occurs in the phrase, "They believe for a while, and in time of testing fall away" (Luke 8:13).

Robert Shank seeks to make the most of this word in Luke's account to convince his readers that the parable is describing real salvation that is later forfeited:

The use of the word [believe] in verse 12 establishes its meaning as it is employed in the parable. It is clearly a believing unto salvation: "Lest they should believe and be saved." No warrant is present for assigning a different meaning to the word as it appears in verse 13, and any exegesis which requires it is obviously prejudiced. Those who "for a while believe" are depicted by Jesus as making a sincere beginning in the life of faith. Language and context forbid any other conclusion. Their subsequent fall does not obviate the fact that their believing, while it continued, was actual saving faith.[119]

There are, however, several reasons why we are compelled to discard Shank's interpretation. First, his argument itself is very weak. We have just noted how the wording found in the text (*believe*) can mean something other than saving faith in the Bible.

The fact that the word *believe* occurs with the idea of believing unto salvation in verse 12 can hardly be considered proof that its meaning should be the same in verse 13. The way in which verse 13 qualifies the faith of those depicted is designed to clarify that they "believed" short of being saved.

Their "belief" is qualified in two ways. Their faith is merely the passing whim of those who receive the Word immediately with excitement but believe only "for a while." Besides that, they have no root—that is, no depth or conviction that would result in perseverance. On the contrary, "when tribulation or persecution arises on account of the word, immediately they fall away" (Mark 4:17).

Second, Shank's interpretation ignores the fact that in the parable the goal is not to sprout from the earth but to bear fruit. A sower does not obtain anything from all his labor until he gathers fruit.

When we read the Lord's explanation of the parable, we can tell that becoming a productive fruit-bearing plant is what should be taken to symbolize spiritual life:

Now the parable is this: The seed is the word of God. The ones along the path are those who have heard. Then the devil comes and takes

---

119 Robert Shank, *Life in the Son* (Bloomington: Bethany House Publishers, 1989), 32–33.

away the word from their hearts, so that they may not believe and be saved. And the ones on the rock are those who, when they hear the word, receive it with joy. But these have no root; they believe for a while, and in time of testing fall away. And as for what fell among the thorns, they are those who hear, but as they go on their way they are choked by the cares and riches and pleasures of life, and their fruit does not mature. As for that in the good soil, they are those who, hearing the word, hold it fast in an honest and good heart, and bear fruit with patience. (Luke 8:11–15)

Only those represented by the good soil actually yield the sower any fruit, and all who produce useful fruit do so "with perseverance" (v. 15, NASB). In the words of Mark, only the seeds that were sown on the good soil yielded a crop:

And other seeds fell into good soil and produced grain, growing up and increasing and yielding thirtyfold and sixtyfold and a hundredfold. (Mark 4:8)

To yield a hundredfold, or sixtyfold, or even thirtyfold is extraordinary. What the parable aims to get across is that all believers bear fruit in abundance, although not all yield as much fruit as others. But there aren't any Christians whose productivity remains at zero.

Third, Shank's interpretation requires those portrayed in the parable as rocky soil and those pictured as thorn-infested soil to be people who at first hear the message of Christ in an honest and good heart. But Luke reserves this designation to contrast those depicted by the good soil from the others by saying, "These are the ones who have heard the word in an honest and good heart" (Luke 8:15 NASB).

The parable does not represent three kinds of people who start out well. In both cases where there was failure, we do not find the problems creeping in later on. In both cases, the plants were doomed to never yield any fruit right from the start, because neither one got off to an adequate start.

Jesus explains that the seed sown on the rocky soil stands for "the one who hears the word and immediately receives it with joy" (Matt. 13:20). It is a person who casually takes up the idea of following Christ, apart from giving the matter enough serious thought and without having any real commitment to still follow when there happens to be a price to pay.

When Christ denounces that "these have no root" (Luke 8:13), he is exposing the fact that they never had the conviction needed to remain loyal to him if it ever came to suffering for being Christians. It is those who are superficial that *immediately* fall away when tribulation or persecution arises on account of the word (Matt. 13:21).

The seeds that fell among the thorns are said by Jesus to represent "those who hear, but as they go on their way they are choked by the cares and riches and pleasures of life" (Luke 8:14). Just as in the previous case, the seeds fall on soil that had not been readied for planting. The soil could only have become productive if a prior work had been performed to remove the rocks and thorns. But no such work had been carried out on this soil.

This represents people whose hearts are already taken by the love of riches, the cares of this world, and the pleasures of this life. Still attached to these kinds of things, never having renounced them, these people show great interest for the Gospel and profess to follow Christ, believing that the good seed will be able to coexist and grow adequately among the thorns.

But their attempt to reconcile worldliness and Christianity proves itself abortive, and it is only a matter of time before the competing interests will suffocate their initial enthusiasm for the things of God. As a result, nothing can ever be harvested from them because they "bring no fruit to maturity" (Luke 8:14, NASB).

To insist that the rocky soil represents people who experienced salvation and then lost it would entail some unacceptable implications. If such were the case, the parable would teach us that people can be saved without being willing to suffer for the sake of Christ. It would also mean that uncommitted people could stay saved as long as they never have to go through persecution, although they would become lost the moment a trial of any kind arose.

In the same way, if that which was sown among the thorns represents people who were saved and then lost, the message of the parable ends up being that people can be saved by means of an association with the Gospel without ever having to renounce their love for sin. And they will continue saved as long as their internal reality does not culminate in their abandoning the church, as in the long run it inevitably must.

Such implications cannot be harmonized with the teachings of Jesus, who insisted that we cannot be his disciples unless we are willing to deny ourselves, suffer hostilities for his sake, and take up our cross (a reference to martyrdom) to follow him. He even likens the decision to follow him to undertaking the building of a tower or the decision to go to war, because these are projects that should not be embarked upon hastily (Luke 14:25–33).

In these illustrations, Jesus is driving home the point that following him requires us to count the cost beforehand and consider if we are willing to finish what we start. A person who is only willing to follow Christ so long as it is never necessary to pay a price is not really a disciple. Even if favorable circumstances allow such a person to remain in church, uncommitted Christianity is nothing more than self-deception.

God knows it when other loves control the heart. Not every Christian is called to go through the same trials, but all are called to the same faith, and nobody can be a disciple who is unwilling to displease father, or mother, or spouse, or children, or siblings, and even forego one's own life (Luke 14:26).

Last, it should be noted that the parable of the sower is found in the three synoptic Gospels, and the interpretation Shank advocates depends completely on the phrase "they believe for a while," which is peculiar to the Gospel of Luke. As a result, besides holding to a thesis that does not fit the evidence from the text of Luke, he creates a conflict between Luke on the one side and Matthew and Mark on the other.

The idea that the same parable has a different meaning in Luke than in the other two Gospels is extremely unconvincing. The reader of Mark and Matthew will not find anything to lend the impression that the rocky soil and the thorny ground are intended to represent people who experienced genuine salvation. According to Matthew's account, those represented by the good soil are distinguished from the rest as being the only ones who *understand* the message of Christ (Matt. 13:23).

Therefore, the evidence shows that the parable underscores that the ones who fall away are those who never had a good start. In the words of Gregorius Nazianzenus (written around AD 350), they are those "who never were sown upon the firm and unshaken rock, but upon dry and barren land; these are they who come to the word in a superficial way, and are of little faith; and because they have no depth of earth, suddenly arise, and looking to please others, after a short assault of the evil one, and a little temptation and heat, are withered and die."[120]

---

120 Gregorius Nazianzenus, quoted by John Gill, *The Cause of God and of Truth*, Part 4, Chapter 5, Section 17, The Ultimate Christian Library (Rio, Wisconsin: AGES Software, 2000), 837.

There are several people in the Bible whose lives turned out that way. They seem to start well, but then we lose all hope that they may have died saved. Of course, these cases are also elicited by some as biblical evidence that the saints can fall away. However, as we have already noted, there are people who make a profession of faith without ever having been born again. They are welcomed into the church (as was Simon Magus) and in some cases admitted into the ministry (as was the case of Judas).

For this reason, Berkhof points out what is really necessary in order to prove the doctrine that salvation can be lost from the cases of apostasy found in the Bible:

Again, it is said that Scripture records several cases of actual apostasy... But these instances do not prove the contention that real believers, in possession of true saving faith, can fall from grace, unless it be shown first that the persons indicated in these passages had true faith in Christ, and not a mere temporal faith, which is not rooted in regeneration. The Bible teaches us that there are persons who profess the true faith, and yet are not of the faith.[121]

Arthur Pink reinforces this same truth:

In order to make good his objection the Arminian must do something more than point to those who made a credible profession and afterwards falsified and renounced it: he must prove that a person who is truly regenerated, born from above, made a new creature in Christ, then apostatised.[122]

It should be no trouble conceding that Berkof and Pink's challenge is reasonable. No one, as far as I know, appeals to the case of Simon Magus as evidence against the doctrine of the perseverance of the saints. Before we jump to the conclusion that the Bible intends to teach that salvation can be overturned by giving us real-life examples, we would need to have enough evidence to conclude that the Scriptures actually do present cases of people who had truly been regenerate before their departure.

Is there this kind of evidence in any particular case? Although there is no attempt to convince us that such evidence exists regarding Simon Magus, many believe that there is evidence in some other cases. Therefore, we need to look into them.

121 Louis Berkhof, *Systematic Theology* (Lexington: 2015), 529–530.
122 A. W. Pink, *Eternal Security* (Grand Rapids: Baker Book House, 1979), 101.

KING SAUL

A number of authors have argued that it is possible to demonstrate from the Bible that King Saul experienced a real conversion. Saul comes to a tragic end, but he appears to start out very well. Early on, Saul demonstrated humility (1 Sam. 15:17) and respected the prophet Samuel. He encouraged the true religion in Israel and cut off the mediums and the necromancers from the land (1 Sam. 28:9).

Besides the good impression from these external indicators, what is presented as real proof of internal godliness is what we find in 1 Samuel 10:9–10:

> When he turned his back to leave Samuel, God gave him another heart. And all these signs came to pass that day. When they came to Gibeah, behold, a group of prophets met him, and the Spirit of God rushed upon him, and he prophesied among them. (1 Sam. 10:9–10)

The argument purports that this text proves Saul was really converted because it says that God changed Saul's heart and that the Spirit of God rushed upon him, causing him to prophesy. But does this description really prove that much? When the Bible says that God changed Saul's heart, it does not specify in what regard, and it would be pure conjecture to say that the meaning here is regeneration.

Nothing in the context points in that direction. There is no indication that this was a turning point in his life whereby he became devoted to God. And the Bible shows God changing people's hearts in several ways that are unrelated to conversion. God swayed the heart of the chief of the eunuchs, making him favorable toward Daniel (Dan. 1:9). God acted upon the hearts of the neighboring nations, preventing them from coveting the land of the Israelites while they kept the religious festivals three times a year (Exod. 34:24).

On some occasions, the Bible even says that God changed people's hearts in a negative sense. In Psalm 105:25, the Bible says of the Egyptians that "He turned their hearts to hate his people, to deal craftily with his servants." On that same note, God changed the heart of Pharaoh to once again pursue the people of Israel after he had broken down and allowed them to leave:

And I will harden Pharaoh's heart, and he will pursue them, and I will get glory over Pharaoh and all his host, and the Egyptians shall know that I am the LORD." And they did so. When the king of Egypt was told that the people had fled, the mind of Pharaoh and his servants was changed toward the people, and they said, "What is this we have done, that we have let Israel go from serving us?" So he made ready his chariot and took his army with him, and took six hundred chosen chariots and all the other chariots of Egypt with officers over all of them. And the LORD hardened the heart of Pharaoh king of Egypt, and he pursued the people of Israel while the people of Israel were going out defiantly. (Exod. 14:4–8)

On at least these two occasions when the Bible speaks of God changing people's hearts, it wasn't to get them to do what is morally right.[123] So we cannot lay hold of that statement about Saul as proof of regeneration. Then what kind of change are we to understand God brought about in Saul's heart? The text does not answer that question, but it seems most likely that it had to do with God making him into the kind of energetic and capable leader that Israel would need as king.

In the very next chapter of 1 Samuel, we see the Spirit of God stirring Saul up to act in response to the Ammonite aggression:

And the Spirit of God rushed upon Saul when he heard these words, and his anger was greatly kindled. He took a yoke of oxen and cut them in pieces and sent them throughout all the territory of Israel by the hand of messengers, saying, "Whoever does not come out after Saul and Samuel, so shall it be done to his oxen!" Then the dread of the LORD fell upon the people, and they came out as one man. (1 Sam. 11:6–7)

According to the book of Proverbs, "the king's heart is a stream of water in the hand of the LORD; he turns it wherever he will" (Prov. 21:1). What is certain is that God molds and changes the hearts of all kings, whether they are converted or not.

If Saul really was a saved man, at what point are we to believe that he fell from a state of grace? As early as in 1 Samuel 13, we hear Samuel's stern reproof:

The LORD has sought out a man after his own heart, and the LORD has commanded him to be prince over his people, because you have not kept what the LORD commanded you. (1 Sam. 13:14b)

---

123 See also Zechariah 8:10 and 2 Samuel 24:1.

If Saul were a righteous man, why would he have been told that he was going to be replaced and that this time God had sought out a man after his own heart?

But there is still the second statement about Saul. We also read that "the Spirit of God rushed upon him, and he prophesied among them" (1 Sam. 10:10). Later on, we read that the Spirit of the Lord departed from Saul and that an evil spirit from the LORD tormented him (1 Sam. 16:14).

But it would be a clear mistake to interpret these words in the sense that Saul received the Holy Spirit in the same sense as in Acts chapters 2 and 10, 1 Corinthians 12, and Romans 8. It is easy to tell that the Holy Spirit's interaction with Saul cannot be equated with the baptism in the Holy Spirit by the simple fact that the Spirit of the Lord "rushed upon" him on more than one occasion (1 Sam. 10:10 and 11:6).

Not only so, but the usage of this expression in the Bible is of a completely different kind of operation. On three occasions, it is said that "the Spirit of the LORD rushed upon" Samson, investing him with extraordinary strength and courage to subdue a lion and to battle the Philistines (Judg . 14:6, 19; 15:14).

On two of these occasions, we can ascertain that Samson was in flagrant disobedience to God's commandments. On the other hand, we have good reason to believe that David was converted before he was anointed to be king of Israel, but the Bible informs us that it wasn't until that time that "the Spirit of the LORD rushed upon David":

> Then Samuel took the horn of oil and anointed him in the midst of his brothers. And the Spirit of the LORD rushed upon David from that day forward. (1 Sam. 16:13)

This happens to David at the very same time when the Spirit the LORD departs from Saul (v. 14). Clearly, something else is going on here. This all strengthens the notion that the expression has more to do with an enablement for a mission.

The fact that Saul prophesied does not prove he was converted any more than prophesying proves that Balaam and Caiaphas were converted. We know that they were wicked men, even though they were compelled to prophesy by the Holy Spirit:

> And Balaam lifted up his eyes and saw Israel camping tribe by tribe. And the Spirit of God came upon him, and he took up his discourse

and said, "The oracle of Balaam the son of Beor, the oracle of the man whose eye is opened." (Num. 24:2–3)

But one of them, Caiaphas, who was high priest that year, said to them, "You know nothing at all. Nor do you understand that it is better for you that one man should die for the people, not that the whole nation should perish." He did not say this of his own accord, but being high priest that year he prophesied that Jesus would die for the nation. (John 11:49–51)

Not only so, but on one occasion, Saul sent several groups of soldiers to capture David, but they could not because the Spirit of the Lord rushed upon them, and they all prophesied. It would not be reasonable to postulate that they were all converted, to a man, or that they all had a conversion experience right then and there. When they failed to bring David in, Saul went personally in his obsession to kill David, but overcome by the Spirit of God, he also prophesied:

Then Saul sent messengers to take David, and when they saw the company of the prophets prophesying, and Samuel standing as head over them, the Spirit of God came upon the messengers of Saul, and they also prophesied. When it was told Saul, he sent other messengers, and they also prophesied. And Saul sent messengers again the third time, and they also prophesied. Then he himself went to Ramah and came to the great well that is in Secu. And he asked, "Where are Samuel and David?" And one said, "Behold, they are at Naioth in Ramah." And he went there to Naioth in Ramah. And the Spirit of God came upon him also, and as he went he prophesied until he came to Naioth in Ramah. And he too stripped off his clothes, and he too prophesied before Samuel and lay naked all that day and all that night. Thus it is said, "Is Saul also among the prophets?" (1 Sam. 19:20–24)

Here, we find conclusive evidence that the fact that Saul prophesied cannot be taken as an indication that his heart was right with God. This occurred while he was out to kill David. His heart was in direct rebellion against God. "Everyone who hates his brother is a murderer, and you know that no murderer has eternal life abiding in him" (1 John 3:15).

An adequate knowledge of the Bible completely demolishes the theory that Saul gave evidence of having been converted. And since there is no biblical evidence that Saul was ever saved, it is unthinkable that the biblical account of Saul's life was designed to serve as an object lesson of how salvation can be lost. Using it to that end is simply an overreach.

JUDAS ISCARIOT

When a biblical example is sought to prove that salvation can be lost, Judas Iscariot is who gets summoned more than anyone else. For example, in his *Systematic Theology*, first published in 1893, the Arminian theologian John Miley admits that the proofs in favor of the doctrine of the perseverance of the saints are plausible and that the most natural interpretation of some biblical texts would lead us to embrace it. Nevertheless, he feels constrained to reject it due to what is known to have taken place in the case of Judas:

> Some texts of Scripture seem, on the face of them, to favor it, but a deeper insight finds them entirely consistent with the conditionality of final perseverance. "My sheep hear my voice, and I know them, and they follow me; and I give unto them eternal life; and they shall never perish, neither shall any man pluck them out of my hand." Such is the assurance from the divine side; but it is entirely consistent with a conditioning fidelity on the human side. The case of Judas is an illustration. From the divine side these words pledged to him all that they pledged to the others given to the Son by the Father; yet there was in him, and therefore in them, the possibility of apostasy.[124]

He then proceeds to cite three more texts used to substantiate the doctrine of the perseverance of the saints (Rom. 11:29; Phil. 1:6; and 1 Pet. 1:5) but dismisses them, reaffirming that "Judas, one of those given to the Son, was lost."[125]

Persuaded that Judas was once saved but then lost, Miley brings this conviction to bear on his interpretation of every text in the Bible where he sees evidence for the doctrine of the perseverance of the saints. As a result of this imposition, he tries to find another way to interpret the four texts that he takes the trouble to discuss and reasons that they must not constitute conclusive proofs that the saints infallibly persevere.

Just as Miley did, many others have interpreted everything in the Bible according to this unchallenged notion. But are they justified in working backward from their premise that Judas actually is a case of a person who lost his salvation? What evidence is there to so conclude?

---

124 John Miley, *Systematic Theology*, Volume II (Peabody, MA: Hendrickson Publishers, 1989), 269.
125 Ibid., 270.

Those who claim that Judas experienced genuine salvation and then lost it build their case on two passages from the Gospels. In Matthew 10:1–4, the evangelist reports that Jesus gave his twelve apostles, including Judas, the authority to cast out unclean spirits and to cure all manner of sickness or infirmity. We can safely say that Judas was not excluded as the only one of the twelve unable to perform miracles. Otherwise, when Jesus announced that he would be betrayed by one of their number, we could presume that they would all have turned to Judas instead of becoming sorrowful and asking Him one after another, "Is it I?" (Mark 14:19).

All the evidence indicates that Jesus did not treat Judas any differently than the other apostles during his earthly ministry. Judas too was sent out to preach, perform miracles, and administer baptism. This is reason enough for some to conclude that Judas must have been a believer, at least for a time, because they maintain that Jesus would not give this kind of power and participation in holy things to an insincere man.

Isn't it true that the Bible sets high spiritual standards for ministers? Can we believe that the Lord himself knowingly placed someone who was unqualified in the office of an apostle?

The second passage claimed as evidence of Judas having had a real conversion (the text Miley appeals to) is John 17:12:

> While I was with them, I kept them in your name, which you have given me. I have guarded them, and not one of them has been lost except the son of destruction, that the Scripture might be fulfilled.
>
> (John 17:12)

Picirilli adduces from this verse that Judas was clearly one of those given to Jesus by the Father:

> The pronoun "them" can have as its antecedent nothing other than "those whom You gave me." This goes far to demonstrate (1) that "giving" them to Jesus does not guarantee their perseverance, since the son of perdition is clearly both among "them" and now lost, and (2) that his prayers for them were not therefore unconditionally efficacious.[126]

However, in reality, this verse proves nothing of the sort. Picirilli is reading into the verse a connotation that it would not have had in its first-century usage. This same grammatical structure, "Not one of them has been lost except [Greek: εἰ μὴ] the son of destruction," occurs several times in the New

---

126 Robert E. Picirilli, *Grace, Faith, and Free Will* (Nashville: Randall House, 2002), 190.

Testament. It takes no more than a cursory look at them to confirm that, in reality, this is no argument at all:

> "I assure you that there were many widows in Israel in Elijah's time, when the sky was shut for three and a half years and there was a severe famine throughout the land. Yet Elijah was not sent to any of them, but [εἰ μὴ] to a widow in Zarephath in the region of Sidon. And there were many in Israel with leprosy in the time of Elisha the prophet, yet not one of them was cleansed—only [εἰ μὴ] Naaman the Syrian."
>
> (Luke 4:25–27, NIV)

No one would take these verses to prove that the widow of Sidom was one of the widows of Israel, much less that Naaman was one of the lepers in Israel! What they show is precisely the opposite. When the text says that Elijah was not sent to any of the widows in Israel "but [εἰ μὴ] to a widow in Zarephath in the region of Sidon," the meaning is that the only exception was someone who was not part of the group just referred to—in other words, someone who was not one of the widows of Israel.

And when Jesus said that in Elisha's time not one of the lepers of Israel was cleansed "but only [εἰ μὴ] Naaman the Syrian," once again, he means to point out that the only exception was to be found in a person who was not part of the aforementioned group.

There is an abundance of other examples of this structure in the New Testament. Paul said, "I saw none of the other apostles except [εἰ μὴ] James the Lord's brother" (Gal. 1:19), and James, the Lord's brother, was not one of the apostles.

In Philippians 3:9 Paul states his desire to "be found in him, not having a righteousness of my own that comes from the law, but that which comes through faith in Christ, the righteousness from God that depends on faith."

Now we know very well that the righteousness from God that depends on faith is not a righteousness of our own. Still, other examples of this same way of expressing contrast are found in Matthew 12:24, Acts 27:22, and in Revelation 21:27.

Therefore, it is totally unfounded to teach that the grammar of John 17:12 indicates that Judas was among those given to Jesus by the Father. The very opposite is the case. When Jesus makes this remark about Judas in this way, his intention is to make it understood that Judas was *not* one of those under his protection. Jesus had just finished saying that he had not lost any of those who had been given to him by the Father, and before anyone had the notion of contradicting him by pointing to Judas, Jesus anticipates the objection showing that the fall of Judas was not due to a failure on his part but took place "that the Scripture might be fulfilled."

So Jesus underscores the fact that Judas had never been among those given to him, a reality that Christ emphasizes again by calling him the "son of perdition." This title conferred on Judas by our Lord was used in first-century Israel to mean someone who was destined to perdition. So much so that the NIV translators felt that the best way to render its idea in the English language was by translating it as "the one doomed to destruction."

This doesn't mean that Judas was not responsible for his own actions. It is certain that he acted voluntarily and was in no way coerced. But his betrayal was part of God's plan. That is why he, an unbeliever from the beginning, had been chosen to be an apostle. He was put in the right place at the right time because he had a role to carry out and thus fulfill the Scriptures.

That brings us back to the first argument set forth in an effort to convince that Judas was temporarily saved. "If Judas had not been sincere," it is said, "then why did Jesus choose and ordain him to be an apostle?"

The answer is actually quite simple: "That the Scripture might be fulfilled." The fact that Judas was an apostle and did miracles does not constitute evidence that he ever had a genuine conversion. As our Lord has foretold, many on that day will say, "Did we not prophesy in your name, and cast out demons in your name, and do many mighty works in your name?" But the answer they will hear is, "I never knew you; depart from me, you workers of lawlessness" (Matt. 7:22–23).

The truth is that there is no real evidence indicating that Judas was ever saved. Furthermore, that perspective is at odds with biblical passages that demonstrate clearly that Judas never had a true conversion. Jesus reveals that Judas was an unbeliever in John chapter 6, which narrates events that transpired long before the betrayal:

"But there are some of you who do not believe." (For Jesus knew from the beginning who those were who did not believe, and who it was who would betray him.) And he said, "This is why I told you that no one can come to me unless it is granted him by the Father."... Jesus answered them, "Did I not choose you, the Twelve? And yet

WILL I MAKE IT TO HEAVEN?

one of you is a devil." He spoke of Judas the son of Simon Iscariot, for he, one of the Twelve, was going to betray him.   (John 6:64–71)

It should be noted that in Jesus's statement the verb is in the present tense: "There are some of you who do not believe" (v. 64). John adds that, among others, Jesus had Judas in mind. Judas was one of those who did not believe, and Jesus knew it. In fact, "Jesus knew from the beginning who those were who did not believe" (v. 64). The indication is that those referred to did not believe from the beginning, and Jesus had known it all along. After all, the text does not say that Jesus knew from the beginning who those were who would lose their faith.

This conclusion becomes inescapable when Jesus immediately adds that there were unbelievers in their midst because "no one can come to me unless it is granted him by the Father" (v. 65). Jesus explains that this statement has everything to do with the case at hand, for it is the very reason why he stated that no one can come to him unless it is granted him by the Father. Such words allow for no other interpretation. The unbelievers who were present had never come to Christ, for that had never been granted to them by the Father.

Next, referring directly to Judas, Jesus declares, "Did I not choose you, the Twelve? And yet one of you is a devil" (v. 70). Once more, the verb is in the present tense ("is a devil"). At this point, the whole argument that Jesus would never allow an unbeliever to function as an apostle falls apart. The biblical witness is conclusive. At this point in time, Jesus knew Judas was an unbeliever, just as he had always known, even at the time when he chose them twelve in number.

Jesus returns to this reality in John chapter 13:

Jesus said to him, "The one who has bathed does not need to wash, except for his feet, but is completely clean. And you are clean, but not every one of you." For he knew who was to betray him; that was why he said, "Not all of you are clean."... "For I have given you an example, that you also should do just as I have done to you... If you know these things, blessed are you if you do them. I am not speaking of all of you; *I know whom I have chosen*. But the Scripture will be fulfilled, 'He who ate my bread has lifted his heel against me.'"
(John 13:10–18; emphasis added)

Here, Jesus refers to Judas as one who, in distinction from the eleven, was not spiritually clean. He then clarifies that he does not pronounce blessedness upon all of them in as much as he knew very well whom he had chosen. Again, the indication is that Judas was an unbeliever from the time he had been chosen and his inclusion among the apostles was for the purpose of fulfilling the Scripture.

In yet another passage, John goes out of his way to expose how Judas was actually a hypocrite, even during the time when he accompanied Jesus without raising any suspicions from the others:

> But Judas Iscariot, one of his disciples (he who was about to betray him), said, "Why was this ointment not sold for three hundred denarii and given to the poor?" He said this, not because he cared about the poor, but because he was a thief, and having charge of the moneybag he used to help himself to what was put into it.   (John 12:4–6)

John's reporting that Judas "was a thief" and that he "used to help himself" to the contents of the moneybag is very powerful. The verb tense employed in Greek carries the idea of prolonged action (hence, the translation "used to") and signifies that stealing from Jesus had been his habitual course of action.

With all this biblical information about Judas, we may marvel that there are still people who believe he serves as an example of someone who was genuinely converted and apostatized. These exposés of Judas's real character included in the fourth Gospel are not merely incidental. John's purpose is to make it known that Judas had never been a real follower of Christ. In doing so, he provides us a lesson on the nature of those who abandon the way. It is true that Judas's problems went undetected by the eleven while they interacted with him, but John would have us know that they were already present at that time and that the Lord Jesus was never fooled, not even for a moment.

OTHER APOSTATES

The application of what can be learned here goes beyond the case of Judas. Just as in his case, others may infiltrate the community of believers and remain therein for some time without having experienced a new birth. However, sinners will not remain indefinitely in the congregation of the righteous.

That is why there are other cases of apostasy, like Hymenaeus, Alexander, Philetus, and Demas. We know very little about these individuals. The only information we find in Scripture about Demas is that he was a ministry companion of the apostle Paul (Phil. 24) who deserted him "in love with this present world" (2 Tim. 4:10). These words would not be unfit to describe Judas Iscariot.

As to the others, Paul wrote the following assessment to Timothy:

> Holding faith and a good conscience. By rejecting this, some have made shipwreck of their faith, among whom are Hymenaeus and Alexander, whom I have handed over to Satan that they may learn not to blaspheme. (1 Tim. 1:19–20)

From this, we learn that Hymenaeus and Alexander had rejected a good conscience and "made shipwreck of their faith." In 2 Timothy, there is another mention of Hymenaeus:

> And their talk will spread like gangrene. Among them are Hymenaeus and Philetus, who have swerved from the truth, saying that the resurrection has already happened. They are upsetting the faith of some. But God's firm foundation stands, bearing this seal: "The Lord knows those who are his," and, "Let everyone who names the name of the Lord depart from iniquity." (2 Tim. 2:17–19)

With these additional insights, we are able to reconstruct that Hymenaeus, Alexander, and Philetus had been part of the church for a time, possibly having labored along with the apostle Paul. However, Paul had personally taken measures to see them excluded from the church due to their involvement with doctrinal aberrations.

Nothing in these verses proves that any of them had been genuine believers. It certainly could not be deduced from the words, "a good conscience, which some have rejected and suffered shipwreck in regard to their faith" (1 Tim. 1:19, NASB). By speaking in this way, Paul is not implying that they had possessed true saving faith. He is merely saying that they strayed as a result of having rejected a good conscience and repudiated doctrines that they had once believed and that are integral to the Christian faith.

As opposed to what some have argued, the depiction of having rejected "a good conscience" is not tantamount to saying they had previously possessed a good conscience. The same Greek word is used in Acts 13:46, where Paul and Barnabas censured the Jews who were unwilling to convert and embrace the truth:

It was necessary that the word of God should be spoken to you first; but *since you reject it*, and judge yourselves unworthy of everlasting life, behold, we turn to the Gentiles.

(Acts 13:46, NKJV; emphasis added)

Hymenaeus and Alexander had certainly heard over and over that they should have a good conscience before God, but it was a message that they rejected, and they departed from the doctrinal orthodoxy in which they had been instructed.

We later find Paul denouncing these men for actively opposing the truth by propagating error. He asserts that "they destroy the faith of some" (2 Tim. 2:18, NIV). But Paul wants to make it clear that he is not suggesting that they could effectively overthrow the faith of the elect. Therefore, he immediately adds, "Nevertheless, God's solid foundation stands firm, sealed with this inscription: 'The Lord knows those who are his'" (v. 19 NIV).

Those who belong to the Lord (and God knows who they are) remain uncorrupted in their faith, for God's solid foundation, which is inseparably linked to his eternal purpose, cannot be shaken. We must not forget this. When we consider the other cases of apostasy in the Bible, we are dealing with people about whom we know very little. Nothing is presented that should cause us to conclude that they had certainly been real Christians. Incidentally, the Bible does not provide us with as much negative information about these other individuals as it does concerning Judas either. Even so, in view of what Paul says in this text, and considering the teaching of Scripture as a whole, we can confidently affirm that if we had a way of obtaining more information about each case, what would come forth is that they too had been false disciples from the beginning, just like Judas.

The same truth applies to people we know personally who abandon the faith. We should interpret what we observe in light of what the Bible teaches instead of interpreting the Bible according to our impressions regarding our own experiences. We cannot read other people's hearts, and we are not in a position to make any categorical pronouncements about the reality of their conversions.

That is something we must keep in mind every time we see people who used to profess faith abandoning their profession and commitment to Christ. There are always those who are ready to rise up and protest against the doctrine of the perseverance of the saints, objecting, "I know a person who abandoned the faith, and I *know* that he or she was truly converted."

But if I may ask, how can that really be known? Can we really know for sure that somebody else was saved by the external signs of a new life? Do we find infallible proofs of salvation in things such as faithful worship attendance, long prayers, Bible knowledge, scrupulous honesty, tithing, denouncement of immorality, and opposition to vice? Did not many Pharisees have such marks? We do well to recall the Bible's concern to unmask Judas, remembering that up to the moment of his betrayal the disciples never suspected that he was actually an unbeliever in their midst.

God alone weighs the human heart. "The heart is deceitful above all things, and desperately sick; who can understand it?" (Jer. 17:9). Only God scrutinizes the heart and can judge its thoughts. It is not for us to pretend certainty as to the spiritual condition of others.

The subtle danger of self-deception is a recurring theme in the New Testament. There are people who are not saved who become part of the visible church. Jesus often spoke about this. On one such occasion, he warned of this danger by means of a parable:

> The kingdom of heaven may be compared to a king who gave a wedding feast for his son, and sent his servants to call those who were invited to the wedding feast, but they would not come. Again he sent other servants, saying, "Tell those who are invited, See, I have prepared my dinner, my oxen and my fat calves have been slaughtered, and everything is ready. Come to the wedding feast." But they paid no attention and went off, one to his farm, another to his business, while the rest seized his servants, treated them shamefully, and killed them. The king was angry, and he sent his troops and destroyed those murderers and burned their city. Then he said to his servants, "The wedding feast is ready, but those invited were not worthy. Go therefore to the main roads and invite to the wedding feast as many as you find." And those servants went out into the roads and gathered all whom they found, both bad and good. So the wedding hall was filled with guests. But when the king came in to look at the guests, he saw there a man who had no wedding garment. And he said to him, "Friend, how did you get in here without a wedding garment?" And he was speechless. Then the king said to the attendants, "Bind him hand and foot and cast him into the outer darkness. In that place there will be weeping and gnashing of teeth." For many are called, but few are chosen.   (Matt. 22:2–14)

This parable of Christ teaches that there are more lost people than only those who reject the Gospel invitation outright. There are also those who infiltrate themselves among God's people without being clothed with a wedding garment—that is, without having been covered with the righteousness of Christ. The Bible makes it very clear that a person is not saved by the simple fact of being joined to a Christian church. Nowhere is this plainer than in the words of John the apostle:

> They went out from us, but they were not of us; for if they had been of us, they would have continued with us. But they went out, that it might become plain that they all are not of us.   (1 John 2:19)

The people here denounced must have shown externally convincing signs of conversion, or they would never have been accepted into the fellowship of an apostolic church.

In their epistles to the Christian communities, the New Testament treated their first readers as Christians based on their profession of faith, but it would be a mistake to conclude on that basis that they intend to convey that their readers were all unquestionably saved individuals. It is not uncharacteristic of them to call upon their addressees to examine themselves, to see whether they were truly in the faith. For instance, after addressing the members of the Corinthian church as saints, Paul exhorted them to spiritual self-examination in order to confirm the authenticity of their professed faith:

> Examine yourselves, to see whether you are in the faith. Test yourselves. Or do you not realize this about yourselves, that Jesus Christ is in you?—unless indeed you fail to meet the test!   (2 Cor. 13:5)

Paul did not write these words to those in a backslidden condition. He was challenging people who were active church members in a church that he had planted.

MAKING OUR CALLING AND ELECTION SURE

In his second epistle, the apostle Peter charges all of us to make our calling and election sure:

> For this very reason, make every effort to supplement your faith with virtue, and virtue with knowledge, and knowledge with self-control, and self-control with steadfastness, and steadfastness with godliness, and godliness with brotherly affection, and brotherly affection with love. For if these qualities are yours and are increasing,

177

they keep you from being ineffective or unfruitful in the knowledge of our Lord Jesus Christ. For whoever lacks these qualities is so nearsighted that he is blind, having forgotten that he was cleansed from his former sins. Therefore, brothers, be all the more diligent to make your calling and election sure, for if you practice these qualities you will never fall. For in this way there will be richly provided for you an entrance into the eternal kingdom of our Lord and Savior Jesus Christ. (2 Peter 1:5–11)

This exhortation is meant to spur the reader to self-examination. Peter's concern is that there should be spiritual growth in terms of faith, virtue, knowledge, self-control, steadfastness, godliness, brotherly affection, and love. He expresses deep concern over those who do not appear to be growing in these areas. But instead of voicing a fear that such people could end up losing their salvation out of negligence, what he says next shows that he fears there may be people in the churches who are not actually converted. Thus, he summons us to "be all the more diligent" to make our "calling and election sure" (v. 10).

This is important. He is not calling into question whether salvation is lasting in those who have been called; what he is questioning is if all who profess Christianity have truly been called. *Calling* is a technical term for conversion wrought by God (cf. 1 Cor. 1:26; Eph. 4:1, 4:4; 2 Tim. 1:9). So the entreaty of 2 Peter 1:10 is for us to confirm the authenticity of our past conversion. And when we confirm that we have truly been called, by extension, we confirm our election, as well. Whoever has been called must be one of the elect, for the Bible tells us that "those whom he predestined he also called" (Rom. 8:30).

But how can we confirm our calling and election? Peter shows us the way. Confirmation of one's conversion comes from manifesting the characteristics listed in 2 Peter 1:5–6. We perceive, therefore, that in Peter's way of thinking, the way we can confirm the fact that we have truly been saved is by persevering and growing in grace. It is those who "practice these qualities" who "will never fall," for this is the way that God provides us "an entrance into the eternal kingdom of our Lord and Savior Jesus Christ" (v. 11).

On the other hand, those who are indifferent to such spiritual duties simply fail to confirm their calling and election. They are not said to lose their salvation. What is invalidated is their profession of having been called and their claim to be among God's elect.

For Peter, this was a pertinent message especially in view of the fact that some church people were becoming corrupted by the doctrines of false teachers. His final words sum up the message of the epistle:

> You therefore, beloved, knowing this beforehand, take care that you are not carried away with the error of lawless people and lose your own stability. But grow in the grace and knowledge of our Lord and Savior Jesus Christ. To him be the glory both now and to the day of eternity. Amen. (2 Pet. 3:17–18)

Peter describes the false teachers who had sprung up in the church in the strongest of terms. He says they are "like irrational animals, creatures of instinct, born to be caught and destroyed" (2 Pet. 2:12). They are denounced as greed driven deceivers (2 Pet. 2:3) who revel in their deceptions (2 Pet. 2:13), indulge in the lust of defiling passion, and despise authority (2 Pet. 2:10).

> They have eyes full of adultery, insatiable for sin. They entice unsteady souls. They have hearts trained in greed. Accursed children! Forsaking the right way, they have gone astray. They have followed the way of Balaam, the son of Beor, who loved gain from wrongdoing. (2 Pet. 2:14–15)

We know that their teaching promoted sensuality (2 Pet. 2:2). It is universally recognized that 2 Peter and Jude address the same problem, unmasking the same false teachers. Jude characterizes them as "ungodly people, who pervert the grace of our God into sensuality and deny our only Master and Lord, Jesus Christ" (Jude 1:4). They somehow twisted the concept of grace into a license to sin, apparently distorting the intended meaning of some passages from Paul's epistles (2 Pet. 3:16).

Those who teach the possibility of apostasy of true saints believe these false teachers and their victims serve as biblical examples confirming their doctrine. However, Peter and Jude do not share the opinion that these defectors had previously been saved.

Peter spells out the kind of people who were being dragged into error by the lawless teachers. He warns that they "entice unsteady souls" (2 Pet. 2:14). He tells us that by "speaking loud boasts of folly, they entice by sensual passions of the flesh those who are barely escaping from those who live in error" (2 Pet. 2:18). The profile of their victims is otherwise rendered as "people who are just escaping from those who live in error" (NIV).

So according to Peter, the false teachers were only successful in alluring away from the Christian community those who were near the kingdom but who had not yet evidenced a clear-cut break from a life of error. They were barely escaping when they found themselves enticed by the message of licentiousness.

Regarding the false teachers themselves, although they were openly violating God's laws at the time when the epistles of Peter and Jude were written, Peter recognizes that for some time they had conformed to the norms of Christianity:

> For if, after they have escaped the defilements of the world through the knowledge of our Lord and Savior Jesus Christ, they are again entangled in them and overcome, the last state has become worse for them than the first. For it would have been better for them never to have known the way of righteousness than after knowing it to turn back from the holy commandment delivered to them. What the true proverb says has happened to them: "The dog returns to its own vomit, and the sow, after washing herself, returns to wallow in the mire." (2 Pet. 2:20–22)

It is clear that for a time they had abstained from the immoral practices to which they now wholeheartedly returned. Otherwise, they never would have achieved leadership positions within the church. What remains to be considered is if they had experienced an inward transformation or if their change was merely outward in nature.

Peter asserts that they had "escaped the defilements of the world through the knowledge of our Lord and Savior Jesus Christ" (2 Pet. 2:21). Some see these words as proof that they had saving faith and sincere repentance.

There are difficulties with this interpretation. First, it is at odds with Jude's equally inspired evaluation of these same false teachers. Jude states that they were reprobates who crept in unnoticed—that is, they managed to get in without their hypocrisy being detected:

> For certain people have *crept in unnoticed* who long ago were designated for this condemnation, ungodly people, who pervert the grace of our God into sensuality and deny our only Master and Lord, Jesus Christ. (Jude 1:4; emphasis added)

Furthermore, the idea that Peter wishes to characterize the false prophets as having had a saving knowledge of Christ, only to subsequently fall back into a state of perdition, does not fit with what Peter himself says.

Peter concludes his observations about the false teachers with an analogy: "What the true proverb says has happened to them: 'The dog returns to its own vomit, and the sow, after washing herself, returns to wallow in the mire'" (v. 22). Although washed, a sow returns to wallowing in the mire because that is her nature. For a pig to keep itself clean would require transforming it into a new creature whose nature was averse to filth. If this were done, there would be no going back to wallowing in the mud. But such had never taken place in these individuals, who are depicted as having ever been pigs and dogs.

Both the pig and the dog were disdained in the Mediterranean cultures of the first century. Peter speaks of the false prophets as never having been anything other than inwardly filthy and detestable, even while they were externally washed by the interruption of their grossly sinful lifestyle. No interpreter can afford to ignore this part of Peter's assessment.

Therefore, when Peter says that they had "escaped the defilements of the world through the knowledge of our Lord and Savior Jesus Christ" (v. 21), it is better to take these words as referring to the fact that their contact with the message of Christ initially drew them away from the immorality and other sins that they shamelessly practiced as pagans. But as they were unhappy with the restrictions imposed upon them by Christian morality, they were attracted and seduced by the idea that they could be Christians without being encumbered by God's moral laws. Thus, they began to champion a falsification of Christianity and turned away "from the holy commandment delivered to them" (v. 21).

Discarding all efforts to observe God's biblical commandments, they not only went back to practicing evil openly but also encouraged others to do the same. They ended up in a worse state than they had been in at first (v. 20). They were now sinning against light, which made them even more guilty, just as is the case of all who hear the message of Jesus but remained unconverted (cf. Mat. 10:14–15; 11:21–24; Luke 12:48).

We know that the knowledge of Christ and his teachings about justice and the coming judgment have inhibited many unconverted people from practicing wrong things. The puritan Matthew Henry, commenting on this passage, provides a most insightful observation:

> Some men are, for a time, *kept from the pollutions of the world, by the knowledge of Christ*, who are not savingly renewed in the spirit of their mind. A religious education has restrained many whom the grace of God has not renewed: if we receive the light of the truth, and have a notional knowledge of Christ in our heads, it may be of some present service to us; but we must receive the love of the truth, and hide God's word in our heart, or it will not sanctify and save us.[127]

Albert Barnes offers these equally insightful comments:

> The meaning of the proverbs here quoted is, that they have returned to their former vile manner of life. Under all the appearances of reformation, still their evil nature remained, as really as that of the dog or the swine, and that nature finally prevailed. There was no thorough internal change, any more than there is in the swine when it is washed, or in the dog. This passage, therefore, would seem to demonstrate that there never had been any real change of heart, and of course there had been no falling away from true religion...

> No matter how clean the swine is made by washing, this would not prevent it, in the slightest degree, from rolling in filth again. It will act out its real nature. So it is with the sinner. No external reformation will certainly prevent his returning to his former habits...

> This passage is often quoted to prove "the possibility of falling from grace, and from a very high degree of it too." But it is one of the last passages in the Bible that should be adduced to prove that doctrine. The true point of this passage is to show that the persons referred to never "were changed;" that whatever external reformation might have occurred, their nature remained the same; and that when they apostatized from their outward profession, they merely acted out their nature, and showed that in fact there had been "no" real change. This passage will prove—what there are abundant facts to confirm— that persons may reform externally, and then return again to their

---

127 Matthew Henry, *Commentary on the Whole Bible, Vol. 10, Galatians to Revelation*, The Master Christian Library (Rio, WI: Ages Software Inc., 2000), 930.

former corrupt habits; it can never be made to prove that one TRUE Christian will fall away and perish.[128]

There is yet one more biblical passage presented by the opponents of the Reformed doctrine that merits our attention. This passage is Hebrews 6:4–12, where many believe there is proof that true Christians have indeed fallen away. It will be examined in the next chapter as part of a broader analysis of the message of Hebrews.

128 Albert Barnes, *Barnes' Notes on the Bible, Volume 17—James–Jude*, The Master Christian Library (Rio, WI: Ages Software Inc., 2000), 413–415.

7

The Message of Hebrews

"Avoid those evil excrescences which bring forth deadly fruit, of which whoever tastes dies; for they are not the Father's planting;" for if they "were, the branches of the cross would appear, and their fruit would be incorruptible; whereby through his sufferings he hath called you, being his members, for the head cannot be born, or be, without the members."[129]   (Ignatius, AD 110)

Behold, they that are enlightened, and have tasted, fall... He that has these things falls; but he that has charity, or love cannot fall.[130]
                                              (Macarius Aegyptus, AD 350)

The book of Hebrews adds greatly to our understanding of the relationship between faith, perseverance, and salvation. There are strong indications that it was written during a turbulent time when the pressure to forsake Christianity was intense. Apparently, some Jews within the Christian community were tempted to go back to Judaism as a means of evading persecution while at the same time continuing to serve the God of Abraham.

The main purpose of the epistle to the Hebrews is to show the superiority of the New Covenant over the Old Covenant and to prove that with the coming of Christ the form of worship prescribed in the Old Covenant has expired, rendering it now unacceptable as way to approach God. In light of this fact, the author of Hebrews exhorts his readers to persevere in the Christian faith in spite of all the hardships, warning that those who apostatize and abandon the Christian church will incur eternal perdition.

Written as a word of exhortation (Heb. 13:22), the epistle serves as an example for all times of the biblical approach to addressing those who profess Christianity in times of trial. When persecution sets in, it exposes the unbelievers among the professing Christians, just as the hot sun exposes the

---

129 Ignatius, quoted by John Gill, *The Cause of God and of Truth*, Part 4, Chapter 5, Section 3, The Ultimate Christian Library (Rio, Wisconsin: AGES Software, 2000), 809.

130 Macarius Aegyptus, quoted by John Gill, *The Cause of God and of Truth*, Part 4, Chapter 5, Section 14, The Ultimate Christian Library (Rio, Wisconsin: AGES Software, 2000), 832.

plants with no root in the parable of the sower. For those who may never have experienced true conversion, this becomes the hour of truth, and it is crucial to speak to them frankly about the condition of their souls and their eternal destiny:

> Why, then, does the Writer bother to warn his readers? He wants them to give attention to the danger of apostasy, in which men believe themselves to be truly saved when they are not. The consequence is that eventually they fall away, in spite of once having made a fair profession of faith in Christ. Such people need to be warned of their condition while they are still receptive towards spiritual things, so that they might turn to Christ in true repentance and faith before it is too late.[131]

At the same time, it is also true that real believers are not immune to temptations. The desire to escape suffering continues to be natural in those who have been saved and possess a sincere commitment to follow Christ at any cost. In times of trial, they too need encouragement.

As noted in the previous chapter, warning against the danger of apostasy is one of the means by which God providentially preserves the souls of his saints. So as we interpret Hebrews, the question is not whether the warnings are intended for real Christians or for nominal Christians, as if only one of the two were within the scope of their application. The same message can bring spiritual benefit to those in either condition. After all, the fact that somebody is being tempted to abandon Christ is no proof that a true conversion has never taken place.

So assuming there may be both kinds of people in our midst, as we ourselves hold fast the confession of our hope without wavering, it is perfectly legitimate to consider how to stir up one another to love and good works, encouraging one another (Heb. 10:23–25). The reality that the saints must persevere or perish makes it totally appropriate to remind them of this fact in order to boost them on in the right direction.

There is no justification in concluding, as some commentators do, that all those addressed in the warning passages must necessarily be true Christians because they are treated as such. While it is true they are called "holy brothers, you who share in a heavenly calling" (Heb. 3:1), for instance, it is simply a mistake to see this as anything more than an acknowledgment that they professed to be believers. No doubt many of the Hebrews were truly saved, but it is just as certain that there were unbelievers among them as well.

---

131 Edgar Andrews, *A Glorious High Throne: Hebrews Simply Explained* (Darlington, England: Evangelical Press, 2003), 105.

Biblical authors writing under divine inspiration were not omniscient[132] and would not necessarily know whether their readers were saved or not. So it was incumbent upon them, just as it is on us, to treat those who have made a credible profession of faith as brothers and sisters in Christ.

Just as Philip was blameless when he unwittingly baptized the unconverted Simon Magus (Acts 8:13), so should we not impugn anyone's conversion, unless we have a good reason for doing so. The mere fact that someone is struggling with temptations along the way is certainly not enough to warrant such a call. Out of concern, we may charge those who are wavering to examine themselves as to whether they are truly in the faith (2 Cor. 13:5), but it would be overly hasty to conclude that someone's faith is spurious, unless that person has indeed apostatized.

In the same way, the author of Hebrews is willing to give the vacillating the benefit of the doubt. He calls them "brothers" without really knowing how many and which among them were truly converted. Yet while doing so, he rallies all of them to make their calling and election sure.

By his own admission, this tension is in his mind as he writes: "Though we speak in this way, yet in your case, beloved, we feel sure of better things—things that belong to salvation" (Heb. 6:9).

THE FIRST WARNING PASSAGE

Having made these preliminary considerations, we are now ready to examine the warning passages in Hebrews and their implications as to the doctrine of the perseverance of the saints. The epistle wastes no time getting to its subject. From the outset, it embarks on the mission of persuading its readers to retain their allegiance to Christianity by reminding us of who Jesus is. He is declared to be the Son of God, the heir of all things, the Creator of the universe (Heb. 1:2). He is shown to be the one who upholds the universe by the word of his power, being the radiance of the glory of God and the exact expression of God's own nature (Heb. 1:3).

The author next proceeds to demonstrate by way of contrast how Jesus is superior to angels in that he is the very Son of the Father (Heb. 1:5) whom the angels are commanded to worship (1:6) and the Creator God who laid the foundation of the earth in the beginning and who will reign over all creation forever (Heb. 1:8–12).

---

132 See 1 Cor. 1:16, Gal. 4:20; 2 Cor. 12:2–3; Col. 1:23; 1 Thess. 3:8.

In keeping with these facts, the epistle argues that rebelling against the leading of the Lord Jesus Christ and despising the New Covenant of which he is the mediator is even worse than the offense of those who previously rejected what was delivered through Moses, the angels, or the prophets. His reasoning is from the lesser to the greater:

> Therefore we must pay much closer attention to what we have heard, lest we drift away from it. For since the message declared by angels proved to be reliable and every transgression or disobedience received a just retribution, how shall we escape if we neglect such a great salvation? It was declared at first by the Lord, and it was attested to us by those who heard, while God also bore witness by signs and wonders and various miracles and by gifts of the Holy Spirit distributed according to his will. (Heb. 2:1–4)

In this first warning passage, it is really important for us to grasp the level of commitment to the Christian faith that is being demanded. The author urges each Christian to determine to remain faithful at any cost, for he understands that those who lack an unshakable commitment are in grave danger. They are, in effect, neglecting so great a salvation, whereas "we must give the more earnest heed to the things we have heard, lest we drift away" (Heb. 2:1 NKJV).

It is unacceptable to take the position that says, "I'm in for now, and depending on how things go, I may or may not stay in." It is imperative that we take a once-for-all stand that says, "I will remain loyal to Christ, come what may!" This is not the only passage where the author's dissatisfaction over the lack of commitment he senses in his audience spills over. Further ahead (Heb. 5:11–14), the writer protests his readers' indifference to spiritual growth as evidenced by how little progress they had made in a considerable period of time. There appeared to be a lack of dedication, a disinterest in pursuing deeper knowledge of biblical truths.

Rebukes of this order yield insight into the mind of the author of Hebrews. Some who professed faith in Christ were actually quite superficial in their commitment. Their attachment to the truths of the Gospel was not deep enough to prevent them from turning away when faced with the mounting opposition that was coming upon the church.

That is why the epistle calls upon all within the visible church to take an inventory regarding how committed they really were, forcefully exhorting the fickle to waste no time in taking a definitive stand for Christ. In a manner of speech, it is saying, "How long will you hesitate between two opinions?" (1 Kings 18:21) If Jesus is the Messiah, commit to following him with all your heart and never look back! He insists that his readers must be resolute, because anything short of wholehearted loyalty is unacceptable to God. And it would be an error to nurture hope of eternal life in those who profess faith but still desire to keep their options open in case they ever decide it has become more expedient to turn back.

THE SECOND WARNING PASSAGE

Chapter 3 presents us with the second warning passage. The chapter explores how Christ is superior to Moses. We are instructed to consider Jesus, the apostle and high priest of our confession (Heb. 3:1), and realize that he "has been counted worthy of more glory than Moses—as much more glory as the builder of a house has more honor than the house itself" (Heb. 3:3).

This identification of Jesus as the Creator God who is "the builder of all things" (Heb. 3:4) becomes a strong argument for our being faithful unto him. After all, what was the example of Moses if not one of being faithful to God in all things (Heb. 3:5)? But sadly, the Scriptures also narrate how in the days of Moses many of the Hebrews resisted his leadership.

The author sees in this a parallel between what occurred when Moses led the exodus and when Jesus came introducing the New Covenant. He points out that the same resistance to God's leading was happening again. Through Jesus, a new exodus of sorts was underway, one in which he was leading his people to a celestial Promised Land.

But tragically, in the days of old, not all who went out under the guidance of the divinely designated prophet and lawgiver actually entered into the Promised Land. In the same way, not all who purported to follow the leadership of Christ would arrive at the Eternal Home, and for the same reason: unbelief.

To Hebrew readers, this approach is devastating. Their whole lives they had denounced the wickedness of their ancestors in rebelling against Moses's leadership. Would they now vacillate in following the One to whom Moses pointed? The One who is greater than Moses?

When writing to the mostly gentile church in Corinth, Paul takes up the same line of reasoning, drawing lessons for Christians from the Israelites' mistakes:

I want you to know, brothers, that our fathers were all under the cloud, and all passed through the sea, and all were baptized into Moses in the cloud and in the sea, and all ate the same spiritual food, and all drank the same spiritual drink. For they drank from the spiritual Rock that followed them, and the Rock was Christ. Nevertheless, with most of them God was not pleased, for they were overthrown in the wilderness. Now these things took place as examples for us, that we might not desire evil as they did. Do not be idolaters as some of them were; as it is written, "The people sat down to eat and drink and rose up to play." We must not indulge in sexual immorality as some of them did, and twenty-three thousand fell in a single day. We must not put Christ to the test, as some of them did and were destroyed by serpents, nor grumble, as some of them did and were destroyed by the Destroyer. Now these things happened to them as an example, but they were written down for our instruction, on whom the end of the ages has come. Therefore let anyone who thinks that he stands take heed lest he fall. (1 Cor. 10:1–12)

What Paul points out is that in spite of all the benefits they had received and of all the external identifications with Christ (1 Cor. 10:1–4), most of those who went out from Egypt with Moses were not pleasing to God (1 Cor. 10:5). But why? Because although they had witnessed the power of God, they were still rebellious unbelievers in their hearts.

There is no doubt that the individuals under scrutiny had never experienced saving grace. The author of Hebrews recalls God's woeful evaluation of those insubordinate souls: "They always go astray in their heart; they have not known my ways" (Heb. 3:10). The sad reality is that many Israelites who rejoiced in being delivered from Egyptian slavery were not interested in freedom from the slavery of sin. They ended up dying in the desert for their unbelief and its consequent disobedience.

Paul asserts that this should put us on alert: "Therefore let anyone who thinks that he stands take heed lest he fall" (1 Cor. 10:5). In other words, anyone who considers himself a follower of Christ needs to beware so as not to fall according to the bad example of the Israelites.

This is the same concern as we find voiced in Hebrews 3. There may be people in the Christian community who will reveal themselves to be unbelievers despite all their external associations with the people of God. For the attentive reader, it becomes evident that this is precisely what Hebrews chapter 3 is warning against, particularly in verses 6 and 14. As was noted in the previous chapter, these verses oblige us to discard any hypothesis that a true Christian will ever apostatize. We can only gain from turning our attention to them once more:

> But Christ as a Son over His own house, whose house we are if we hold fast the confidence and the rejoicing of the hope firm to the end... For we have become partakers of Christ if we hold the beginning of our confidence steadfast to the end. (Heb. 3:6–14, NKJV)

The first of these two verses establishes that any assumption on our part that we are presently the house of God is only confirmed as a reality in the case of those of us who "hold fast the confidence and the rejoicing of the hope firm to the end." The second verse denies that anyone who fails to hold the faith steadfast to the end was ever a partaker of Christ.

Since according to the book of Hebrews the legitimacy of one's conversion is only admitted on the grounds of perseverance, there is no margin left for the idea that the warning passages imply that there is a possibility that true saints will commit apostasy. Readers are not so much being put on guard against *developing* an unbelieving heart. The exhortations are instead a caution against the very real danger of *possessing* an unbelieving heart (just like the Hebrews from the time of the exodus) despite having made a profession of faith and having become externally identified with Christ.

Such an internal condition will end up causing a person to depart from the living God, just as the warning goes on to spell out:

> Take care, brothers, lest there be in any of you an evil, unbelieving heart, leading you to fall away from the living God. But exhort one another every day, as long as it is called "today," that none of you may be hardened by the deceitfulness of sin. For we share in Christ, if indeed we hold our original confidence firm to the end. (Heb. 3:12–14)

The big issue in the book of Hebrews is whether or not we possess real faith. True faith is proven by the fruits of sanctification and perseverance. The lack of these betrays a heart of unbelief. At the time of Moses, those who believed obeyed. The reason why people were excluded from the Promised Land was their unbelief. "The word which they heard did not profit them, not being mixed with faith in those who heard (it)" (Heb. 4:2, NKJV). "So we see that they were unable to enter because of unbelief" (Heb. 3:19).

The same truth continues to apply today. Those who rebel are the unbelievers in our midst. Such were those who left Egypt led by Moses yet whose bodies ended up falling in the wilderness (Heb. 3:16–17). However, all who believe enter the Promised Land. The question that is left hanging before each reader is, "What about you? What kind of follower are you?"

Entrance into the eternal paradise is promised to every Christian. Nevertheless, the epistle alerts us that while "a promise remains of entering his rest, let us fear lest any of you seem to have come short of it" (Heb. 4:1, NKJV).

So what exactly determines whether someone enters the promised rest or falls short of it? As the epistle goes on to explain, the same truth is reaffirmed—that is, that just as in the days of Moses, those who do not possess real faith are the ones who end up failing, whereas those who truly believe go on to enter the longed-for rest:

> For indeed the gospel was preached to us as well as to them; but the word which they heard did not profit them, not being mixed with faith in those who heard it. For we who have believed do enter that rest...Let us therefore be diligent to enter that rest, lest anyone fall according to the same example of disobedience. (Heb. 4:2–11, NKJV)

These words constitute a summons to self-examination, of the sort, "Examine yourselves, to see whether you are in the faith" (2 Cor. 13:5), besides being an exhortation to persevere and not give up due to the difficulties. The formula is quite simple: (1) those who did not benefit from the Word received were those who heard it without faith, while (2) those who hear it and actually believe *do* enter the promised rest.

In summary, this warning passage not only teaches that apostates do not enter into the eternal rest, but also teaches that the only ones who apostatize are those who had never become partakers of Christ by faith.

THE THIRD WARNING PASSAGE

Chapter 5 resumes the apology for the superiority of Christ, showing how Jesus meets all the requirements to be our high priest as he is the fulfillment of Psalm 110's prophecy of an unchanging priest according to the order of Melchizedek.

But before delving any deeper into this subject, the author digresses into another exhortation. Concerned that his readers may find such matters difficult to understand, he reprimands the way in which some of them were squandering opportunities to grow in their understanding of Christian doctrine, as was evidenced by how slowly they were making progress (Heb. 5:11–14). His desire was to see them moving beyond a comprehension of merely the elementary principles of the teaching of Christ (Heb. 6:1), yet he fears that might not be possible in the case of all his readers.

"This we will do," he says, "if God permits" (6:3). This way of putting it suggests that their proceeding in the right direction might actually be impossible, being prevented by the Lord God himself. The cause for this fear is then shared in the following verses (Heb. 6:4–6), where we come across the most frightening warning found in the book.

His grave pronouncement makes it clear that certain people who are still alive in this world are already beyond being forgiven or given a second chance. This is the case of those who fall away after having graciously received some very special privileges that the author goes to the trouble of spelling out very carefully and in detail:

> For it is impossible to restore again to repentance those who have once been enlightened, who have tasted the heavenly gift, and have shared in the Holy Spirit, and have tasted the goodness of the word of God and the powers of the age to come, if they then fall away, since they are crucifying once again the Son of God to their own harm and holding him up to contempt. (Heb. 6:4–6)

These solemn verses have been the cause of much debate down through the centuries, even causing the canonicity of the epistle to the Hebrews to be temporarily impugned by some Christians. It is easy to discern that the text signifies that there is a risk of falling in such a way that repentance becomes an impossibility, ruling out all hope of forgiveness. The reality of this danger is underscored in chapter 12:

> See to it…that no one is sexually immoral or unholy like Esau, who sold his birthright for a single meal. For you know that *afterward*, when he desired to inherit the blessing, he was rejected, for *he found no chance to repent*, though he sought it with tears.
> (Heb. 12:15–17; emphasis added)

Ambrose, Aquinas, Erasmus, and some others have tried to escape this conclusion by suggesting that the word *impossible* in Hebrews 6:4 denotes no more than an improbability. However, there is no linguistic evidence to support such a conclusion.

Others have sought a way out by proposing that we should translate the word *crucifying* in verse 6 in a temporal sense, making it mean that it is only impossible to restore them again to repentance *as long as* they proceed crucifying once again the Son of God to their own harm. But there is no justification for translating the verse in such a way, firstly because it is highly improbable in light of the relevant grammatical considerations, and secondly because it constitutes an obvious subversion of the text's clearly intended meaning.

As F. F. Bruce rightly noted:

> To say that they cannot be brought to repentance so long as they persist in their renunciation of Christ would be a truism hardly worth putting into words. The participle "crucifying" is much more appropriately taken as causal than as temporal in force; it indicates *why* it is impossible for such people to repent and make a new beginning.[133]

This element in the text may be unpleasant, but it is unavoidable.

What will prove even more difficult, though, is reaching a consensus on the meaning of the privileges cited and the nature of the fall the author has in mind. Controversies run as far back as the Patristic period, when it became the battleground in the controversy with the Novatians, who understood the text as a statement to the effect that there can be no forgiveness to people who fell after having been baptized. They specifically took the expression "those who have once been enlightened" as meaning those who had received baptism.

Owen informs us that in some churches the definition adopted for the words *fall away* came to be very broad indeed, making readmission into church impossible for all those who fell into any notorious sin after having been baptized:

> But upon flagitious and scandalous crimes, such as murder, adultery, or idolatry, in many churches they would never admit those who had been guilty of them into their communion any more. Their greatest and most signal trial was with respect unto them who, through fear of death, complied with the Gentiles in their idolatrous worship in the time of persecution.[134]

---

133 F. F. Bruce, *The Epistle to the Hebrews* (Grand Rapids, Michigan: Eerdmans Publishing Co., 1981), 124 (emphasis in original).

134 John Owen, *Exposition on Hebrews*, vol. 21 of The Works of John Owen (Rio, WI: Ages Software Inc., 2000), 82–83.

Other churches and their leaders recognized the harm in such a practice, but being uncertain as to whether or not they could effectively refute the Novatian interpretation, they opted for rejecting the authority of the epistle altogether rather than risk damage to their congregations from the misuse of this particular passage.

The Reformed commentator Simon Kistemaker explains how this issue cast doubt on the canonicity of Hebrews in some circles, keeping it from gaining full acceptance throughout the Western church until the fourth century:[135]

> Novatian, a native of Phrygia in Asia Minor, used Hebrews 6:4–6 against all Christians who had fallen away because of these persecutions. Novatian was of the opinion that it was impossible for them to come to repentance; they were cut off from the church and denied readmission. The application of this Scripture passage in the rigorous manners of the Montanists and the Novatians did not meet with approval in the church. Because of these schismatic movements and their abuse of this particular passage, the Epistle to the Hebrews was not placed among the canonical books of the New Testament in the West.[136]

In retrospect, it is easy to see that belief in the inspiration and canonicity of Hebrews was not misplaced and that the error lied totally in the Novatians' misguided interpretation of the chapter 6 warning passage. Just how unjustified they were in their rigor can be seen in the fact that the Bible elsewhere recounts real cases of baptized Christians who committed grievous sins, but whose repentance was deemed enough for their continued acceptance and/or reinstatement in the church (1 Cor. 5:1–13; 2 Cor. 2:5–11; Luke. 22:32–34).

As Owen observed,

> And so usually doth it fall out, very unhappily, with men who think they see some peculiar opinion or persuasion in some *singular text* of Scripture, and will not bring their interpretations of it unto the analogy of faith, whereby they might see how contrary it is to the whole design and current of the word in other places.[137]

---

135 Simon Kistemaker, *Hebrews New Testament Commentary* (Grand Rapids, MI: Baker Book House, 1989), 13–14.

136 Ibid., 13.

137 John Owen, *Exposition on Hebrews*, vol. 21 of *The Works of John Owen* (Rio, WI: Ages Software Inc., 2000), 83–84 (emphasis in original).

If instead of insisting on their point of view that they based solely on their interpretation of an obscure passage in Scripture, they had been cautious enough to reject any position that was in blatant conflict with the rest of the biblical message, they would have recognized the wisdom crystalized in the old adage to the effect that whoever preaches a doctrine that can only be supported by one biblical passage may find, under more careful investigation, that it actually isn't found in any biblical passages at all.

We should keep this lesson in the back of our minds today as well. We do well not to raise a doctrinal edifice on top of Hebrews 6 that puts it at odds with the teaching of the Bible as a whole and then endeavor to overcome the difficulties by means of a tidal wave of biblical reinterpretation, forcing everything else to rearrange itself in order to achieve the appearance of harmony.

That is exactly what happens when this passage is used as a proof text for the doctrine that salvation can be lost, expecting all other biblical passages to follow suit and step in time.

So what is the real meaning of this warning? There are currently four ways of interpreting this controversial passage. The interpretation that has received greatest support among Reformed Christians maintains that the text describes people who have been ingratiated with an enormous measure of the truth but who, short of experiencing a true conversion, end up turning their backs on the light with which they were endowed.

According to this view, the ones who are portrayed as falling away have never experienced regeneration, although they may have professed the Christian faith for a time before openly repudiating Christianity. This interpretation sees the passage as a warning against a real possibility of falling away that is pertinent to people in the visible church who are contemplating abandoning their profession of faith. They are warned that a person who apostatizes after having received the degree of privilege and enlightenment described becomes irremediably condemned.

A few who follow this line of interpretation believe that the kind of blessing here described is so great that it must involve personally witnessing the miracles of Jesus or the apostles, so that only people living in those days could qualify.

In contrast with the first interpretation, a minority among the Reformed believe that genuine Christians are described in the text, but maintain that in no way does this understanding lend support to the possibility of Christians losing their salvation because they see the warning as merely hypothetical in nature. The passage is perceived as intending to point out what the implications would be if a believer did fall away, although such a thing could never happen.

According to this view, its role can be described as strengthening our resolve to persevere as believers by calling our attention to the fact that apostasy on our part would result in an irreversible separation from the grace of God.

In the Arminian camp, the predominant view is that the passage is a warning to true believers of a very real possibility of falling away and ending up eternally lost. Those who defend this view arrive naturally at this conclusion, since they are convinced that the author's selection of words cannot be anything other than a description of genuine believers and that his dire tone is incompatible with a mere supposition about an impossibility.

The interpretation that concludes our rundown of current views on Hebrews 6, which also happens to be the most recent, is that of the Arminians who regard perseverance as unnecessary for final salvation. They believe the text has in mind saved individuals who fall away by apostasy but who experience no loss of salvation by doing so. It is claimed that the only loss envisioned is the forfeiting of spiritual growth and the attainment of a greater degree of honor to be enjoyed throughout eternity.

It should be recognized from the outset that none of these interpretations are free from difficulties and that they all run into objections, as will be noted ahead. Nevertheless, by examining the text carefully and objectively, it is not beyond our capacity to identify which one is able to respond to its critics satisfactorily, besides holding on faithfully to the analogy of faith.

To this end, we must consider three crucial questions around which the debate revolves:

1. Does falling away entail eternal perdition or nothing more than the loss of rewards?

2. Is there a real possibility of falling away, or is that only a hypothetical supposition?

3. Is the description intended to single out true Christians?

DOES FALLING AWAY ENTAIL ETERNAL PERDITION OR NOTHING MORE THAN THE LOSS OF REWARDS?

The weakest of the four views is clearly the one that claims it is possible for Christians to fall in the way described and still remain saved. This interpretation is part of the erroneous doctrinal system that was rejected in chapter 1 of this book. According to that vein of thought, the book of Hebrews as a whole exhorts Christians to persevere not because perseverance is essential to salvation but in order to secure a greater number of rewards in the kingdom of God. As was observed in chapter 1, this approach does not do justice to the warning passages of Hebrews 2, 3, 4, and 10.

We find the same thing to be true as we look at Hebrews chapter 6, where those who fall away find that their "end is to be burned" (Heb. 6:8), having come under the curse of God. The language is reminiscent of John the Baptist proclaiming, "Every tree therefore that does not bear good fruit is cut down and thrown into the fire." (Matt. 3:10).

It is inconceivable to speak in such a way of people who enter the blessedness of eternal life. Moreover, a clear distinction is made between this end (to be burned) and salvation since the author expresses that he is confident of "better things—things that belong to salvation" (Heb. 6:9) in the case of his readers, although he feels compelled to write to them in these terms.

We should, therefore, reject this interpretation because it ignores the grave nature of the condemnation the text pronounces upon those who fall away, besides the fact that it is patently at odds with the rest of Holy Scripture.

IS THERE A REAL POSSIBILITY OF FALLING AWAY, OR IS THAT ONLY A HYPOTHETICAL SUPPOSITION?

The main difficulty in reading this passage as nothing more than a supposition is found in the fact that the author goes so far as to actually question whether his readers will be able to go on and progress beyond the elementary teachings of Christ. Although he is inclined to believe better things in their case (Heb. 6:9), his manner of speaking seems to indicate that in his mind the question as to whether or not his readers will persevere is still unsettled. He says, "This we will do if God permits" (Heb. 6:3), and next tells us that the cause for such reservations is that "it is impossible to restore again to repentance those who have once been enlightened," etc., "if they then fall away" (Heb. 6:4–6).

Though grammatical considerations of themselves may not be conclusive, aorist participles as employed in verses 4–6 are not normally used when speaking of something that is hypothetical, which favors the idea that there have been real cases of people who met this description and then fell away, finding themselves beyond all hope of being renewed unto repentance.

If that is what the author intends to say, then there must be a real possibility for people who match the description to actually fall away, as uncommon as such a thing may be. If it has happened before, we have good reason to fear that others may also wander down that same road of no return.

IS THE DESCRIPTION INTENDED TO SINGLE OUT TRUE CHRISTIANS?

The most widely held interpretation among Reformed Christians is attacked by critics for denying that the characteristics cited in verses 4 and 5 apply exclusively to Christians. According to these verses, repentance is out of the question for someone who falls away after having been enlightened, tasted the heavenly gift, shared in the Holy Spirit, and tasted the goodness of the Word of God, as well as the powers of the age to come.

Many have become persuaded that these things are inseparably linked to a real conversion. For instance, Homer Kent feels comfortable defending that the text presents a hypothesis that can never materialize but dismisses the notion that those described could be anything other than true Christians, saying he is doubtful "whether the same description if found elsewhere would ever be explained by these interpreters in any other way than full regeneration."[138]

Naturally, this opinion is shared by those who believe this passage constitutes evidence that saints can apostatize. Indeed, their doctrine depends totally on identifying those who are here stated to have fallen away as people who had unmistakably been regenerate and justified. After all, the fact that people abandon their profession of faith in Christianity does not prove that salvation may be lost unless it can be confirmed that some individuals who have done so had truly been saved. But in this case, the Arminians display great confidence.

After expounding his interpretation of each attribute found in verses 4 and 5, Picirilli concludes the following:

Of these four clauses as a whole, then, we may say that one would

---

138 Homer A. Kent, *The Epistle to the Hebrews: A Commentary* (Grand Rapids, MI: Baker Book House, 1972), 112.

be hard put to find a better description of genuine regeneration and conversion. Either of them will stand by itself in this respect. The four together provide one of the finest statements about salvation, from its experimental side, that appears anywhere in the Scriptures.[139]

According to this point of view, the sense of these verses would essentially be that it is impossible to renew unto repentance those who fall away after having been saved. For sake of argument, if we assume this to be the correct meaning of the text, and assuming that people thus described do fall away, then the text would really be teaching that true Christians can fall away unto perdition.

However, that is not all it would be teaching. It would also mean that there can never be forgiveness or a second chance for any Christian who crossed that line, a detail that Arminians are rarely willing to incorporate into their belief system. With very few exceptions, the concept on the loss of salvation taught in Arminian churches is that salvation can be regained if lost. At the end of the day, salvation becomes somewhat like a revolving door in a world of repeated regeneration.

Hebrews chapter 6 allows for no such thing. It narrows the options down to just two: (1) either the text has nothing to do with a saved person losing his or her salvation, or (2) it teaches that salvation can be lost but only *once*, never to be regained, which is in blatant conflict with the doctrine of the vast majority of those who appeal to this passage as evidence that saints can fall from grace.

But before rushing to any conclusions, it is needful to carefully look into the meaning of the words used to describe those who are said to have fallen away. The impossibility of repentance applies to those who fall away after having (1) once been enlightened, (2) tasted the heavenly gift, (3) shared in the Holy Spirit, and (4) tasted the goodness of the Word of God and the powers of the age to come (Heb. 6:4–5).

Some contend that these words can only be taken to mean that we are dealing with people who had come to possess eternal life. Could they be right?

In spite of the confidence with which this thesis is advanced, an objective investigation shows that it falls short of any real proof. Even more significantly, the immediate context militates strongly for us to conclude the very opposite, as do other relevant passages of Scripture. We must begin,

---

139 Robert E. Picirilli, *Grace, Faith, and Free Will* (Nashville: Randall House, 2002), 219.

therefore, by examining the meaning of the words themselves that make up this detailed description.

In the early church, it became popular to interpret the clause "those who have once been enlightened" as synonymous with those who had once been baptized. This is due to the fact that from Justin Martyr onward receiving baptism became increasingly referred to as receiving enlightenment. But there is no convincing reason to read this understanding back into Hebrews since, as far as we can tell, baptism was never spoken of in these terms in the first century.

Instead, we find that both in the New and in the Old Testament the term enlighten is used to speak of the transmission of spiritual truth. Consequently, "those who have once been enlightened" are those who received instruction in the Gospel and understood it, having received enough light to become persuaded as to its veracity. That a full enlightenment is meant can be gathered from the use of ἅπαξ, which is here translated as "once."

One thing about which the words "those who have once been enlightened" are completely silent, however, is regarding the manner in which such people reacted to the light they were given. They do not tell us whether or not the light met with acceptance in the heart. Having one's eyes open in this way is not the same as being saved, although it is an indispensable step for true conversion to come about.

The second thing we are told about those who cannot repent is that they are people "who have tasted the heavenly gift." Several views are set forth as to what the "heavenly gift" is: the Lord Jesus (John 6:32–35), salvation or the forgiveness of sins (Rom. 6:23), the Lord's Supper (1 Cor. 11:23), or simply the teaching of spiritual truth (Eph. 4:7–11). Kistemaker suggests that it would be improper to limit the meaning to any one single idea since the word *gift* is used for such a broad range of ideas in the New Testament:

> Suppose that someone has attended the worship services of the church, has made profession of faith, has been baptized, and has taken part in the active life of the church; he has tasted the broken bread and taken the cup offered to him at the celebration of the Lord's Supper. Then this new convert has indeed tasted the heavenly gift.[140]

---

140 Simon Kistemaker, *Hebrews New Testament Commentary* (Grand Rapids, MI: Baker Book House, fourth printing, 1989), 158.

But even if we identify the "heavenly gift" as salvation or as a reference to Jesus himself, we still will not have arrived at a reason to conclude that we are speaking of people who were saved. Several commentators highlight the fact that "tasted" is not the same as "received." When Jesus declared himself to be the true bread from heaven, sent by the Father, his message was poignant:

I am the living bread that came down from heaven. If anyone eats of this bread, he will live forever. And the bread that I will give for the life of the world is my flesh. (John 6:51)

Yet what we find in Hebrews doesn't go quite so far. The word *taste* is frequently used to indicate an experimental sensing the flavor without the commitment of ingesting:

The expression of "tasting" is metaphorical, and signifies no more but to make a trial or experiment; for so we do by tasting naturally and properly of that which is tendered unto us to eat. We taste such things by the sense given us to discern our food, and then either receive or refuse them, as we find occasion. It doth not therefore include eating, much less digestion and turning into nourishment of what is so tasted; for its nature being only thereby discerned, it may be refused...It is therefore properly to make an experiment or trial of any thing, whether it be received or refused, and is sometimes opposed to eating and digestion, as Matthew 27:34 ["they offered him wine to drink, mixed with gall, but when he tasted it, he would not drink it"].[141]

This great gift, however, was not received. It was not feasted on, but only **tasted**, sampled. It was not accepted or lived, only examined.[142]

Those who are determined to equate "tasted the heavenly gift" with receiving salvation routinely present verses where "taste" indicates much more than an evaluation or test. For instance, in Hebrews 2:9 (emphasis added), we read, "But we see him who for a little while was made lower than the angels, namely Jesus, crowned with glory and honor because of the suffering of death, so that by the grace of God he might *taste death* for everyone."

---

141 John Owen, *The Nature and Causes Of Apostasy from the Gospel*, vol. 7 of *The Works of John Owen* (Rio, WI: Ages Software Inc., 2000), 39–41.

142 John F. MacArthur, *The MacArthur New Testament Commentary: Hebrews* (Chicago: Moody Press, 1983), 143 (emphasis in original).

When Jesus went so far as to "taste" death for everyone, he obviously did more than get a small "taste" of what it means to die without actually dying. He drank the cup to the last drop. So no one is contesting the fact that the word *taste* can have a more complete meaning. But it would be insincere and arbitrary to claim this *must* be the word's meaning here, omitting the fact that the same Greek word is also used to signify an undecided trial procedure, as it does in Matthew 27:34:

> The word "tasted," which is repeated, can mean to "perceive the flavour of, partake of, enjoy, feel, make trial of, experience." Although the word can be used of genuine spiritual experience (e.g. Ps. 34:8; 1 Pet. 2:3), it can equally signify something temporary or superficial.[143]

This is all that is needed to bring down the attempts at using this attribute as proof that those here described *can only be* regenerate people. All we can say for certain is that they felt a taste of the heavenly gift. We cannot go beyond what the inspired text actually says. This leaves us having examined two of the characteristics here listed without having run into anything that could only be said of someone who had been saved.

The words "have shared in the Holy Spirit" are sometimes taken to mean that these people received the Holy Spirit within, in the sense of becoming the temple of the Holy Spirit. This reading is not necessary, nor probable. The Greek term here translated as "shared" or "partakers" (NKJV) is never used in that sense. It is a word used to denote association, as the Greek scholar Kenneth Wuest points out:

> Those unsaved Hebrews had become participators or partakers of the Holy Spirit in that they willingly cooperated with Him in receiving His pre-salvation work of leading them step by step toward the act of faith in Messiah as high priest...The word *metechos* in no way indicates that these Hebrews possess the Holy Spirit as a permanent indweller such as a saved person today does.[144]

We may perceive the force of this term by its usage in 1 Corinthians:

> Consider the people of Israel: are not those who eat the sacrifices participants in the altar? What do I imply then? That food offered to

143 Edgar Andrews, *A Glorious High Throne: Hebrews Simply Explained* (Darlington, England: Evangelical Press, 2003), 166.

144 Kenneth S. Wuest, "Hebrews Six in the Greek New Testament," *Bibliotheca Sacra* 119, January 1962, 48.

idols is anything, or that an idol is anything? No, I imply that what pagans sacrifice they offer to demons and not to God. I do not want you to be participants with demons. You cannot drink the cup of the Lord and the cup of demons. You cannot partake of the table of the Lord and the table of demons. (1 Cor. 10:18–21)

According to this passage, one should not go to a pagan temple and partake in its rituals because by doing so one becomes a participant or partaker with demons. This is true whether one really believes in the pagan religion or not, whether one participates wholeheartedly, skeptically, or even cynically. By the same standard, the act of partaking in the Lord's table brings one into association with the Lord, even if done in an unworthy manner, which exposes the undiscerning to judgment (1 Cor. 11:29–33).

So what would be necessary for a person to "have shared in the Holy Spirit"?

Partakers (Greek, *metochos*) has to do with association, not possession. These Jews had never possessed the Holy Spirit, they simply were around when He was around... It is possible to have an association with the **Holy Spirit**, to share in what He does, and not be saved.[145]

Sharing in the Holy Spirit implies that this is done in fellowship with other believers. And the Spirit of God manifests himself in various spiritual gifts given to the members of the church (1 Cor. 12:7–11).[146]

"Put simply, this means that the Spirit 'inhabits' the true believer, but may merely 'operate' upon the unregenerate."[147] Indeed, the Holy Spirit came upon unsaved men such as Balaam, Saul, and Caiaphas causing them to prophesy, or to cast out demons and to cure diseases, as in the case of Judas (Luke 9:1). Moreover, if we understand the working of the Holy Spirit in the history of redemption, we can easily see how since the coming of Christ a personal involvement with the Christ's church would be one way in which a person may be said to "have shared in the Holy Spirit."

---

145 John F. MacArthur, *The MacArthur New Testament Commentary: Hebrews* (Chicago: Moody Press, 1983), 144.

146 Simon Kistemaker, *Hebrews New Testament Commentary* (Grand Rapids, MI: Baker Book House, fourth printing, 1989), 159.

147 Edgar Andrews, *A Glorious High Throne: Hebrews Simply Explained* (Darlington, England: Evangelical Press, 2003), 166.

Last of all, the Sacred Text describes these individuals who fall irremediably as people who "have tasted the goodness of the word of God and the powers of the age to come." Once more, we find that their experiences are of an external kind but of great importance. They had a sufficient measure of contact with the good word of God and with the powers of the age to come to render their rejection of Christianity a deliberate sin for which there is no attenuating degree of ignorance. They could never claim that the truth of the Christian message had not been objectively proven to them.

"The powers of the age to come" can be identified with the "signs and wonders and various miracles" (Heb. 2:4) by which God himself bore witness to the Christian Gospel. Such miraculous events announced the arrival of the messianic era and provided a sample of the power that will bring to pass the coming resurrection, along with the inauguration of new heavens and new earth.

Those who took part in the Christian movement in those first days had the singular opportunity of experiencing in firsthand the dramatic evidence to the effect that Jesus and his apostles truly spoke from God. Those who personally witnessed the accompanying supernatural phenomena could not plead ignorance as to whether or not God was really at work in their midst. Therefore, to publicly repudiate the Christian faith in the face of incontrovertible attestation by the operation of the Holy Spirit put them in the position of blaspheming against him, resulting in the impossibility of forgiveness in their case.

It is those who have been intellectually convinced of the truth who are at risk of so doing. It may be that hearing the Word they receive it immediately with joy, but having no root in themselves, when tribulation or persecution arises on account of the Word (as was going on when the book of Hebrews was written), they immediately fall away (Mark 4:16–17).

The repeated use of the word *tasted* may well be a deliberate way of highlighting the lack of a full-fledged commitment:

Hereof they are said to "taste," as they were before of the heavenly gift. The apostle, as it were, studiously keeps himself to this expression, on purpose to manifest that he intendeth not those who by faith do really receive, feed, and live on Jesus Christ as tendered in the word of the gospel, John 6:35, 49–51, 54–56. It is as if he had said, "I speak not of those who have received and digested the spiritual food of their souls, and turned it into spiritual nourishment, but of such as have so far tasted of it as that they ought to have desired it as sincere milk, to have grown thereby; but they had received such an experiment of its divine truth and power as that it had various effects upon them."[148]

Recalling all these spiritual privileges, we can come to an understanding of what kind of people the author of the epistle has in mind. He is speaking of those who fall away after they have heard the Gospel and comprehended its message, after they were given incontestably persuasive confirmation of its truth (perhaps including miraculous signs), and became fully convinced that the Gospel is indeed true. Such a great degree of privilege immensely compounds the guilt of disavowing the Gospel of Christ.

Having reached the end of our analysis of the characteristics ascribed to the apostates of Hebrews 6:4–6, it should be underscored that we did not come across any of the New Testament's technical terms for saved individuals, such as *saints*, *born again*, *regenerate*, *redeemed*, *justified*, *sanctified*, *adopted*, *forgiven*, *sealed*, etc. All have been carefully avoided.

We thus fail to find anything that would compel us to conclude that the subjects being described were in fact true Christians. The words selected by the Holy Spirit in this description are not even of the sort we would expect to find if the intent were to identify saved people. A lengthy list would not be needed if that had been the point.

On the other hand, if the goal was to specify the degree of revelation that someone would need to experience in order to make their rejection of Christ unpardonable, then such a list makes perfect sense. It is a topic that must be treated very cautiously. We know that great privilege engenders greater accountability. From everyone who has been given, much shall be required (Luke 12:48).

But what we find in Hebrews 6 is that there is a line that, if crossed, will cause a person to become hopelessly lost so that repentance and forgiveness are now utterly impossible. Any inconsequential statement about a matter of this nature carries the potential to do great harm. For instance, imagine the implications of a statement like, "It is impossible to renew unto repentance those who come to understand the Gospel and then fall away." Or, "It is impossible to renew unto repentance those who receive baptism and then fall away."

---

148 John Owen, *The Nature and Causes Of Apostasy from the Gospel*, vol. 7 of *The Works of John Owen* (Rio, WI: Ages Software Inc., 2000), 43.

This was essentially the Novatian interpretation, and history stands to show how much chaos can result from their shallow understanding of the text. So while the author seeks to warn against an unpardonable sin, he is careful to avoid giving the impression that there is no second chance for all people who fall away in general. Such a condemnation applies only to those who fall away after having received the great degree of light he has taken the trouble to set forth in detail.

It is not surprising, therefore, that he goes to the trouble of carefully enumerating a series of privileges, all of which are grandiose. His concern is that misunderstanding at this point would cause readers to lump more people into this condition than they should and drive many needlessly into despair. The point must be made that the only people who find themselves in this irremediable condition are those who fall away after receiving this full measure of light and this profound partaking in the operation of the Holy Spirit.

At the same time, the author is equally careful to avoid using any of the technical terms that would denote salvation, or any terms that could only refer to regenerate people, because we should not suppose that one would need to go as far as being regenerate in order to make his opposition to the Gospel the deliberate and conscious sin for which there can be no forgiveness.

Let us consider the issue from a practical perspective. We know that many people have heard the Gospel proclaimed for years without being converted. They may have understood its message so well that they would be able to evangelize other people, but they have not as of yet been converted. They may even be experiencing a profound conviction of sin and become persuaded that the Gospel is true, but still, they remain hardened.

All these factors aggravate their sin of rebellion, but would anyone dare say that they are already beyond the reach of God's grace? One could not do so on the basis of Hebrews 6:4–6 precisely because the privileges therein described are so rich that we would be unable to affirm that they had all been enjoyed by such people. In fact, the privileges mentioned in the text point to a degree of experience and illumination that is so profound that we would not even be apt to categorically assert that they were all experienced in the case of someone who abandoned the church after having been an active member for a considerable length of time.

That is the usefulness of this very detailed list. It does not allow us to recklessly shut the door of repentance in anyone's face. At the same time, however, it has a grave message for those who are being tempted to apostatize. It brings to bear just how dangerous it is to consciously reject the truth by pointing out that doing so leaves no room for repentance, depending on the amount of light that one has received.

And would any professing Christian dare assure himself not to take the risk as personal? Can people in the visible church truly be sure they have not received the measure of privilege that is here specified?

At one time, the apostle Paul was a persecutor of the church. He rejected the Christian faith and sought to stamp it out. But even though he was formerly a blasphemer and a persecutor and an insolent opponent, he was shown mercy because he had acted ignorantly in unbelief (1 Tim. 1:13).

Paul recognized that his sin would have been far worse had he been opposing the truth of God consciously at that time. But he was not sinning deliberately after receiving the knowledge of the truth (cf. Heb. 10:26). He truly believed in his heart that he was pleasing God by assailing the church. No doubt he knew something of the Christian Gospel, but his mind was convinced that it was a false message. Likewise, there are many other enemies of the truth who know not what they do. This does not make them blameless in their error, but it does leave an open door for repentance and mercy.

This is precisely the point of contrast. Although opposition to the truth is always an extremely serious sin, one is generally allowed to repent and obtain mercy. But once someone has enjoyed all the benefits listed in Hebrews 6:4–5, a decision to turn on Christ becomes much more flagrant, ruling out the possibility of being renewed unto repentance.

The text declares that "it is impossible to restore again to repentance" those who find themselves in such a condition. We should not overlook how different this is from saying that it is impossible to renew their repentance. Indeed, there is no statement here to the effect that they had ever repented:

> "**To renew them again to repentance**" means to restore them unto their previous condition of interest wherein they came very close to being converted. Here we find an emphasis on the fact that although they had been reached by so many blessings and were not far from the Kingdom, they had not crossed the line of repentance. They had been in that state of mind confronted by the hymnist, "So near to the Kingdom, yet what dost thou lack?" In light of their apostasy, the divinely

inspired author asserts that it is impossible to renew them unto their previous spiritual condition which afforded them enough light to allow for repentance. Their mental attitude was now set and unchangeable. They can never be restored in order that they might repent.[149]

The reality for these people is utterly tragic. Previously they had been in a vantage point from whence repentance would have been permissible. Since they proceeded to fall away, they are now denied the possibility of repentance and nothing can ever be done to reverse this fact and take them back to their prior condition of opportunity. It is impossible to restore them again unto repentance.

At this point, before going any further, it must again be underscored that the line—which, if crossed, will permanently disallow for repentance—is drawn short of experiencing true conversion, and this is a matter of utmost importance.

If the text we are considering teaches anything, it is that those who fall away after having been granted the degree of privilege that it delineates cannot be subsequently forgiven. Forgiveness is beyond such people because when that much light is received, it greatly increases a person's responsibility and aggravates the error of rejecting Christ's claim upon our lives. So by teaching us that these people cannot be forgiven, the Bible here also teaches the kind of person who cannot be forgiven. It would be a flat-out contradiction of the text to say that there is no opportunity for repentance even in the case of those who have not gone so far as to taste the amount of revelation and illumination therein described.

THE BLASPHEMY OF THE HOLY SPIRIT

This all leads us to another crucial question: is there any other passage of Scripture that relates to people committing this selfsame sin that could shed some light by comparing Scripture to Scripture and letting the Bible interpret itself? Indeed, there is. The parallel is found in the blasphemy of the Holy Spirit committed by the enemies of Christ.

It can be incontrovertibly demonstrated that their act constituted the same sin of which we read in Hebrews 6, which makes it abundantly clear that it is possible to commit the unpardonable sin without ever having been converted.

---

149 Aníbal Pereira dos Reis, *Pode o Crente Perder a Salvação?* (São Paulo, Brazil, Edições Caminho de Damasco, 1978), 213 (emphasis in original).

This fact completely rules out the interpretation that the characteristics found in Hebrews 6:4–5 are things that belong to a genuine salvation experience.

Let us elaborate on this step-by-step. The unpardonable sin is identified by Jesus:

> Therefore I tell you, every sin and blasphemy will be forgiven people, but the blasphemy against the Spirit will not be forgiven. And whoever speaks a word against the Son of Man will be forgiven, but whoever speaks against the Holy Spirit will not be forgiven, either in this age or in the age to come. (Matt. 12:31–32)

Jesus's statement is categorical to the effect that the sin that had just been committed by the Pharisees (Matt. 12:22–24) cannot be forgiven for all eternity. Furthermore, he emphasized that this particular sin is the *only* sin that is unforgivable. This point is all the more confirmed by cross-referencing with Mark's rendition of the words spoken by our Lord:

> "Truly, I say to you, all sins will be forgiven the children of man, and whatever blasphemies they utter, but whoever blasphemes against the Holy Spirit never has forgiveness, but is guilty of an eternal sin"— for they had said, "He has an unclean spirit." (Mark 3:28–30)

If blasphemy against the Holy Spirit is the only sin that cannot be forgiven, and if the sin of Hebrews 6 cannot be forgiven, then we are constrained by logical necessity to admit that the two must be one and the same. This connection is recognized by interpreters from all points of view. However, not all seem to perceive that this association establishes the fact that these Pharisees had certainly attained the degree of spiritual illumination described in Hebrews 6, despite having ever been obstinate enemies of Christ. If such were not the case, there would still be hope for them, just as there is still hope for all those who repudiate Christ short of having received all the privileges examined above.

For instance, Stanley Outlaw, who argues that Hebrews 6:4–6 proves the loss of salvation, comments as follows:

> Since there is only one sin which cannot be forgiven, the sin against the Holy Spirit, this then must be at least one manifestation of this awful sin... Therefore, the sin against the Holy Spirit can be committed by both unsaved people, who constantly and willfully reject the obvious

truth of the Gospel, and by saved people who also constantly and willfully turn their back on Christ to the point of final apostasy.[150]

But if this sin can be committed by unbelievers, as Outlaw cannot help but concede, then there is no escaping the fact that it is possible for people to receive all the privileges necessary to render their betrayal of the truth an "eternal sin" while still in unbelief, apart from ever having experienced a true conversion. So there is simply no room left for the argument that the privileges of Hebrews 6 are distinctive marks of true Christians.

It is not hard to see the similarity between the sin committed by the Pharisees and the sin the Hebrews would commit if they apostatized. The Pharisees sinned when their jealousy drove them to say that the Spirit working in Jesus was demonic. Jesus distinguished between this particular blasphemy against the Holy Spirit and a blasphemy against the Son of Man, which could be forgiven.

The reason lies in the fact that the deity of the Son was veiled by his incarnation. But not even for a moment could they pretend to ignore that the power by which Jesus performed miracles and cast out demons was truly divine. They knew the good Word of God enough to tell that no one could possibly do the signs that Jesus was doing unless God was with him (John 3:2). They could not deny that Jesus was performing authentic miracles (John 9:18; 11:47–48; Acts 4:16).

But instead of fearing, as did Nicodemus (John 7:50), they dared to blaspheme. They sinned against light. They suppressed any outcry from their consciences. They were so set on keeping others from following Christ that they pronounced words of blasphemy against God even while they were fully aware their words weren't true. It was the fact that they had received the benefit of so much light that caused their sin to be "eternal." Once committed, their sin could never be forgiven.

It is not just anybody who is in the position to commit this unpardonable sin. Blurting out the same words as the Pharisees uttered, without having received as much understanding as they had, would be a qualitatively different sin. But when we consider the Hebrews who are warned against apostasy, we recognize that many of them could have reached the same level of privilege as the Pharisees had. And for as many as found themselves in this highly enlightened condition, the act of turning on Christ, after all that

---

150 W. Stanley Outlaw, *The Book of Hebrews* (Nashville: Randall House Publications, 2005), 125.

they had been allowed to know and experience, would not be the same as what goes on when other unbelievers despise Christ and reject his Gospel.

Quite the contrary, it would be the same sin as that of the Pharisees in its essence. They had witnessed the working of the Holy Spirit that vindicated Christ and his message. As a result, they had come to a full knowledge of the truth. At this point, they could no longer repudiate Christ without treating what they knew to be true as a lie, without treating the working of the Spirit as the activity of the devil, the father of lies.

The author of Hebrews points out that by doing so these people would be "crucifying once again the Son of God to their own harm and holding him up to contempt" (Heb. 6:6). Owen helps us understand why:

> "They crucify him again to themselves." They do it not really, they cannot do so; but they do it to themselves morally...They approved of and justified the fact of the Jews in crucifying him as a malefactor; for there is no medium between these things. The Lord Christ must be esteemed to be the Son of God, and consequently his gospel to be indispensably obeyed, or be supposed to be justly crucified as a seducer, a blasphemer, and a malefactor; for professing himself to be the Son of God, and witnessing that confession unto his death, he must be so received or rejected as an evil-doer. And this was done by these apostates; for, going over to the Jews, they approved of what they had done in crucifying of him as such an one.

> They did it [they crucified Christ again] by declaring, that having made trial of him, his gospel and ways, they found nothing of substance, truth, or goodness in them, for which they should continue their profession. Thus that famous or infamous apostate, Julian the emperor, gave this as the motto of his apostasy, "I have read, known, and condemned" your Gospel...

> Now, no man living can attempt a higher dishonor against Jesus Christ, in his person or in any of his ways, than openly to profess that upon trial of them they find nothing in them for which they should be desired..."They crucify him again;" they do it as much as in them lieth, and declare that they would actually do it if it were in their power.[151]

---

151 John Owen, *The Nature and Causes Of Apostasy from the Gospel*, vol. 7 of *The Works of John Owen* (Rio, WI: Ages Software Inc., 2000), 67–69.

With these facts in mind, let us return our focus to the controversies over Hebrews 6. While the vocabulary describing the privileges received by the apostates is insufficient to prove that they had ever been saved, the words of Jesus about the blasphemy of the Pharisees prove conclusively that a person need not experience regeneration before being capable of committing this sin.

THE POINT OF THE WARNING ILLUSTRATED

But there is still another proof that Hebrews 6:4–6 is not referring to true Christians who fall away. When we read this passage in its context, we notice that it is followed up immediately with an illustration:

> For land that has drunk the rain that often falls on it, and produces a crop useful to those for whose sake it is cultivated, receives a blessing from God. But if it bears thorns and thistles, it is worthless and near to being cursed, and its end is to be burned. (Heb. 6:7–8)

What a poignant illustration! Or is it? Actually, the picture we are given here is totally inadequate as an illustration of how true believers may lose their salvation. If that had been what the author was talking about, he would have used an appropriate illustration to drive home that point.

But he does not speak of land that yields good fruit for some time and then stops doing so. Instead, he speaks of land that was surrounded by all the external conditions that could have contributed for the land to become productive but which, nevertheless, yielded up no fruit when harvest time came around. Thorns and thistles are all that ever sprang up from this land.

We are left with a perfect illustration of what goes on in the case of people who receive great privileges but who neglect them, frustrating any expectation that true conversion will come about. We may additionally note that analogies like this are always used throughout the Bible to censure those who remain unconverted in spite of receiving great external blessings, which should have moved them unto repentance (cf. Isa. 5:1–7; Matt. 3:10; Luke. 13:6–9). So this illustration in verses 7–8 only makes sense if that is what the context (verses 4–6) is really about.

The case for this interpretation becomes even more solid as we move on to the next verse:

Though we speak in this way, yet in your case, beloved, we feel sure of better things—*things that belong to salvation.*

(Heb. 6:9; emphasis added)

At this point, the author assures us that although he is writing in these dire terms, he is optimistic as to his readers and is not leaning toward the idea that they are of the kind that ends up being cursed and whose end is to be burned. Instead, he is confident "of better things" in their case, specifically, of "things that belong to salvation"—that is, "things that accompany salvation" (NASB):

This verse...makes even more clear that the various spiritual experiences rehearsed in 6:4–5 do not necessarily "accompany salvation." Although these experiences sound like the genuine article, they do not necessarily imply the presence of saving faith.[152]

Again, the context militates against the Arminian interpretation. If the things that "accompany salvation" are better things, it must be because none of the things that had already been mentioned are inseparable from salvation. All this goes to show that there is no support to be found in Hebrews 6 for the doctrine that saints can and do apostatize.

THE FOURTH WARNING PASSAGE

In conclusion, we will examine Hebrews 10:23–39, where we find the last of the warning passages that requires our attention:

Let us hold fast the confession of our hope without wavering, for he who promised is faithful. And let us consider how to stir up one another to love and good works, not neglecting to meet together, as is the habit of some, but encouraging one another, and all the more as you see the Day drawing near. For if we go on sinning deliberately after receiving the knowledge of the truth, there no longer remains a sacrifice for sins, but a fearful expectation of judgment, and a fury of fire that will consume the adversaries.

Anyone who has set aside the law of Moses dies without mercy on the evidence of two or three witnesses. How much worse punishment, do you think, will be deserved by the one who has spurned the Son of God, and has profaned the blood of the covenant by which he was sanctified, and has outraged the Spirit of grace? For we know him who

---

152 Edgar Andrews, *A Glorious High Throne: Hebrews Simply Explained* (Darlington, England: Evangelical Press, 2003), 171 (emphasis in original).

213

said, "Vengeance is mine; I will repay." And again, "The Lord will judge his people." It is a fearful thing to fall into the hands of the living God.

But recall the former days when, after you were enlightened, you endured a hard struggle with sufferings, sometimes being publicly exposed to reproach and affliction, and sometimes being partners with those so treated. For you had compassion on those in prison, and you joyfully accepted the plundering of your property, since you knew that you yourselves had a better possession and an abiding one. Therefore do not throw away your confidence, which has a great reward. For you have need of endurance, so that when you have done the will of God you may receive what is promised. For, "Yet a little while, and the coming one will come and will not delay; but my righteous one shall live by faith, and if he shrinks back, my soul has no pleasure in him." But we are not of those who shrink back and are destroyed, but of those who have faith and preserve their souls. (Heb. 10:23–39)

There is much similarity between this exhortation and the previous ones in the book. Its goal is clearly to reinforce what has already been set forth, thus enriching our grasp of the book's message as a whole.

At the outset, we notice how verses 26–27 tie in so closely with what we have just analyzed in 6:4–6. The words "deliberately after receiving the knowledge of the truth" seem to correspond with the idea of being once enlightened, having tasted the heavenly gift, having shared in the Holy Spirit, and having tasted the goodness of the word of God and the powers of the age to come.

If drawing this correlation is accurate, then we find here yet another proof that the privileges listed in chapter 6 do not signify conversion but instead a full measure of understanding. "The knowledge of the truth" (or "full knowledge," as in Young's Literal Translation) is the translation of the Greek word ἐπίγνωσιν, which is stronger than γνωος (knowledge), and conveys the idea of a more profound and complete knowledge. Receiving this type of knowledge puts one in a position of much-greater responsibility.

Calvin touches on this:

The clause, "after having received the knowledge of the truth," was added for the purpose of aggravating their ingratitude; for he who willingly and with deliberate impiety extinguishes the light of God kindled in his heart has nothing to allege as an excuse before God. Let us then learn not only to receive with reverence and prompt docility of mind the truth offered to us, but also firmly to persevere in the knowledge of it, so that we may not suffer the terrible punishment of those who despise it.[153]

It should also be noted that "go on sinning deliberately" is not the same as committing a deliberate or willful sin. This text has been horribly abused by those who use it to teach that saints become lost every time they sin deliberately. That is an affront to the whole biblical teaching about justification and is very far from what the author of Hebrews has in mind.

If that were the case, we would all perish. Since we all sin, we would promptly wind up with no hope of salvation, there no longer remaining a sacrifice for our sins. But the words carry the idea of prolonged persistence in error and can only apply to continuous and obstinate rebellion.

There can be no doubt that apostasy from the Gospel is what is envisioned here, just as throughout the whole epistle. The Hebrews are exhorted not to forsake meeting together as a church, as some end up doing (Heb. 10:25). Abandoning the church, living aloof from the Christian community and apart from being subject to its discipline is flagrant disobedience to the commandment of Christ, who instituted his church on earth.

Those who persist in like negligence and rebellion against the law of God are said to "go on sinning" (Heb. 10:26). Those who do so "willfully after receiving the knowledge of the truth" (NASB) bear an even greater guilt:

> But there is a vast difference between particular fallings and a complete defection of this kind, by which we entirely fall away from the grace of Christ. And as this cannot be the case with any one except he has been already enlightened, he says, *If we sin willfully, after that we have received the knowledge of the truth*; as though he had said, "If we knowingly and willingly renounce the grace which we had obtained."

> And that the Apostle here refers only to apostates is clear from the whole passage...He denies, then, that any sacrifice remains for them who renounce the death of Christ, which is not done by any offense except by a total renunciation of the faith.[154]

---

153 John Calvin, *The Commentaries on the Epistle of Paul the Apostle to the Hebrews, The John Calvin Collection* (Rio, WI: Ages Software Inc., 2000), 214.

154 Ibid., 213.

The common elements in this exhortation of chapter 10 and the previous ones are striking. There is always this tension between an optimistic credence, given the addressees' profession of faith, and caution. We may recall how in chapter 6 the author immediately follows up the warning against apostasy with the reassurance to his readers that although he was writing in those terms he remained, as of yet, persuaded of better things in regards to them—that is, of their salvation (Heb. 6:9).

He states why he is inclined to be so persuaded, citing the external evidence of love for Christ that they had been displaying by serving the saints (Heb. 6:10). This kind of outward behavior is an indication of conversion but is not proof. More than anything of the sort, conversion is confirmed as genuine by persevering in the faith unto the end.

If there is any shortcoming in this pivotal criterion, if we find someone giving up and turning back along the way, then it becomes obvious that no regeneration had ever taken place, no matter what external signs may have been feeding our hopes (Heb. 3:14). Fully aware of this, he proceeds, saying,

> But we want each one of you to demonstrate the same earnest concern with regard to the realization of your hope until the end, so that you will not become sluggish, but imitators of those who with faith and steadfast endurance inherit the promises. (Heb. 6:11−12)[155]

This amounts to making your calling and election sure.

Now, as we get to chapter 10, we find the author once more recognizing that there are external aspects in the behavior of his intended readers that would lead to the conclusion that they are indeed saved. For instance, he mentions how they had "endured a hard struggle with sufferings" after they had been enlightened (Heb. 10:32), even to the point of cheerfully holding up under the plundering of their property out of confidence that they had a better and an enduring heavenly possession (Heb. 10:34).

But then once again, he shows himself cautious, perceptive of the fact that he can do no more than look at the external aspects of their lives. He therefore goes on in verses 38 and 39 to emphasize that it is by persevering that we confirm whether we have truly been called or not:

---

155 William L. Lane, trans. of Hebrews 6:11−12, *Word Biblical Commentary*, Volume 47a, Hebrews 1−8 (Columbia: Nelson Reference & Electronic, 1991), 130.

THE MESSAGE OF HEBREWS

But my righteous one shall live by faith, and if he shrinks back, my soul has no pleasure in him. But we are not of those who shrink back and are destroyed, but of those who have faith and preserve their souls. (Heb. 10:38–39)

There are three essential questions that get to the heart of Hebrews 10:23–39:

1. What are we instructed to do?

2. What will happen to those who fail to do so?

3. Why is it that some will persevere and others will not?

WHAT ARE WE INSTRUCTED TO DO IN HEBREWS 10:23–39?

There is a list of imperatives in the passage. We are commanded to hold fast without wavering to our Christian faith (Heb. 10:23), to not neglect the assembling of ourselves with fellow believers (Heb. 10:25), and to not abandon our confidence (Heb. 10:35). Besides these individual measures, we are told to consider how to stir up one another to love and good works (Heb. 10:24), exhorting one another (Heb. 10:25).

All these orders point back to the same truth: we must persevere in the faith (Heb. 10:36); we absolutely must not shrink back through apostasy (Heb. 10:38). We must persevere as individuals, and we should strive to encourage our fellow Christians to persevere. These instructions apply to every Christian and remind us that the perseverance of the saints, though made certain by the grace of God, involves the conscious effort of the saints toward that end.

WHAT DOES THE PASSAGE SAY WILL HAPPEN TO THOSE WHO FAIL TO HEED THE DIVINE COMMAND TO ACT IN THIS WAY?

Some of the harshest words of condemnation in the Bible are pronounced against those who do not persevere in the faith. Apostates are warned that they will find no remission for their sins, be it in Judaism or anywhere else, for without Christ there no longer remains a sacrifice for sins (Heb. 10:26). Instead of pardon, all they are left with is a fearful expectation of judgment and the fury of a fire that will consume them as enemies of God (Heb. 10:27).

Professing faith in Christ for a time and then repudiating the Christian faith is a grave offense, comparable to trampling on Christ and scorning his

Gospel (Heb. 10:29). We are assured that such an affront deserves a much-worse punishment than the death penalty meted out to those who rejected the law of Moses (Heb. 10:28–29). The message is outright scathing: those who depart "draw back to perdition" (Heb. 10:39, NKJV).

ACCORDING TO THIS PASSAGE, WHY IS IT THAT SOME WILL END UP PERSEVERING WHILE OTHERS WILL NOT?

This is an often-neglected question that is immensely important. There can be no doubt that this text teaches the necessity of perseverance and affirms the condemnation of apostates. But alongside these doctrines, we also find here the conviction that all who possess genuine faith will persevere. This truth can be seen in verses 37–39:

> For, "Yet a little while, and the coming one will come and will not delay; but my righteous one shall live by faith, and if he shrinks back, my soul has no pleasure in him." But we are not of those who shrink back and are destroyed, but of those who have faith and preserve their souls. (Heb. 10:37–39)

As he concludes his admonition, the writer quotes from the prophecy of Habakkuk. His source is evidently not the original Hebrew but the Greek Septuagint translation. In place of the phrase "Behold the proud, His soul is not upright in him," the Septuagint introduces the explanation: "If he shrinks back, my soul has no pleasure in him."

Detecting how relevant this particular phrase is to his message, the author of Hebrews uses it, reordering it so as to highlight his point:

> Though it tarries, wait for it; Because it will surely come, It will not tarry. Behold the proud, His soul is not upright in him; But the just shall live by his faith. (Hab. 2:3b–4, NKJV)

> For, "Yet a little while, and the coming one will come and will not delay; but my righteous one shall live by faith, and if he shrinks back, my soul has no pleasure in him." (Heb. 10:37–38)

The quotation presupposes familiarity with the text of Habakkuk in which a contrast is made between two types of people: (1) the righteous or just person who lives by faith, and (2) the proud, whose soul is not upright. To the author of Hebrews, this partition of humanity into two categories has everything to do with those who profess to be Christians. There are two types of followers in the Christian fold:

1. There are the righteous, who *shall live*—that is, who will not perish. These shall live, and that by faith. Sadly, though, not all followers are of this kind.

2. There are also followers who shrink back and in whom God has no pleasure.

But what is the key difference between those who shall live and those who shrink back? The difference is whether or not faith is present in the individual. As the writer puts it, "But we are not of those who shrink back and are destroyed, but of those who have faith and preserve their souls" (Heb. 10:39).

This turns out to be an all-important statement. "We are not of those who shrink back," he says. No, we are not that type of follower! What kind are we? We are "of those *who have faith* and preserve their souls." By drawing this distinction, our author makes it clear that "those who have faith" do not shrink back. They are not liable to do so.

Consistent with the rest of Scripture, here it once more turns out that the ones who shrink back and are destroyed are those who are devoid of faith. By shrinking back, they give proof of their unbelief, for "those who have faith" are the same as those who "preserve their souls."

This flow of thought carries us right into Hebrews chapter 11, where the history of God's people is now shown to illustrate over and over that faith is the distinguishing mark of the overcomers. Believers prove to be faithful. It was by faith that the God's people of old "gained approval" (Heb. 11:2, NASB).

Faith was what made the difference between Cain and Abel. By faith Abel. By faith Enoch. By faith Noah. By faith Abraham. By faith Sarah. By faith Isaac. By faith Jacob. By faith Joseph. By faith Moses. By faith Rahab.

The same was true in the case of Gideon, Barak, Samson, Jephthah, David, Samuel, and the prophets. They all lived by faith and died in faith (Heb. 11:13). And how was it that their faith became evident? Just as the genuine character of Abraham's faith was revealed through his obedience to God (James 2:23), so too was the reality of each of these individuals' faith made manifest in their lives.

True faith always yields fruits. The faith of Moses showed forth when he chose "rather to be mistreated with the people of God than to enjoy the fleeting pleasures of sin" (Heb. 11:25) and in the way "he considered the reproach of Christ greater wealth than the treasures of Egypt" (Heb. 11:26). Others had their faith attested by the fact that they underwent torture, "refusing to accept release, so that they might rise again to a better life" (Heb. 11:35).

Still, others demonstrated that they were of those who have faith when they proved themselves willing to suffer mocking and flogging, and even chains and imprisonment (Heb. 11:36); by being stoned, sawn in two, or killed with the sword (Heb. 11:37); when they went about in sheep or goatskins, being destitute, afflicted, mistreated (Heb. 11:37), wandering about in deserts and mountains, and in dens and caves of the earth (Heb. 11:38). All this they preferred to endure rather than shrinking back!

That is what biblical faith does. Faith—real faith—will prove itself in this way over and over again, if need be. The point has been made: "Those who have faith" "are not of those who shrink back and are destroyed" (Heb. 10:39).

All this is meant to lead us to reflect upon what kind of follower we are. Are we of those who will shrink back and be destroyed, or are we of those who have faith and preserve their souls? Let us be like Abraham and Moses! May we never be like unbelieving Esau (Heb. 12:16). God forbid we prove to be no better than the unbelievers who rebelled in the desert. Let us prove to be imitators of those who through faith and steadfast endurance inherit the promises (Heb. 6:12). Those who have faith become heirs of the righteousness that comes by faith. This we are taught by the book of Hebrews.

8

To God Alone Be the Glory

Whereas it is the will of God, that all whom he loves should partake of repentance, and so not perish with the unbelieving and impenitent, he has established it by his almighty will. But if any of those whom God wills should partake of the grace of repentance, should afterwards perish, where is his almighty will? And how is this matter settled and established by such a will of his?[156]   (Clement of Rome, AD 69)

Therefore, we are preserved, not by the power of free will, but by the clemency of God.[157]   (Jerome, AD 390)

Perseverance is neither of man that willeth or runneth; for it is not in the power of man, but it is of God that showeth mercy, that thou canst fulfill what thou hast begun.[158]   (Ambrose, AD 380)

One of the great challenges we face as Bible students is that of maintaining our objectivity and not allowing our concepts and prejudices to rule over our interpretation. Conscious or unconsciously, we all bring preconceived ideas into our reading of the Sacred Text. Our outlook, shaped by our culture and our times, can hinder us from "seeing" what is written in the Bible. This is certainly one of the causes of the doctrinal differences that divide Christians into differing camps, and even churches and denominations.

The Bible most certainly contains concepts that are contrary to our natural thinking. One that proves to be among the most difficult for us to fully appreciate is the concept of grace in salvation. What could be more natural than to believe that salvation is by works? The voice of our culture comes across in the popular saying, "God helps those who help themselves." Without the light of divine revelation, who would ever question this rationale and come up with a doctrine that attributes salvation in its totality to the grace of God?

156 Clemens Romanus, quoted by John Gill, *The Cause of God and of Truth*, Part 4, Chapter 5, Section 1, The Ultimate Christian Library (Rio, Wisconsin: AGES Software, 2000), 807.

157 Jerome (Hieronymus), quoted by John Gill, *The Cause of God and of Truth*, Part 4, Chapter 5, Section 22, The Ultimate Christian Library (Rio, Wisconsin: AGES Software, 2000), 848.

158 Ambrose (Ambrosius Mediolanensis), quoted by John Gill, *The Cause of God and of Truth*, Part 4, Chapter 5, Section 20, The Ultimate Christian Library (Rio, Wisconsin: AGES Software, 2000), 844.

We buck against the concept of grace in salvation even when we encounter it in the authoritative pages of Holy Scriptures. As soon as we realize that the Bible teaches that salvation is by grace, our natural leaning is to seek ways to relegate God's grace a partial role in salvation while ascribing ourselves an equally important role.

The doctrinal systems that arise from this approach always portray salvation as resulting from a joint venture of sorts between God and the sinner. It is emphatically stated that God's grace is absolutely necessary for salvation since, strictly speaking, no sinner could ever merit eternal life. Nevertheless, the idea that grace alone is what brings about salvation is not embraced. Short of this, an element of human cooperation in salvation is snuck in which is not wrought by the grace of God.

It is easy to confirm this fact if we make the following observation. When this approach is adopted, it is invariably maintained that the role performed by God's grace in salvation is not a sufficient cause to ensure a person's salvation. Instead of believing that God endows those he saves with a special measure of grace that makes their salvation certain, it is believed that the same measure of grace is given indiscriminately to all. In other words, God performs exactly the same role toward the salvation of everybody.

But since not all people are saved, as the Bible clearly teaches, this way of thinking leads inescapably to the conclusion that what makes the difference between those of us who inherit eternal life and those of us who perish is not in what God does for us in his grace. So where is it then?

That which makes all the difference is to be found in what we do for ourselves. In this way, we are safeguarded a vital role in our own salvation that God's grace does not provide for us. In fact, the truth is that it all comes down to our performance. If we do for ourselves that which God's grace does not do for us, in that case—and only in that case—will our salvation turn out to be a success.

When salvation is thought of in this way, grace is not understood as effectively saving anyone. It only goes up to a certain point, stopping short of actually saving. Its designed effect is limited to making salvation possible unto all. Being insufficient to make the salvation of any individual certain, the role of grace is merely to contribute toward salvation by placing conversion and perseverance within each person's reach.

But grace does not guarantee these results. It is left to the individual to complete the good work that God began by adding his or her own contribution—that is, by doing that which the grace of God does not go so far as to accomplish. Therefore, whenever salvation becomes a reality, it can be said that it only came to pass because, in addition to all that was done by the grace of God, the saved person also did *his* part or *her* part accordingly.

This is precisely the kind of system that is to be found in the Roman Catholic concept that the grace of God performs a partial, albeit indispensable, role in salvation. The Catholic system carefully distinguishes itself from pelagianism by affirming original sin and the absolute necessity of the grace of God in salvation, but it does not attribute salvation to grace alone because it considers works and merit as the means of attaining and maintaining the salvation that grace makes possible.

It was for this very reason that the Reformers' motto included the words *Sola Gratia* (grace alone). They realized that it was not enough to confess that salvation is by grace. The word *alone* made all the difference. Catholicism admits that faith has an indispensable role in salvation, but rejects the teaching that salvation is through faith alone (*Sola Fide*). In this same way, a number of religious groups (including the Roman Catholic Church) are ready to say that we can only be saved with the aid of God's enabling grace, but are not ready to join the Reformers in affirming that we are saved by grace alone (*Sola Gratia*). Recognizing that salvation is impossible apart from grace is not the same as recognizing that it is grace alone that makes salvation become a personal reality.

Resistance against the doctrine of the perseverance of the saints arises precisely due to the lack of a clear comprehension of what it means for salvation to be by grace alone. It is not surprising that so many cults and apostate forms of Christianity teach that salvation can be lost and vehemently attack the idea of eternal security. This is no coincidence. It is the logical outworking of their belief in salvation based on merit though good works.

Believing as they do that sinners must save themselves by means of their works, they naturally assume that those who have already achieved enough merit to be presently saved must still live out the rest of their lives as a probation period throughout which they will need to continue to prove their worthiness. For anyone who thinks along these lines, nothing seems more obvious than that salvation can be lost.

In a book entitled *Can Believers Lose Their Salvation?* author Aníbal Pereira dos Reis (a former Roman Catholic priest turned Baptist preacher) accurately identified the heart of the matter, pointing out that the believer's security is eternal because it is God who is the Savior:

> My salvation is not secured by my works. It could never come from them. That would be an effect far greater than the cause, putting it into the realm of impossibility. It would make salvation dependent on man. A self-salvation is what would occur.

> When the pseudo-Christian sects, such as Catholicism, suppose it is possible for the Christian to fall away, they are building upon an anti-evangelical foundation because they hang salvation upon human works instead of on God, the Only Savior. If the saved can become lost by sinning, what this means, in effect, is that salvation is unstable because it varies according to one's works, which is contrary to the Gospel. That is simply not the Eternal Gospel![159]

At length, we will see that the biblical concept of salvation by grace alone and the doctrine of the perseverance of the saints are inseparable. The first cannot exist without the latter. If salvation is by grace alone, then the doctrine of the perseverance of the saints comes as part of the package. That is why it is a doctrine that can be found exclusively among the churches that preach the biblical message of salvation by grace alone (*Sola Gratia*).

And yes, there are evangelicals who use the terminology of salvation by grace alone but who believe in the possibility of salvation being lost. Notwithstanding, this is due to their inconsistency. There remains in their reasoning a measure of the same anti-evangelical way of thinking, which is typical of pseudo-Christianity and from which they need to break free.

It is totally possible to demonstrate that there is nothing unfair about this criticism. The evangelicals who oppose the doctrine defended in this book do so because they fail to see perseverance as something graciously granted by God. As a rule of thumb, the attacks brought against the doctrine presented in this book labor to prove that salvation is conditional. Every effort is concentrated on demonstrating that the believer is not unconditionally secure.

Yet nothing is more obvious than the fact that there are conditions in salvation. To be saved, one must believe in the Gospel, with perseverance.

---

159 Aníbal Pereira dos Reis, *Pode o Crente Perder a Salvação?* (São Paulo, Brazil, Edições Caminho de Damasco, 1978), 59.

But where do faith and perseverance come from? What role does grace play in salvation? Should we attribute only a part of salvation or its totality to the grace of God? That is the key issue in the debate concerning security or the loss of salvation.

The root cause of the ongoing debate is that many Christians presuppose that those who fulfill the conditions for salvation do so of themselves. They do not envision a special impartation of divine grace given to those who fulfill the conditions. They believe instead that some people stand out from the rest because they qualify themselves for salvation by doing their part and meeting the divinely prescribed conditions.

Guy Duty's book *If Ye Continue* is a typical example. He repeatedly makes the case that salvation is conditional, appealing to several biblical passages that use the word *if* as proof. However, his unquestioned assumption is that those who meet the conditions do so on their own. Not even for one moment does he question this underlying premise. Therefore, he unwittingly circumvents the real issue at hand.

The debate here is not between those who believe that salvation is conditional and those who believe that salvation is unconditional. No one promoting the doctrine of the perseverance of the saints is claiming that salvation is unconditional. The difference lies in the fact that its detractors deny that the people who actually fulfill the conditions for salvation do so because this is granted unto them by the grace of God.

Indeed, Duty turns out to be so superficial in his understanding of the matter that he even accuses Arthur Pink of inconsistency for stating that we do not contribute anything to our own salvation in one book and that repentance is a condition for salvation in another.[160] What he fails to grasp is that as a Calvinist, Pink maintains that people do not repent unless repentance is granted unto them by God (see Acts 11:18; 2 Tim. 2:25).

Therefore, presupposing that those who meet the conditions for salvation do so without it being granted unto them by divine grace, Duty thinks of salvation in terms of a great test to which God subjects people to in order to see who will pass. Some of his statements are quite revealing. For example, he says, "God tests everyone. All must be proved to determine if they are worthy to enter the Kingdom of God."[161]

---

160 Guy Duty, *If Ye Continue* (Minneapolis: Bethany House Publishers), 64.
161 Ibid., 110.

It is of importance to observe how merit surfaces as the basis for salvation in these words. The test is to determine who is *worthy* of entering the kingdom. And how must we prove ourselves worthy? Duty's answer comes forth in unambiguous terms:

> God gave Abraham an everlasting covenant and an everlasting kingdom "because" he obeyed God's covenant conditions. God also gives us an eternal covenant of life if we "do the works of Abraham."[162]

This statement betrays a profound confusion regarding the biblical doctrine of salvation by grace through faith. Instead of believing that we are totally unworthy, he believes that we must prove ourselves worthy. Instead of understanding that God grants salvation by means of the gift of faith—which, in turn, results in works—he supposes that works are the basis for someone's inclusion in the covenant of life.

In his approach, merit takes the place of grace and works the place of faith. The fact that a book with statements of this kind is acclaimed in many evangelical churches should be alarming. It makes one wonder whether the words "by grace through faith" have not been completely emptied of their meaning in some circles. The truth is that there are many churches and seminaries where Duty's book has been deemed a reference tool, the reading to recommend to anyone who is unconvinced that salvation can be lost.

Let us consider yet another example of his anti-evangelical way of thinking:

> Two men asked Jesus what they must do to inherit eternal life. One asked: "What good thing shall I do, that I may have eternal life?" Jesus replied: "If thou wilt enter into life, keep the commandments" (Matt. 19:17). The other inquirer asked: "Master, what shall I do to inherit eternal life?" Jesus directed him to the commandment: "Thou shalt love the Lord thy God with all thine heart, and with all thy soul, and with all thy strength, and with all thy mind; and thy neighbour as thyself." Then Jesus added: "This do, and thou shalt live [eternally]."[163]

The way Duty puts things at this point intimates that salvation is by the works of the law. His error here flows from his failure to recognize that Jesus was not preaching the Gospel to these two men. What Jesus did was preach the law unto them. But in no way was he preaching the law as the method of

---

162 Ibid., 38.
163 Ibid., 73.

salvation. He was employing what is called the "theological use" of the law—namely, Jesus was confronting them with the requirement of the law for the purpose of making them recognize that they were incapable of inheriting life by means of their own righteousness.

The law needs to be held up before the eyes of every individual who believes in his own capacity of attaining salvation by keeping its commandments until the person comes to realize how impossible this really is. When this is done, the law causes sinners to despair in relation to their self-righteousness and engenders the recognition that their only hope of being saved is by the grace of God apart from their merit.

In this way, the law is instrumental in preparing people to hear the Gospel, as it causes them to understand their guilt before God (Rom. 3:19–20). This is a legitimate use of the law. But the law is not the Gospel, and insinuating that Jesus meant that sinners can inherit eternal life by keeping the commandments goes contrary to everything that the Bible teaches.

This failure to distinguish between the law and the Gospel is just one example of how Duty lacks an adequate understanding of salvation by grace. Yet as he approaches the end of his book, he defends himself by dismissing any cause for concern on this matter:

> I have given repeated emphasis throughout this book that we cannot earn or merit our salvation, no matter how many conditions we keep. It is only by God's underserved grace that we are saved.[164]

I suppose that is meant to silence any objection against his missteps in this crucial area, but frankly, it is simply not enough. Tagging this disclaimer at the end of his work after all that was written above it only serves to convince the theologically informed reader of a serious communication breakdown.

Although Duty says that "it is only by God's underserved grace that we are saved," he most definitely does not mean what the Reformers meant. He is merely using their vocabulary without grasping its true meaning. This should be a warning to us all. There is a subtle danger in the Arminian doctrine. It teaches people to repeat the right words; however, it does not lead them unto an accurate understanding of their meaning. Without realizing it, people can end up speaking in terms of grace while thinking in terms of merit and works.

---

164 Ibid., 177.

SALVATION IS BY GRACE ALONE

Many Arminians do not perceive any conflict between their system and the doctrine of salvation by grace alone. But the conflict exists. When an Arminian says he believes in salvation by grace, what he means is that salvation is impossible without some measure of the grace of God, but what is not being said is that salvation as a whole (including the individual's conversion and perseverance) is a work wrought by divine grace.[165]

For the Arminian, it is as if grace opened up the way for us and invited us, but did no more. In contrast, in the biblical perspective, grace not only opens up a way, it also causes someone who was spiritually dead to rise up, enter the way, and follow it all the way to the end. The Bible presents it all as the working of God's grace, from beginning to end, so that salvation is the result of grace alone and not the added result of grace and human cooperation.

The Bible shows us that fallen humanity is dead in sin and has no desire to seek God: "As it is written: 'None is righteous, no, not one; no one understands; no one seeks for God'" (Rom. 3:10–11). Furthermore, in an unregenerate condition, we lack the ability to please God: "Those who are in the flesh cannot please God" (Rom. 8:8).

Incapable of pleasing God, instead of finding ourselves free to choose between resisting Christ or yielding to him, as long as we are in the flesh, we are enslaved by sin. In the words of Christ, "Everyone who commits sin is a slave to sin" (John 8:34). Or, as Jeremiah put it, "Can the Ethiopian change his skin or the leopard its spots? Neither can you do good who are accustomed to doing evil" (Jer. 13:23, NIV).

For this reason, in order for anyone to be saved, God must do more than simply provide an opportunity for salvation and invite the sinner to accept the gift of eternal life. If God did no more than that, no one would be converted, for people love the darkness rather than the light (John 3:19), and we would all reject the Gospel.

---

165 The Arminian view of conversion is that God grants all people prevenient grace to make their conversion possible, but this grace is not enough to make anyone's conversion unavoidable. The Arminian doctrine does not maintain that the human heart is effectively opened by God to receive the Gospel, nor that faith, repentance, and perseverance are bestowed upon each believer by God. These elements are considered to be within the realm of human cooperation and are seen as conditions that must be met on our part, and without which God's grace alone is impotent to save.

228

But God, in his grace, does more than just send out an invitation. He himself draws some people and gives them to Christ—that is, he converts them. God overcomes sinners and saves them, unilaterally removing their natural resistance to conversion. He takes the heart of stone out and puts a heart of flesh in its place (Ezek. 36:26). We would never have chosen to open our hard hearts to the Gospel; however, God does this for us. He is the One who opens our hearts, and as a result, we are sure to believe.

This is how we find God acting to bring about salvation in the Bible, as in the case of Lydia:

> Now a certain woman named Lydia heard [us]. She was a seller of purple from the city of Thyatira, who worshiped God. The Lord opened her heart to heed the things spoken by Paul.
>
> (Acts 16:14, NKJV)

God does not limit himself to knocking on the door of our hearts, as some are fond of saying. He opens the door of the heart of those whom he saves. He does not depend on sinners being willing to believe in order to save them, "for it is God who works in you to will and to act according to his good purpose" (Phil. 2:12, NIV). God mightily converts sinners, causing them to desire Christ, granting them faith and repentance.

Jesus taught that without this powerful work of conversion on God's part nobody would be saved. On one occasion, some Jews were unbelieving and murmured against Jesus because of his claims, even after having seen him working miracles. John's Gospel recounts how Jesus responded:

> Jesus answered them, "Do not grumble among yourselves. No one can come to me unless the Father who sent me draws him. And I will raise him up on the last day." (John 6:43–44)

In this passage, Jesus stated in no uncertain terms that sinners are utterly incapable of converting themselves and coming to God unless they are drawn by God. Moreover, Jesus makes it equally clear that when God acts in this way, drawing a sinner unto Christ, the sinner will invariably be converted.

The effect of God's drawing is not just to make conversion a possibility. It renders conversion a guaranteed result. This fact is often overlooked in the text, so it should be emphasized. Arminians seek to deal with this passage by saying that it teaches no more than their concept of prevenient grace, namely that conversion is impossible unless God's Spirit acts upon people, enabling conversion.

But they hasten to add that the Spirit of God moves equally upon all people in this way, indiscriminately. They agree that no one can come to Christ unless the Father makes this possible through the work of the Spirit, but they claim that the Father performs this work on all people. They thus reduce God's work to an effort at converting people that can be stifled by human will and which, indeed, often results in failure.

Not only does this portray God as being frustrated in achieving his ends, which the Bible discards as nonsense (Job 42:2), but also it is a flat contradiction of what is explicitly stated in the text of John chapter 6. Reading verses 43–44 in their context, we find that the surrounding verses clarify Jesus's point:

> It is written in the Prophets, "And they will all be taught by God." Everyone who has heard and learned from the Father comes to me.
> (John 6:45)

Jesus is not speaking of a divine operation that may or may not result in conversion. He is speaking of an efficacious work. He is teaching that when God acts in this manner toward someone, the person will infallibly come to Christ. As he had said moments earlier, "All that the Father gives me will come to me" (John 6:37).

Once it is true that *everyone* who has heard and learned from the Father *comes* (v. 45), there are none whom God draws that he fails to convert. Every individual who undergoes the divine drawing unto Christ comes to faith in him—no exceptions. Indeed, the positive result of God's operation on those whom he draws is so certain that Jesus even said that the reason some were unbelievers is because they had not received this work of God in their lives:

> "But there are some of you who do not believe...This is why I told you that no one can come to me unless it is granted him by the Father."
> (John 6:64–65)

According to Jesus, those Jews who did not believe in him are those to whom it was not granted by the Father. This makes it all the more evident that the working of God without which no one can come to Christ is not performed equally upon all.

What we find, therefore, is that the free and sovereign grace of God is responsible for the salvation of the individual, even down to the act of conversion to Christ. Believing in Christ is needful. The Bible declares that whoever believes will be saved but whoever does not believe will be condemned (Mark 16:16). So believing is definitely a condition for salvation. But how does the believer come to faith? Is faith granted as a gift, or does the person generate his or her own faith?

Anibal dos Reis had no doubts as to the biblical answer:

It is grace on God's part for anyone to even desire salvation. The sinner is incapable of even wanting salvation. Furthermore, believing in Christ depends on grace. "Such is the confidence that we have through Christ toward God. Not that we are sufficient in ourselves to claim anything as coming from us, but our sufficiency is from God," (2 Cor. 3:4–5). In the sinner's condition of complete inability, what works could be performed to obtain salvation? Let the adversaries of the doctrine of the infallible perseverance of the saints turn back three pages in the Holy Scripture and read: "For by grace you have been saved through faith. And this is not your own doing; it is the gift of God, not a result of works, so that no one may boast" (Eph. 2:8–9). That's it! Faith itself, according to this text, is to be understood as a gift of God's grace.[166]

If our faith as believers came from ourselves, if it were the result of our own decision, then there would be something for which we could boast. We could boast of having done our part to be saved, setting ourselves apart from the others sinners who perish. But when it is understood that our faith was given to us by divine grace, no grounds are left for boasting on our part; quite the contrary, "let the one who boasts, boast in the Lord" (1 Cor. 1:31).

PERSEVERANCE IS BY GRACE ALONE

The same principle applies to the believers' perseverance. Just like believing in Christ, persevering in the faith is also a condition for salvation. But upon reading the Bible, we discover that perseverance is equally a gift of God, granted to all whom he saves, out of no other consideration than his free grace. Jesus is the founder and perfecter of our faith (Heb. 12:2). He Who creates faith in us initially is also the One who sustains and preserves it all

---

166 Aníbal Pereira dos Reis, *Pode o Crente Perder a Salvação?* (São Paulo, Brazil, Edições Caminho de Damasco, 1978), 240.

the way to its consummation on that day when we, being with the Lord, will walk no longer by faith but by sight (2 Cor. 5:1–8)!

> Our perseverance flows from God's preserving us. It does not depend on the will of man, but on the sustaining grace of God... The Christian life as a whole, from its beginning with regeneration, through its development, all the way to the moment of departure unto beatific glory depends on the grace of God. "It depends not on human will or exertion, but on God, who has mercy" (Rom. 9:16). The clear and categorical teaching of the Holy Scriptures is that "by grace you have been saved" (Eph. 2:5; 8), and that includes conversion, progressive sanctification and final salvation. This final salvation is the culmination of perseverance.[167]

This is the reason why Augustine entitled his work on this topic *Donum Perseverantiae* (the Gift of Perseverance). He recognized that perseverance is not the achievement of one's own will but a gift from God. It is not a way in which we contribute to our salvation; it is something we receive:

> This grace He placed "in Him in whom we have obtained a lot, being predestinated according to the purpose of Him who worketh all things." And thus as He worketh that we come to Him, so He worketh that we do not depart.[168]

God does this, and it is the only reason why any Christian perseveres unto the end at all.

John Bunyan illustrated the truth that perseverance is by grace most beautifully in his classic *The Pilgrim's Progress*:

> Then I saw in my dream, that the Interpreter took Christian by the hand and led him into a place where was a fire burning against a wall, and one standing by it always, casting much water upon it to quench it; yet did the fire burn higher and hotter.
>
> Then said Christian, What means this?
>
> The Interpreter answered, this fire is the work of grace that is wrought in the heart; he that casts water upon it, to extinguish and

---

167 Ibid., 142–145.

168 Augustine, *Augustin: Anti-Pelagian Writings, The Gift of Perseverance*, ed. Philip Schaff, Volume 5 of *The Nicene and Post-Nicene Fathers, Series 1*, The Master Christian Library (Rio, WI: Ages Software Inc., 2000), 1240.

put it out, is the devil; but if that thou seest the fire notwithstanding burn higher and hotter, thou shalt also see the reason of that. So he had him about to the backside of the wall, where he saw a man with a vessel of oil in his hand, of the which he did also continually cast, but secretly, into the fire.

Then said Christian, What means this? The Interpreter answered, This is Christ, who continually, with the oil of His grace, maintains the work already begun in the heart: by the means of which, notwithstanding what the devil can do, the souls of His people prove gracious still. And in that thou sawest that the man stood behind the wall to maintain the fire, this is to teach thee that it is hard for the tempted to see how this work of grace is maintained in the soul.[169]

This marvelous picture captures the biblical concept of perseverance perfectly. The devil is constantly throwing at Christians all that would have the effect of extinguishing their faith, if it weren't for what the grace of God does on their behalf. Although it is not easily perceptible to us, it is the grace of Christ that makes all the difference. The perseverance of the saints is not the fruit of what the saints do for themselves but of that which Christ does for them continually.

Christ never ceases to pour out the oil of his grace upon his elect. This does not merely make it possible for them to persevere but also guarantees that they will persevere, that they will never turn back in the way, for the effect of this work of grace in their lives is ongoing and ever intensifying.

Bunyan understood that the perseverance of the saints is certain not due to anything in the saints themselves, as if it depended on their constancy, but as the assured result of God's outpouring of his grace. For this cause, we should not say that we have a part in our own salvation. God, and God alone, is Savior. He saves us without any help from us.

God certainly saves us in a way that involves human decisions, but not in such a capacity that makes us responsible for the success of our own salvation. We turn to God voluntarily, but God works in us to will. We believe and persevere so that our decisions are consequential. However, God's hand is behind all that we do. He, by his grace, is the one who converts us unto himself and who grants us the gift of perseverance.

---

169 John Bunyan, *The Pilgrim's Progress* (Grand Rapids, MI: Baker Book House, July 1991), 38–39.

The Bible gives ample testimony that this perspective on perseverance is correct. Let us consider a few examples:

> I give thanks to my God always for you because of the grace of God that was given you in Christ Jesus, that in every way you were enriched in him in all speech and all knowledge—even as the testimony about Christ was confirmed among you—so that you are not lacking in any spiritual gift, as you wait for the revealing of our Lord Jesus Christ, who will sustain you to the end, guiltless in the day of our Lord Jesus Christ. God is faithful, by whom you were called into the fellowship of his Son, Jesus Christ our Lord. (1 Cor. 1:4–9)

In this passage, Paul first highlights how the Corinthians were Christians because of the grace of God, which had been given unto them. As he gets to verse 8, he turns his focus toward the future and confidently asserts that the Lord "will sustain you to the end, guiltless in the day of our Lord Jesus Christ."

There are two things in this statement that we should carefully consider. First, notice how this work is ascribed to Christ. He is the One who accomplishes it. The Lord Jesus "will confirm you to the end," Paul tells the Corinthians. Second, notice that the result of Christ's acting on their behalf is that they will be guiltless in the day of our Lord Jesus Christ.

In light of this, it is not reasonable to maintain that Christ will confirm them to the end as long as they remain faithful. After all, that is precisely what it means to confirm them to the end. It means that Christ will cause them to remain faithful to the end. And that not because of their faithfulness but because "God is faithful," by whom they "were called" (1 Cor. 1:9). Since God is faithful, he keeps his people faithful.

Paul expresses the same certainty in regard to the final salvation of the Thessalonians:

> But the Lord is faithful. He will establish you and guard you against the evil one. (2 Thess. 3:3)

In this verse, as always, he underscores the faithfulness of God as the key to our final salvation. Because God is faithful, he will establish us and will not allow the devil to ensnare us again with his wiles and traps.

In his first epistle to the Thessalonians, we find this same truth affirmed:

Now may the God of peace himself sanctify you completely, and may your whole spirit and soul and body be kept blameless at the coming of our Lord Jesus Christ. He who calls you is faithful; he will surely do it.   (1 Thess. 5:23–24)

Here, Paul prays for the Thessalonians that they be completely sanctified and kept blameless at the time of Christ's return. This naturally involves perseverance unto the end in faith and sanctification. He directs his prayer toward God, asking that they "be kept blameless."

Then he immediately follows up on his prayer with the categorical assertion: "He who calls you is faithful; he will surely do it" (1 Thess. 5:24). His words leave no margin for uncertainty in the matter. They will be kept blameless, not because of their faithfulness but due to the faithfulness of God. And no one can object that God will only keep them as long as they remain faithful, for the express meaning of the text is that God will keep them blameless.

If the believers had to keep themselves faithful for God to, in turn, keep them, then it would not be God who would be keeping them blameless, at all. The biblical perspective is rather that they will remain faithful because God will keep them and not the other way around.

The guarantees Paul gave the Corinthians and Thessalonians, he also promised to the Philippians:

I thank my God in all my remembrance of you…because of your partnership in the gospel from the first day until now. And I am sure of this, that he who began a good work in you will bring it to completion at the day of Jesus Christ.   (Phil. 1:3–6)

Paul does not say he was hoping for the Philippians to continue in the faith unto the end, nor does he say he is confident they probably would. His conviction is such that he declares himself to be "sure" that the good work of salvation begun by God in them would be completed by God himself. His certainty was bound up in the fact that it is God's work and it does not depend on human constancy.

Paul was equally certain about his own personal future. He did not live apprehensive, uncertain as to his own final salvation due to his own weaknesses. No, he was secure and resting, leaning on the everlasting arms of God:

For this reason I also suffer these things; nevertheless I am not ashamed, for I know whom I have believed and am persuaded that He is able to keep what I have committed to Him until that Day.

(2 Tim. 1:12, NKJV)

The Lord will rescue me from every evil attack and will bring me safely to his heavenly kingdom. To him be glory forever and ever. Amen.

(2 Tim. 4:18, NIV)

We find this truth stated time and again throughout the Bible:

The LORD preserves the faithful.

(Ps. 31:23)

He preserves the souls of His saints.

(Ps. 97:10, NKJV)

For the LORD loves justice; he will not forsake his saints. They are preserved forever.

(Ps. 37:28)

God does this! Jude informs us that he "is able to keep you from stumbling and to present you blameless before the presence" (Jude 1:24). For this reason, as believers, we can and should rejoice together with the apostle that God will also deliver us from every evil deed and bring us safely into his heavenly kingdom.

Being confident of this is not pride. Nor is it presumptuous. There isn't the slightest hint of self-sufficiency in it. Our gaze is fixed on Christ in a spirit that says, "I will not stumble because he is able to keep me from stumbling." He does not keep us as long as we do not slip up, for it is he who "has preserved our lives and kept our feet from slipping" (Ps. 66:9, NIV).

The Psalms are replete with this recognition. From the days of the Old Covenant, the people of God have attributed their triumphs to God. By means of the Psalms, the highest expression of faith is lifted up for the reality that we are kept by God. Not merely kept as long as our feet do not stumble but kept from stumbling. We are kept not only from external threats but also from all evil. We are not only protected for some time but continually, from this time forth and forevermore, for he who keeps Israel will neither slumber nor sleep.

I lift up my eyes to the hills. From where does my help come? My help comes from the LORD, who made heaven and earth. He will not let your foot be moved; he who keeps you will not slumber. Behold, he who keeps Israel will neither slumber nor sleep. The LORD is your keeper; the LORD is your shade on your right hand. The sun shall not strike you by day, nor the moon by night. The LORD will keep you from all evil; he will keep your life. The LORD will keep your going out and your coming in from this time forth and forevermore.

(Ps. 121:1–8)

Now that is what our praise should sound like, giving God all the glory for our safety. Isaiah prophesied that the song of God's redeemed would be a celebration of salvation and divine protection:

In that day this song will be sung in the land of Judah: "We have a strong city; he sets up salvation as walls and bulwarks. Open the gates, that the righteous nation that keeps faith may enter in. You keep him in perfect peace whose mind is stayed on you, because he trusts in you. Trust in the LORD forever, for the LORD GOD is an everlasting rock."

(Isa. 26:1–4)

When reading these words, some will say, "But there it is. The Bible says that the Lord keeps in perfect peace the one whose mind is stayed on him." That is true, but before anyone assumes that God keeps the righteous according to how well they keep themselves, let us read on where we find these most enlightening words: "The path of the righteous is level; you make level the way of the righteous" (Isa. 26:7) and "O LORD, you will ordain peace for us; you have done for us all our works" (Isa. 26:12).

This is the praise that goes up to the Lord from God's people. He receives all the glory. It was he who elected them and transformed them into a "righteous nation," into his own special people. They, in gratitude, exalt and proclaim the virtues of the One who called them out of darkness into his marvelous light. And just as he brought them out of the darkness of sin and unbelief, so does he set up salvation as walls and bulwarks for their security. He stays their mind on him and keeps them in perfect peace. Consequently, they trust in the LORD forever, for the LORD GOD is an everlasting rock!

HELD SECURE IN THE HAND OF GOD

To all these witnesses, our Lord adds his own testimony:

My sheep hear my voice, and I know them, and they follow me. I give them eternal life, and they will never perish, and no one will snatch them out of my hand. My Father, who has given them to me, is greater than all, and no one is able to snatch them out of the Father's hand. I and the Father are one."

(John 10:27–30)

Here we have a passage of Scripture that is conclusive in itself. It teaches the unassailable security of the saints from several angles. First, it says, "I give them eternal life." Eternal life is a gift. It is not earned, but is freely bestowed. Christ's sheep do nothing whatsoever to deserve it.

From that foundational assertion, Jesus proceeds stating that due to this gift "they will never perish." This covers all eternity future. As is the case with two other passages that deny the possibility of saints ever becoming lost again (Heb. 10:17 and John 6:37), the negative grammatical construction used in this passage (οὐ μὴ) is the strongest possible negation in the Greek language to indicate an absolute impossibility.

What this means for someone who is Christ's sheep is that in the future, come what may, he cannot perish under any conceivable circumstances. That is the Lord's promise:

> "For the mountains may depart and the hills be removed, but my steadfast love shall not depart from you, and my covenant of peace shall not be removed," says the LORD, who has compassion on you.
>
> (Isa. 54:10)

All this confirms that the salvation that Christ gives is irreversible and forever: "I give them eternal life, and they will never perish." If our Lord had stopped at that point, his words would already be enough to make it abundantly clear that it is impossible for any of the saved to fall away and be lost.

"Does it make any sense to understand Jesus's words as meaning, 'My sheep, some of whom may indeed perish, will never perish?'"[170] And yet, wishing to make his statement even stronger, Jesus added, "And no one will snatch them out of my hand."

This additional guarantee makes the security of salvation all the more evident. Once called, Christ's sheep will never again be ensnared by the devil. There is no greater power than that of Christ. He is one with the Father (John 10:30). Belonging to Christ means being safe in the omnipotent hands of God. There is no power in the universe that could pry his people from his hand. No one will ever be removed from the divine hands, no matter who may attempt such a feat.

---

170 Anthony A. Hoekema, *Saved by Grace* (Grand Rapids, MI: William B. Eermans Publishing Company, 1994), 239.

With so powerful a statement of our Lord in the Bible, it is surprising that there are Christians willing to defend the thesis that salvation can be lost. Even so, what goes through their minds is understandable. When they read this passage, they do not promptly acquiesce to what it is teaching, because they have been persuaded that other biblical texts teach that the saints can lose their salvation. Besides that, in their way of thinking things must be this way, for otherwise Christians could abandon the faith, go on living in sin deliberately, and continue to be saved, anyway.

However, that is not how things work. Undoubtedly, the Bible does not teach a licentious concept of unconditional security, and that is not what this book is setting forth. But the confusion comes from the fact that these Christians do not conceive of divine grace as the cause of perseverance. They think of perseverance as a condition that Christians fulfill in order to stay in a state of grace. That is why they say things like, "I don't doubt that God will do his part in keeping me, but what if I fail in doing my part?" or, "I know that no one can snatch me out of God's hand, but what if I, of my own choice, choose to remove myself from God's hand?"

In reality, when Christians talk this way, they are importing into the text something that it does not say. They believe they are well-grounded on other biblical texts when doing so, but the effect is to cause the statement of Jesus to lose its absolute character. Jesus did not qualify his statement in the slightest. He simply stated that his sheep will never perish. What they are doing is saying that some of Christ's sheep will perish, doing violence to the text.

Nevertheless, some will insist, "Jesus only promised to protect us as long as we are his sheep. So if anyone ceases to be one of his sheep, this will no longer apply, and that person could perish." This argument too is but a futile attempt to evade what Jesus is really saying.

There are two fallacies in this argument that should be exposed. First, it presumes that someone becomes one of Christ's sheep in the sense spoken by Jesus in John chapter 10 when that person is converted. That is not the case. Verses 3 and 4 indicate that Christ's sheep are already his sheep even before they are called out by him. "Being called" is a technical term in the New Testament for God's mighty work wrought inside a person's being, which results in conversion.[171] It seems that Jesus is using the term

---

171 Cf. Rom. 8:28–30; 1 Cor. 1:24 e 26; 1 Cor. 7:17–18; Gal. 1:15; 2 Thess. 2:14; 2 Tim. 1:9; Heb. 9:15; Rev. 17:14.

in this sense at this point, especially in view of the fact that his sheep begin following him *after* he calls his own sheep by name and leads them out.

At any rate, in verse 16, we find irrefutable proof that those who are Christ's sheep are already his sheep even before they are converted. Our Lord says, "And I have other sheep that are not of this fold. I must bring them also, and they will listen to my voice. So there will be one flock, one shepherd" (John 10:16).

Speaking here of the Gentiles, who were yet to be called, Jesus says, "I have [present tense] other sheep." This does not mean that they are saved before they are converted by the Shepherd, but it does mean that they were already elect unto salvation. That is the reason why Jesus said of the unbelievers, "But you do not believe, because you are not of My sheep" (John 10:26, NASB). It is noteworthy that he did *not* say, "You are not My sheep, because you do not believe." The point is that they were not of the elect, and that is why they would never come to faith.

As the Gospel is proclaimed, it becomes visible who the elect are. The sheep of Christ hear his voice and begin following him (John 10:27). The Bible says that when Paul and Barnabas preached the gospel in Antioch, "as many as had been appointed to eternal life believed" (Acts 13:48, NASB).

The Bible makes it clear that even before they are converted, God already considers those he has elected unto salvation as his own. One instance where we see this is when Paul was in Corinth and things did not seem to be going well. God encouraged him to continue his work in that city, announcing, "Do not be afraid, but go on speaking and do not be silent, for I am with you, and no one will attack you to harm you, for I have many in this city who are my people" (Acts 18:9–10).

God had many people there. They were not, as of yet, converted, but being elect, they were Christ's sheep, and they would be called out to follow him. Knowing that God has a chosen people whom he will convert unto himself served as a great incentive and encouragement to Paul on that occasion and throughout his missionary labors. He informs us that this fact motivated him even when he faced prison and scourging, because in the midst of all the difficulties he remembered that God is sovereign over all things and that in some way he would even use his tribulations for others to obtain salvation. "Therefore," he said, "I endure everything for the sake of

TO GOD ALONE BE THE GLORY

the elect, that they also may obtain the salvation that is in Christ Jesus with eternal glory" (2 Tim. 2:10).

The Bible teaches that specific individuals are chosen for eternal life since "before the foundation of the world" (Eph. 1:4; cf. 2 Tim. 1:9). According to what we learn in Revelation 17:8, their election is so individual and irrevocable that, in contrast with the rest of humanity, their names were written in the Book of Life "from the foundation of the world." Therefore, it is unreasonable to think that Christ's sheep may cease to be his sheep. "It would be utter nonsense for a name to be registered in this Book 'from the foundation of the world' if many centuries later it could be marked out."[172]

The second and more obvious problem that arises from claiming that Christ's sheep could cease to be his sheep and end up perishing is that it makes the words of Jesus lose any real significance. The promise of Jesus is that his sheep will be kept safe so that no one will ever be able to snatch them out of his hand. If this protection only applies to them as long as they continue in the hands of Christ, then Jesus is not actually promising them anything at all.

After all, who would like to snatch Christ's sheep from his hands more than the devil, the enemy of our souls? His tactics are known unto us. By means of doctrines of demons that he spreads, he induces some to apostatize from the faith (1 Tim. 4:1). He is also the dragon who, wishing to see Christians deny the Lord Jesus, conjures up persecution against the people of God in this world (Rev. 13). He is the tempter who through his wiles tries to undo the labors of those who preach the Gospel so that they will have toiled in vain, even in the lives of those who have come to faith in Christ (1 Thess. 3:5).

It was the devil who filled the heart of Ananias to lie to the Holy Spirit (Acts 5:3). Paul recognized that being tempted by him some widows had already strayed after Satan (1 Tim. 5:15). By means of his tactics, the devil is able to mislead many, but not the sheep of Christ, for if any of his tactics (false teaching, persecution, or temptation) resulted in a single sheep of Christ leaving the hands of God, he would obtain a victory in snatching that soul from the hands of God.

Who could deny it? If that did not constitute a triumph of the devil over God, what else would? But nobody can snatch Christ's sheep from his hands.

---

172 Aníbal Pereira dos Reis, *Pode o Crente Perder a Salvação?* (São Paulo, Brazil, Edições Caminho de Damasco, 1978), 107.

On the contrary, the Lord delivers his sheep from every evil attack and brings them safely into his heavenly kingdom.

Still, there are some who teach that Christ's words should be understood as saying something along these lines: "I have good news for my sheep. I know that you fear that the devil may take eternal life from you, even in the case of those who remain faithful unto death. You are worried that he will cancel the salvation of those who resist all his temptations and overcome all the obstacles in the Christian life. Do not worry yourselves about this any longer. It may very well happen that by his cunning and tricks the devil may get you to depart from God, but I will never allow you to be taken forcibly from me against your will."

Now seriously, has anyone ever believed that the devil could unilaterally cancel the eternal life of those who remain faithful to Christ unto the end? If that were all that our Lord was saying, his words would bring no comfort at all. They would be empty words. It would make no difference to anybody if they had simply never even been spoken or if they were removed from the Bible. But what kind of a shepherd would that make out of Christ?

> Doth the veriest hireling in the world deal thus with his sheep,—keep them in case they keep themselves? Nay, to what end is his keeping if they keep themselves? Christ compares himself to be the good shepherd which seeketh out and fetcheth a wandering sheep from the wilderness, laying it on his shoulders, and bringing it home to his fold. How did that poor sheep keep itself, when it ran among the ravenous wolves in the wilderness? Yet by the good shepherd it was preserved.[173]

The notion that whoever preserves oneself will be preserved is most objectionable and must be met with our strongest protest. It amounts to another way of saying, "God helps them that help themselves." Speaking in such a manner about the salvation of sinners threatens the core of the Gospel, which is an acknowledgment that God alone is Savior. We do not save ourselves; it is God who saves us by his grace.

Grace, by definition, is not what we receive as a reward. Our deeds can never become the reason why we receive the grace of God. Grace is given freely, or it is not grace. As Luther put it, "Grace is not the reward for making good use of 'free will.' Divine grace is granted in spite of sin and all that it deserves."[174]

173 John Owen, *The Doctrine of the Saints' Perseverance Explained and Confirmed*, vol. 11 of *The Works of John Owen* (Rio, WI: Ages Software Inc., 2000), 267.
174 Martin Luther, *Nascido Escravo* (São José dos Campos, Brazil: Editora FIEL, 2007), 91.

If we think in terms of meeting conditions in order to receive grace, we have already reversed the proper order. If we say that we receive a measure of grace freely but that we need to fulfill certain conditions to receive more grace, our understanding of grace is still deficient. Saying that it is necessary to meet certain conditions in order to receive saving grace is not far from saying that we have to earn grace by deserving it.

This may harmonize with a theology that teaches that God came down with salvation to a certain point and requires people to cover the rest of the distance, ascending to the point of reaching for themselves the salvation that God made possible. But in no way is this concept consistent with the biblical teaching that it is God who saves us.

We are forgetting that God alone is the One who saves when we say that God makes salvation possible and leaves it to us to do our part for our individual salvation to become a reality. This manner of speaking is no more than an admission that we are unable to save ourselves without some help from God in clearing our path.

What does the Bible mean when it says that God saves us? In everyday language, saying "I will make something possible" does not mean the same as "I will do something." If God does not act in such a way as to make the salvation of his people certain, if all he does is render it possible, then is it really fitting to say that he saves us? If all God does for those who enter into eternal life is what he does for those who end up lost, then the difference between salvation and perdition is to be found in what people do for themselves.

The same is true of perseverance. If God does the same to keep all believers but some persevere while others do not, then what God does on their behalf is not enough to effectively save any of them. If the deliverance from spiritual dangers that God provides for his redeemed is not sufficient to make sure that none of them will perish, then staying saved depends on what we do for ourselves and not on the grace of God alone.

However, what is certain is that God performs a work of grace in the life of his elect that infallibly leads them to fulfill the conditions for salvation. He brings them to faith by his effective call, and he preserves them by granting them perseverance in faith unto the end. So teaches the doctrine of salvation by grace alone (*Sola Gratia*).

CONCLUSION

We should not underestimate how important it is to maintain a proper comprehension of the role grace plays in salvation. It is not merely theoretical. Down through the centuries, it has been a battle of the utmost importance.

During the Middle Ages, it was the church's deviation on this issue more than any other that compromised the vitality of the church and made the Reformation necessary. Since then, many evangelicals have been losing ground that had been reconquered by the Reformers and are no longer stressing that the totality of salvation is accomplished by the grace of God.

We must sound a warning over this, for when we begin to weaken the emphasis that is given to God's grace in salvation, we head in a dangerous direction and run the risk of abandoning the Gospel of grace altogether. In soteriological terms, there are only two religions in the world: the religion of self-salvation and the religion of salvation by grace. The more we take away from grace, the more we approach the heretical confidence in self-righteousness that has been multiplying its casualties since the days of the Pharisees. Therefore, grace is one aspect of Christian doctrine that we dare not tamper with.

This is the reason why the subject of this book is truly important. The perseverance of the saints is one of the so-called *doctrines of grace*. It cannot be rejected while at the same time maintaining intact the concept of "grace alone" in salvation. Adopting the theory of the possibility of apostasy is clearly a step in the direction of a system of self-salvation, because it necessarily implies that a part of salvation will be considered a human accomplishment.

This inevitably causes the glory of salvation to be shared with man. Giving God the glory for something means that we thank him for it and declare, "God did this for me." But we fail to give him the glory if we think of it as something that we did for ourselves. When our creed does not point clearly to God's grace as the sufficient cause of salvation, we rob God of the honor that he is due.

Salvation *is* by grace alone. No one has ever persevered by his or her own strength so as to be congratulated for it. All who have ever persevered, and all who ever will, owe their success entirely to the fact that their perseverance was assured, even guaranteed by the dispensation of special grace. It is hence an impropriety to render unto man that which rightly belongs unto God.

By way of contrast, the doctrines of grace teach us to give God all the glory. *Sola Gratia* results in *Soli Deo Gloria*. The apostle Paul understood this connection. After confidently asserting, "And the Lord will deliver me from every evil work and preserve me for His heavenly kingdom," he concludes, "To Him be glory forever and ever. Amen!" (2 Tim. 4:18, NKJV). Certain as he was that he would arrive safely in the heavenly kingdom, he gives God the glory, for he realizes that his victory is not his own doing. He was absolutely sure that he would win, because he knew that the cause of his triumph was not in himself.

Just like Paul, every true Christian can be assured of never perishing, because that is the promise of God. There is no pride or presumption in having assurance of future salvation, just as there is none in the assurance of present salvation, as long as all trust is deposited in God. So we should glory in the unshakable security of salvation. That is a way in which we glorify God, just as Abraham glorified God when he did not doubt God's promise (Rom. 4:20).

When we think in this way, we realize that we are so weak that we cannot stand on our own, not even for a moment, especially when we take into account that we are up against the devil, the world, and our own flesh. Even so, without wavering in unbelief, we do not doubt God's promise but grow strong in faith, giving glory to God. We are fully assured that what he has promised, he is able also to perform.

> All perseverance can be understood and confessed only as a miracle, a miracle that radically excludes all self-righteousness...Because of this there is no less glorying in perseverance; but what remains besides glorying in the Lord?[175]

As is the case in the new birth, the perseverance of the saints is a miracle:

> We are awed and rejoiced when we learn of how some notorious rebel was brought to the foot of the Cross. But equally interesting, equally wonderful, equally blessed is the story of each Christian's life after conversion....The saint is indeed a marvel of marvels: without strength yet continuing to plod along his uphill course. Think of a tree flourishing in the midst of a sandy desert, where there is neither soil nor water; imagine a house suspended in mid-air, with no visible means

---

175 G. C. Berkouwer, *Faith and Perseverance* (Grand Rapids: Wm. B. Eerdmans Publishing Company, 1979), 24.

of support above or below; conceive of a man living week after week and year after year in a morgue, yet maintaining his vigour; suppose a lone lamb secure in the midst of hungry wolves, or a maid keeping her garments white as she ploughs her way through deep mud and mire, and in such figures you have an image of the Christian life.[176]

We must banish all naturalism from our doctrine of conversion and perseverance. We are not capable of such things, but our sufficiency comes from God. May we learn to deposit all our trust in the grace of God. The hope of every Christian is to enter eternal glory, but not all Christians are counting on certainly making it by the grace of God. Many entertain doubts as to their own final salvation since they suppose that everything ultimately hangs on their unstable will.

But that is precisely the problem. They are not totally confident in regard to the future because the measure of hope they do enjoy is deposited in themselves. Although they are not fully convinced that they will most definitely enter eternal bliss, they enjoy some measure of tranquility because they look unto themselves and figure they have a reasonable chance. Uncertain as to their own future perseverance, they can only remain optimistic to the degree in which they believe themselves sufficiently determined to go on to the end doing their part—that is, doing that which depends upon them.

They can sleep at night even though they do not have the assurance that they will continue saved for the rest of their lives because they don't really consider a failure on their part so likely, and this affords them some comfort. In this way, they show a degree of confidence in themselves pertaining to their own salvation, although they speak in terms of trusting Christ as our only and sufficient Savior. There is, indeed, a great deal at stake in the debate over perseverance.

The belief in the possibility of apostasy of saints has yet another unacceptable ramification when contemplated from the perspective of those who have already finished the race and kept the faith. If perseverance is a gift from God, whoever perseveres has nothing to boast about. But if perseverance depends on how we fare in doing our part, then whoever perseveres unto the end has something to boast about.

The one who makes it may say, "I owe my salvation to what Christ did for me, but it is likewise true that all that he did for me would have been in vain

---

176 A. W. Pink, *Eternal Security* (Grand Rapids: Baker Book House, 1979), 31.

if it had not been for what I did for myself. I persevered. I was faithful unto the end. You'll find there are a lot of people in hell today who received just as much help from God as I did, but their story just didn't turn out quite as good as my own. It looks like I ought to get a little credit too."

Now is that, by any stretch of the imagination, a biblical picture of heaven? It most certainly is not! In heaven, there is no such boasting. The very thought is outrageous. No one gets applauded for making it to heaven. No one will prostrate himself in gratitude for salvation only to hear that his own praise is in order on the grounds that nothing that God did would have resulted in anything, were it not for the person's having done his own part.

Quite the contrary, all the glory belongs to God, as it is written in Psalm 115:1, "Not to us, O LORD, not to us, but to your name give glory, for the sake of your steadfast love and your faithfulness!"

When entering the Promised Land, the Israelites were warned against fancying that they had any merit in the achievement:

> Not because of your righteousness or the uprightness of your heart are you going in to possess their land, but because of the wickedness of these nations the LORD your God is driving them out from before you, and that he may confirm the word that the LORD swore to your fathers, to Abraham, to Isaac, and to Jacob. Know, therefore, that the LORD your God is not giving you this good land to possess because of your righteousness, for you are a stubborn people. (Deut. 9:5–6)

If it mattered so much that they recognized that they were not receiving that land because of anything they had done or merited, how much more does it matter that we understand that we do not make it to the Celestial Kingdom by any contribution of our own, whether works or merit? The lesson contained in the warning they were given applies to us, as well, lest our hearts be lifted up.

Just as God bore Israel "on eagles' wings" and brought them out of captivity and to himself, so has he done the same with us. Just as they were not the ones who decided to be the people of God but were rather a chosen people, the same is true in our case. And just like in their case, we were not chosen to be God's people because we were a better or more logical choice than the rest of humanity in any sense (Deut. 7:6–8).

Far from it, God deliberately chose the foolish of the world to shame the wise, and God chose the weak to shame the powerful. Indeed, God chose the low and despised in the world, even things that are not, to bring to nothing the things that are "so that no human being might boast in the presence of God" (1 Cor. 1:29).

> But by his doing you are in Christ Jesus, who became to us wisdom from God, and righteousness and sanctification, and redemption, that, just as it is written, "Let him who boasts, boast in the Lord."
> (1 Cor. 1:30–31, NASB)

Will any persevere unto the end apart from the Lord bringing it to pass? We have nothing except that which we have received (1 Cor. 4:7). Or has anyone ever put God in the position of owing a reward? Of course not. When did he ever need our help for anything?

> Who has ever given to God, that God should repay him? For from him and through him and to him are all things. To him be the glory forever! Amen.
> (Rom. 11:35–36, NIV)

On the Day of Judgment, this will be made perfectly clear. "The arrogance of man will be brought low and the pride of men humbled; the LORD alone will be exalted in that day" (Isa. 2:17). As goes the song of the redeemed, "Salvation belongs to our God who sits on the throne, and to the Lamb!" (Rev. 7:10). Therefore, to God be all the praise, glory, wisdom, thanksgiving, honor, power, and might, forever and ever! Amen.

The celestial scene in Revelation shows the church triumphant in harmony, giving glory to God. Sadly, on earth, God's people do not enjoy unanimous agreement on the doctrinal matter that has been the subject of this book. But our doctrinal differences will disappear on that Day when we find ourselves all gathered before our Lord's glorious throne. There will be consensus among us then. But that means that some of our views will have changed.

If the thesis of this book proves to be wrong, it will be because it gives too much credit to God in the matter. If that turns out to be the case, Reformed believers as myself will learn that we have conveyed an exaggerated picture of what God does for his people. We will discover that in some measure the success of each glorified saint really depended on how well each person performed his or her role.

But it is my strong conviction that things will not turn out that way. Most assuredly, on that Day, we will all fall down before the One seated on the throne and worship him, casting all our crowns before him and proclaiming, "Worthy are you, our Lord and God, to receive glory!"

In the presence of the Lord, we will all be keenly aware of the fact that it was not we who kept ourselves; we will all know that the devil would have sifted us like wheat had it not been for the intercession of Christ on our behalf, and we will all confess that we would have certainly failed if any part of our salvation had depended on us. God will be greatly exalted on that Day!

Appendix

The Doctrine of Justification
in the Patristic Period

Writings from the first centuries of Christianity confirm that far from preaching novelty, the view of justification advanced by the Reformers is none other than what was taught by early Christian leaders. The following quotes are selected to corroborate this fact as they include all the elements of the Reformed doctrine of justification by faith alone.

1. The sins of the redeemed are imputed to Christ while they, having no righteousness of their own, receive the righteousness of Christ by imputation.

   He gave His own Son as a ransom for us, the holy One for transgressors, the blameless One for the wicked, the righteous One for the unrighteous, the incorruptible One for the corruptible, the immortal One for them that are mortal. For what other thing was capable of covering our sins than His righteousness? By what other one was it possible that we, the wicked and ungodly, could be justified, than by the only Son of God? O sweet exchange! O unsearchable operation! O benefits surpassing all expectation! that the wickedness of many should be hid in a single righteous One, and that the righteousness of One should justify many transgressors![177]
   (Epistle to Diognetus, AD 130)

2. We are clothed with his perfect righteousness from the moment we believe.

   This righteousness is not ours but belongs to God, and in saying this, Paul hints to us that it is abundantly available and easy to obtain. For we do not get it by toil and labor but by believing. Then, since his statement does not seem credible, if the adulterer and homosexual, the grave robber and the magician are not only to be suddenly set free from punishment but to be made righteous, and righteous with

---

177 *The Epistle of Mathetes to Diognetus*, Chapter 9, *Ante-Nicene Fathers*, vol. 1, ed. A. Roberts and J. Donaldson (Albany, OR: Sage Software, 1996), 65.

the righteousness of God, Paul backs up his assertion from the
Old Testament.[178]   (John Chrysostom, AD 347–407)

The purpose of the law was to make man righteous, but it had no
power to do that. But when faith came it achieved what the law
could not do, for once a man believes he is immediately justified.
Faith therefore established what the law intended and brought to
fulfillment what its provisions aimed for. Consequently faith has not
abolished the law but perfected it.[179]
                                         (John Chrysostom, AD 347–407)

Righteousness comes from faith, which means that it too is a gift of
God. For since this righteousness belongs to God, it is an unmerited
gift. And the gifts of God greatly exceed any achievements of our
own zeal.[180]   (John Chrysostom, AD 347–407)

Not only sufficient but superabundant indeed is the righteousness
that comes from faith. This salvation is freely given by the grace of
God through the knowledge of Christ. It can hardly be said to be a
gift of the law. For to know rightly the mystery of his incarnation and
passion and resurrection is the perfection of life and the treasure
of wisdom.[181]   (Theodoret, AD 393–451)

3. Human works are totally excluded in justification, for salvation is by grace.
   To obtain salvation by works would require us to be perfect, having no sin
   at all. Therefore, no work on our part could count toward our salvation.

   God allowed his Son to suffer as if a condemned sinner, so that
   we might be delivered from the penalty of our sins. This is God's
   righteousness, that we are not justified by works (for then they would
   have to be perfect, which is impossible), but by grace, in which case
   all our sin is removed.[182]   (John Chrysostom, AD 347–407)

---

178 John Chrysostom, *Homilies on Romans 2:17, Ancient Christian Commentary on Scripture*, NT vol.
   6, ed. Gerald Bray (Downers, Grove, IL: InterVarsity Press, 2013), 32.

179 John Chrysostom, *Homilies on Romans 7, Ancient Christian Commentary on Scripture*, NT vol. 6,
   ed. Gerald Bray (Downers, Grove, IL: InterVarsity Press, 2013), 107.

180 Chrysostom, *Homilies on the Philippians 12 3:7–9, Ancient Christian Commentary on Scripture*,
   NT vol. 8, ed. Mark J. Edwards (Downers Grove, IL: InterVarsity Press, 1998), 270.

181 Theodoret, *Epistle to the Philippians 3:9–10, Ancient Christian Commentary on Scripture*, NT vol.
   8, ed. Mark J. Edwards (Downers Grove, IL: InterVarsity Press, 1998), 271.

182 John Chrysostom, *Homilies on the Epistles of Paul to the Corinthians 11:5, Ancient Christian
   Commentary on Scripture*, NT vol. 7, ed. Gerald Bray (Downers Grove, IL: InterVarsity Press,
   1999), 252.

4. There are no works that we could possibly perform that would contribute toward our justification. If our works had any role in our justification, salvation would be earned as wages instead of granted as a gift of God.

> And just as there are no crimes so detestable that they can prevent the gift of grace, so too there can be no works so eminent that they are owed in condign judgement that which is given freely. Would it not be a debasement of redemption in Christ's blood, and would not God's mercy be made secondary to human works, if justification, which is through grace, were owed in view of preceding merits, so that it were not the gift of a Donor, but the wages of a laborer?[183]
> (Prosper of Aquitaine, written around AD 450)

> The fact that you Ephesians are saved is not something that comes from yourselves. It is the gift of God. It is not from your works, but it is God's grace and God's gift, not from anything you have deserved.[184]
> (Marius Victorinus, fourth century AD)

> We are saved by grace rather than works, for we can give God nothing in return for what he has bestowed on us.[185]
> (Jerome, AD 347–420)

> Paul shows clearly that righteousness depends not on the merit of man, but on the grace of God, who accepts the faith of those who believe, without the works of the Law.[186]

5. Justification comes through faith alone.

> They are justified freely because they have not done anything nor given anything in return, but by faith alone they have been made holy by the gift of God.[187]

183 Prosper of Aquitaine, *The Call Of All Nations (1, 17)*, *The Faith of the Early Fathers*, Vol. 3, sec. 2044, ed. William A. Jurgens (Collegeville, MN: Liturgical Press, 1979), 195.

184 Marius Victorinus, *Epistle to the Ephesians 1, 2:9*, *Ancient Christian Commentary on Scripture*, NT vol. 8, ed. Mark J. Edwards (Downers Grove, IL: InterVarsity Press, 1998), 134.

185 Jerome, *Epistle to the Ephesians 1.2:1*, *Ancient Christian Commentary on Scripture*, NT vol. 8, ed. Mark J. Edwards (Downers Grove, IL: InterVarsity Press, 1998), 132.

186 Jerome, *Against the Pelagians 2.7*, *Ancient Christian Commentary on Scripture*, NT vol. 6, ed. Gerald Bray (Downers, Grove, IL: InterVarsity Press, 2013), 106.

187 Ambrosiaster, *Commentary on Paul's Epistles*, *Ancient Christian Commentary on Scripture*, NT vol. 6, ed. Gerald Bray (Downers, Grove, IL: InterVarsity Press, 2013), 101.

By "the circumcised" Paul means the Jews who have been justified by their faith in the promise and who believe that Jesus is the Christ whom God had promised in the law. By "the uncircumcised" he means the Gentiles who have been justified with God by their faith in Christ. Thus God has justified both Jews and Gentiles. For because God is one, everyone has been justified in the same way. What benefit then is there in circumcision? Or what disadvantage is there in uncircumcision when only faith produces worthiness and merit?[188]   (Ambrosiaster, fourth century AD)

He did not make us deserving, since we did not receive things by our own merit but by the grace and goodness of God.[189]
                        (Marius Victorinus, fourth century AD)

For he had promised that he would justify those who believe in Christ, as he says in Habakkuk: "The righteous will live by faith in me." Whoever has faith in God and Christ is righteous.[190]
                        (Ambrosiaster, fourth century AD)

For God is just, and therefore he could not justify the unjust. Therefore he required the intervention of a propitiator, so that by having faith in him those who could not be justified by their own works might be justified.[191]   (Origen, AD 184–254)

6. The faith by which we are justified is itself a gift, wrought in our hearts by the grace of God.

All we bring to grace is our faith. But even in this faith, divine grace itself has become our enabler. For [Paul] adds, "And this is not of yourselves but it is a gift of God; not of works, lest anyone should boast" (Eph. 2:8–9). It is not of our own accord that we have believed, but we have come to belief after having been called; and even when

---

188 Ambrosiaster, *Commentary on Paul's Epistles*, Ancient Christian Commentary on Scripture, NT vol. 6, ed. Gerald Bray (Downers, Grove, IL: InterVarsity Press, 2013), 106.

189 Marius Victorinus, *Epistle to the Ephesians 1 2:7*, Ancient Christian Commentary on Scripture, NT vol. 8, ed. Mark J. Edwards (Downers Grove, IL: InterVarsity Press, 1998), 132.

190 Ambrosiaster, *Commentary on Paul's Epistles*, Ancient Christian Commentary on Scripture, NT vol. 6, ed. Gerald Bray (Downers, Grove, IL: InterVarsity Press, 2013), 103.

191 Origen of Alexandria, *Commentary on the Epistle to the Romans 2:112*, Ancient Christian Commentary on Scripture, NT vol. 6, ed. Gerald Bray (Downers, Grove, IL: InterVarsity Press, 2013), 103.

we had come to believe, He did not require of us purity of life, but approving mere faith, God bestowed on us forgiveness of sins.[192]

(Theodoret of Cyrrhus, AD 393–457)

So that you may not be elated by the magnitude of these benefits, see how Paul puts you in your place. For "by grace you are saved through faith." Then, so as to do no injury to free will, he allots a role to us, then takes it away again, saying "and this not of ourselves"... Even faith, he says, is not from us. For if the Lord had not come, if he had not called us, how should we have been able to believe? "For how," [Paul] says, "shall they believe if they have not heard?" (Rom. 10:14). So even the act of faith is not self-initiated. It is, he says, "the gift of God" (Eph. 2:8c).[193]   (John Chrysostom, AD 347–407)

7. The depravity of our fallen nature prevents us from taking the initiative in seeking God, or even choosing him. Only divine grace can produce this change in the heart of a sinner.

These are the true riches of God's mercy, that even when we did not seek it mercy was made known through his own initiative.[194]

(Ambrosiaster, fourth century AD)

[Paul] is speaking not of the first but of the second creation, wherein we are re-created by the resurrection. Completely unable as we are to mend our ways by our own decision on account of the natural weakness that opposes us, we are made able to come newly alive without pain and with great ease by the grace of the One who re-creates us for this purpose.[195] (Theodore of Mopsuestia, AD 350–428)

8. The just cannot boast on any account, since it is only by God's grace that they come to faith and do what is right.

It is not in God's power that anyone should be forced against his will to do evil or good but that he should go to the bad, according to his

---

192 Theodoret of Cyrrhus, *Interpretation of the Fourteen Epistles of Paul, The Faith of the Early Fathers*, Vol. 3, sec. 2163, ed. William A. Jurgens (Collegeville, MN: Liturgical Press, 1979), 248–249.

193 John Chrysostom, *Homilies On Ephesians 2:8, Ancient Christian Commentary on Scripture*, NT vol. 8, ed. Mark J. Edwards (Downers Grove, IL: InterVarsity Press, 1998), 134.

194 Ambrosiaster, *Epistle to the Ephesians 2:4, Ancient Christian Commentary on Scripture*, NT vol. 8, ed. Mark J. Edwards (Downers Grove, IL: InterVarsity Press, 1998), 132.

195 Theodore of Mopsuestia, *Epistle to the Ephesians 2:10, Ancient Christian Commentary on Scripture*, NT vol. 8, ed. Mark J. Edwards (Downers Grove, IL: InterVarsity Press, 1998), 135.

own deserts, when God abandons him. For a person is not good if he does not will it, but the grace of God assists him even in willing. It is not without cause that it is written, "God is the one who works in you to will and to do, of his own good will."[196]   (Augustine, AD 354–430)

We should not suppose, because he said, "For it is God that works in you both the willing and the doing," that he has taken away free will. For if that were so he would not have said above, "Work out your own salvation with fear and trembling." For when he bids them work, it is agreed that they have free will. But they are to work with fear and trembling so that they will not, by attributing the good working to themselves, be elated by the good works as though they were their own.[197]   (Augustine, AD 354–430)

9. Good works have a place in the Christian life, but not in justification. Once someone has been saved through faith, works will inevitably follow.

God's mission was not to save people in order that they may remain barren or inert. For Scripture says that faith has saved us. Put better: since God willed it, faith has saved us. Now in what case, tell me, does faith save without itself doing anything at all? Faith's workings themselves are a gift of God, lest anyone should boast. What then is Paul saying? Not that God has forbidden works, but forbidden us to be justified by works. No one, Paul says, is justified by works, precisely in order that the grace and benevolence of God may become apparent![198]   (Chrysostom, AD 347–407)

---

196 Augustine, *On Two Letters of Pelagius 1:36*, *Ancient Christian Commentary on Scripture*, NT vol. 8, ed. Mark J. Edwards (Downers Grove, IL: InterVarsity Press, 1998), 258.

197 Augustine, *On Grace and Free Will 21*, *Ancient Christian Commentary on Scripture*, NT vol. 8, ed. Mark J. Edwards (Downers Grove, IL: InterVarsity Press, 1998), 258.

198 John Chrysostom, *Homilies on Ephesians 4 2:9*, *Ancient Christian Commentary on Scripture*, NT vol. 8, ed. Mark J. Edwards (Downers Grove, IL: InterVarsity Press, 1998), p. 134.